# THE ELECTION OF POPE LEO XIV

# THE ELECTION OF POPE LEO XIV

*The Last Surprise of Pope Francis*

Gerard O'Connell and Elisabetta Piqué

ORBIS BOOKS
**Maryknoll, New York 10545**

Founded in 1970, Orbis Books endeavors to publish works that enlighten the mind, nourish the spirit, and challenge the conscience. The publishing arm of the Maryknoll Fathers and Brothers, Orbis seeks to explore the global dimensions of the Christian faith and mission, to invite dialogue with diverse cultures and religious traditions, and to serve the cause of reconciliation and peace. The books published reflect the views of their authors and do not represent the official position of the Maryknoll Society. To learn more about Maryknoll and Orbis Books, please visit our website at www.orbisbooks.com.

---

Copyright © 2026 by Gerard O'Connell and Elisabetta Piqué

Published by Orbis Books, Box 302, Maryknoll, NY 10545-0302.

All rights reserved.

No part of this publication may be reproduced or transmitted in any form or by any means, electronic or mechanical, including photocopying, recording, or any information storage or retrieval system, without prior permission in writing from the publisher.

Queries regarding rights and permissions should be addressed to: Orbis Books, P.O. Box 302, Maryknoll, NY 10545-0302.

Manufactured in the United States of America

---

Library of Congress Cataloging-in-Publication Data

Names: O'Connell, Gerard author | Piqué, Elisabetta author
Title: The election of Pope Leo XIV : the last surprise of Pope Francis / Gerard O'Connell and Elisabetta Piqué.
Description: Maryknoll, NY : Orbis Books, [2026] | Includes bibliographical references and index. | Summary: "A daily chronicle by two veteran Vatican correspondents from the death of Pope Francis to the first days of Pope Leo's papacy"— Provided by publisher.
Identifiers: LCCN 2025038686 (print) | LCCN 2025038687 (ebook) | ISBN 9781626986640 trade paperback | ISBN 9798888661185 epub
Subjects: LCSH: Leo XIV, Pope, 1955- | Catholic Church—History—20th century | Popes—Election
Classification: LCC BX1378.8 .O26 2026  (print) | LCC BX1378.8 (ebook) | DDC 282.092—dc23/eng/20250919
LC record available at https://lccn.loc.gov/2025038686
LC ebook record available at https://lccn.loc.gov/2025038687

*For Edwin, Juan Pablo, and Carolina*

# CONTENTS

Acknowledgments  xi

Introduction  xiii

## PART I
### FAREWELL TO POPE FRANCIS

April 21, Monday [Betta]   3
*The Shock*

April 22, Tuesday [Betta]   14
*The Shell Breaks*

April 23, Wednesday [Gerry]   22
*The Goodbye Begins*

April 24, Thursday [Gerry]   29
*A Loose Cannon*

April 25, Friday [Betta]   35
*The* Cartonero *Returns*

April 26, Saturday [Betta]   42
*The Farewell Popemobile*

## PART II
### The Quest for a New Pope

April 27, Sunday [Gerry]   53
*A New Pilgrim Site*

April 28, Monday [Gerry]   62
*We Have a Date*

April 29, Tuesday [Betta]   71
*Not the Favorite*

April 30, Wednesday [Gerry]   82
*Betrayal*

May 1, Thursday [Betta]   90
*An Exhausting Labor Day*

May 2, Friday [Gerry]   99
*Outside Interferences*

May 3, Saturday [Betta]   114
*Counterattack*

May 4, Sunday [Gerry]   123
*Abnormal Sunday*

May 5, Monday [Betta]   130
*Under the Radar*

May 6, Tuesday [Betta])   142
*Great Anxiety*

## PART III
### THE CONCLAVE

May 7, Wednesday [Gerry]    157
*The Hour of Truth*

May 8, Thursday [Gerry]    175
*White Smoke*

## PART IV
### A MISSIONARY POPE

May 9, Friday [Betta]    197
*The Day After*

May 10, Saturday [Betta]    212
*Accepting a Yoke*

May 11, Sunday [Gerry]    221
*Never Again War*

May 12, Monday [Gerry]    232
*Meeting the Press*

May 13, Tuesday [Betta]    240
*@Pontifex*

May 14, Wednesday [Gerry]    248
*Peace, a Priority*

May 15, Thursday [Gerry]    254
*An Unknown Past*

May 16, Friday [Betta]   261
*Descendant of Immigrants*

May 17, Saturday [Gerry]   270
*A Different Style*

May 18, Sunday [Gerry]   278
*Love and Unity*


Conclusion   287

Index   291

# ACKNOWLEDGMENTS

To all the sources—especially the cardinals—
who trusted and helped us write this book.

To Irene Hernández Velasco, a lifelong friend
who inspired us to write it and put us in touch
with our enthusiastic Spanish publisher, Joaquín Palau, at ARPA.

To Robert Ellsberg of Orbis Books, who was the first to agree,
without any hesitation, to publish this book.

To Patrick Dunbar, who helped and advised us
in record time, and in a variety of ways.

To all our friends—it's not possible to mention everyone—
at *La Nación* and at *America Magazine,*
who always enthusiastically supported this project.

To our family.

# INTRODUCTION

We knew this moment would arrive. Although Pope Francis always showed unwavering strength, energy and courage despite his age and advancing ailments, his death was inexorable.

As he himself said in one of the dozens of interviews he granted, he was no Superman. And God called him on the morning of April 21, 2025.

In this book, in the form of a diary, we recount the impact of the death of the first Latin American and first Jesuit pope, not only on the world's 1.4 billion Catholics and on the cardinals who were to elect his successor, but also on us personally, as we had the extraordinary privilege of being his close friends for over twenty-four years.

From that shattering moment, we recount his apotheotic farewell and, set amidst the whirlwind that a papal transition always unleashes for journalists, piece together the path of Leo XIV's election, an outcome that very few had foreseen. It was, for us, Francis's final surprise.

The 2025 conclave—a mega-event religious and spiritual, but also political—unfolded with all the intrigue and intensity characteristic of papal elections, both real and fictional. Feeling ourselves suddenly like pieces in the very puzzle at hand, we describe how certain factions—the rigorists, the diplomats, Italian interests, and a combination of these—maneuvered to defy the harsh arithmetic, only to end up undermining their own cause.

Although it was a *cum clave* (with a key, secret) election, we were able, thanks to different sources, to reconstruct what the pre-conclave preparatory meetings called "general congregations" were like. We detail the events inside the Sistine Chapel where, in under than twenty-four hours, on May 8, Leo XIV—the first US-born pope,

Peruvian by adoption, the first pope "of both worlds," the first Augustinian pope, the first missionary pope—was elected.

The book also covers his first days as the 267th successor of Peter—until his inauguration on May 18—which hint at a pontificate with its own style, distinct from his predecessor's in form, but not in substance.

Writing this book together, and as a married couple, was an immense challenge. But we overcame it as you will see in the following pages....

—Gerard (Gerry) O'Connell and Elisabetta (Betta) Piqué

PART I

# FAREWELL TO POPE FRANCIS

MONDAY, APRIL 21 [BETTA]
*The Shock*

GERRY WAKES ME AT 9:48 am "Betta...the pope...the pope is dead!"

This sentence changes everything. It changes our lives, it changes history. I am semi-paralyzed, but not surprised. We had seen him in such bad shape yesterday, Easter Sunday. Gerry and I were extremely worried. When he made that final outing in the popemobile, we were there in St. Peter's Square. When he passed in front of the Press Office at the beginning of Via della Conciliazione, I had climbed a flowerpot and shouted "Father Jorge!" as I always called him. Gerry also tried to get his attention by waving his arms. But, unlike the hundreds of times in the midst of crowds and on his travels around the world, when he, who always connected visually with people, had seen us and greeted us, this time he did not respond. Accompanied by Juan Cruz Villalón, one of his private secretaries, who cared for him with striking tenderness during his final months of illness, Father Jorge was lost, in another dimension, looking only forward. We returned to the Press Room in anguish. I wanted to burst into tears. He was no longer himself. "Maybe he was saying goodbye," Gerry commented, always the first to grasp the essence.

That's why that Easter Sunday night, which we spent with friends at home—eating the traditional baked lamb—had not been a joyful dinner. Everyone, including Eva Fernández, our friend from the Spanish radio station Cope, was worried. We had seen Francis in very bad shape. And Gerry and I had gone to bed with that in mind. What's more, we barely slept a wink all night, thinking that we would be unable to make our planned trip to Buenos Aires on Tuesday night to attend the May 3 wedding of my niece Isabella, daughter of my brother Enrico. How could we leave with Pope Francis in such bad shape?

So when Gerry abruptly wakes me with the most unwelcome news, although I'm shocked, I'm not really surprised. We'd sensed it coming.

GERRY IS ON THE PHONE with our friend Chris Lamb, a Vatican correspondent for CNN, who was in a taxi heading to the airport to return to his home in London after Easter. During that conversation, the Holy See Press Office sends a cryptic message via telegram at 9:45 AM to permanently accredited journalists:

> A live broadcast will begin shortly from the Chapel of Casa Santa Marta. It will be possible to follow it on the Vatican News and Vatican Media channels.

Gerry and Chris listen together as American Cardinal Kevin Farrell, the *camerlengo* (chamberlain), the person who becomes the highest authority in the Holy See when a pope dies or resigns, announces the news at 9:47 AM. "It is with profound sorrow that I must announce the death of our Holy Father Francis. At 7:35 AM this morning, the Bishop of Rome, Francis, returned to the House of the Father."

As soon as Gerry hears Farrell's voice, he runs to get me. I jump out of bed. Then I send an email to the Argentine newspaper *La Nación*, where I've been a correspondent for more than twenty-five years. I also call Inés Capdevila, one of my bosses and a good friend at the newspaper. "The pope has died!" I tell her. She is shocked. She is in Poland on a trip and sets off the alarm in Buenos Aires where it is 5:00 AM and everything is ready: all that's left is to press a button for the obituary I've written to appear[1] along with dozens of other notes, all prepared months ago and especially since that stressful evening of February 22, when Pope Francis, hospitalized at the Gemelli Hospital since February 14, was for the first time on the verge of death due to an acute respiratory crisis and needed a blood transfusion because of kidney failure.

Gerry immediately calls two of the top editors at *America* magazine, for which he is the Vatican correspondent, but he can't reach them because it's still nighttime in New York. Only executive editor Ashley McKinless answers, and she is stunned by the news. He asks her to alert the other editors at *America* and sends her a brief note announcing the pope's death, which she quickly publishes along with

---

1. Elisabetta Piqué, "El Papa sencillo que rompió moldes y abrió la Iglesia como nunca antes," *La Nación*, April 21, 2025.

the obituary Gerry had updated when the pope was hospitalized on February 14.[2]

A few hours later, Sam Sawyer, SJ, editor-in-chief of *America*, calls him to let him know that *America* will be sending seven members of its team to help cover the papal transition. He tells him they will arrive in Rome on Friday, April 25.

Gerry also calls friends of his who are cardinals on three continents to share the sad news; he wakes some of them up.

He also tries to contact the producers at CTV Canada, with whom he has a contract for the papal transition, just as he had in 2005 when John Paul II died and in 2013 when Benedict XVI resigned. He can't reach anyone. It's after midnight in Toronto. Later, they tell him they'll send a reporter—Geneviève Beauchemin, Quebec bureau chief for CTV National News, with whom he worked when Francis traveled to Quebec on July 29, 2022, during his visit to Canada—and a cameraman. Since they will arrive later, they ask him to be available for live broadcasts and interviews at various times.

Juan Pablo and Carolina, our children, ages 19 and 17, are sleeping. In Italy, it's the traditional Easter Monday "Pasquetta" holiday when the children usually go out for picnics in the parks. Gerry wakes Juampy first, then Caro. "The pope has died. You were lucky to know such a great man," he tells them. For them, too, Pope Francis was always "Father Jorge"—that open, approachable, ever-present priest who would come to our house for dinner whenever he traveled to Rome, and who, because we had gotten along so well, Gerry and I had asked to baptize the children, both of whom had been born in Buenos Aires. He was delighted, and immediately agreed. At Gerry's request, the baptisms took place in the Church of San Ignacio in Buenos Aires—a copy of the Jesuit Church of the Gesú in Rome—the oldest church in Buenos Aires. Father Jorge baptized Juan Pablo first in 2005, and then Carolina in 2007. He gave each of them a small medallion depicting the Virgin of Luján, engraved with the date of their baptism and his initials, "JMB." Lately, he would laughingly call the children "the squatters," because we had told him they were actively participating in the protest occupations of their secondary school, the Liceo Classico Visconti, the oldest in Rome. Instead of being shocked, Father Jorge,

---

2. Gerard O'Connell, "Pope Francis, Trailblazing Jesuit with a Heart for the Poor, Dies at 88," *America*, April 21, 2025.

with his usual openness and youthful spirit, would laugh: "If they don't occupy the school and protest now, when will they?" he would comment. And he would call me the mother of "the revolutionaries."

MY CELL PHONE EXPLODES with WhatsApp messages. After dozens of fake news stories about Pope Francis's recent weeks of hospitalization and convalescence, everyone wants to know if it is true that the pope has died. The news is saying the pope has died. "Is it true?" my friends Sister Lucía Caram and Juan Carlos Cruz ask me from Spain. "Yes," Gerry and I answer.

In fact, it was our friend Cristina Cabrejas, the Vatican expert for the Spanish news agency EFE—an exceptional woman who recently lost her fantastic husband, Antonello Nusca, a photographer who had always worked with Gerry and me on our interviews with Francis—who broke the news about Francis's death. Cristina beat all the other international agencies to the punch. I am truly happy for her.

Our friend Annalisa Bilotta, a doctor at the Salvator Mundi International Hospital in Rome, who has helped us so much during recent weeks in interpreting the brief medical reports issued by the Vatican about Francis, also sends us a WhatsApp message to ask if it is true that the pope has died. When Gerry replies "Yes," she—always very professional—comments, "It happened as I predicted: it could happen at any moment, and it did."

My cell phone is exploding also because I have hundreds of interview requests. But over a month ago, I signed a contract with CNN as a contributor and analyst, giving me exclusivity with them, except for LN+, my newspaper's TV channel. It's logical. Everyone wants to talk to that Argentine journalist, a friend of the pope, a biographer of the pope, who knew him long before he was elected pope—having met him in 2001, more than twenty-four years ago!—and with whom he remained in contact until the end.

I receive hundreds of messages of condolence. "I'm sorry, Betta, I know you loved him very much." "A hug, I can imagine how you feel." "Be strong, Betta, this must be very hard for you." "I share your grief over the passing of our beloved Francisco." "I send you a big kiss, Betta, beyond journalistic concerns." "I'm sorry for your loss; I know the pope meant a lot to you."

Not even when my father died did I receive so many messages.

Gerry's cell phone is also ringing constantly. He receives condolence messages and phone calls, first from his eldest son Edwin in Brussels, then from his sister Fidelma in Ladispoli outside Rome. In addition, he has a surge of interview requests, not only from CTV, but also from various television and radio channels, ranging from the BBC to Al Jazeera, ITV, Channel 4, Sky TV, Australian and Irish television and radio, and several American television channels—too many to handle, which, fortunately, Lisa Manico, the media manager for *America* magazine, helps him filter.

In the midst of the madness and still in my nightgown, I send a few lines to my newspaper[3] and then take a quick shower. A CNN producer calls and asks me to go to their office on Via di Col di Lana. I get ready and fill a backpack with a computer, tripod, selfie stick, makeup, and a brush: it's going to be a long day.

I take a taxi to CNN Rome as the WhatsApp tempest continues. I arrive at the office—for the first time since the 2005 conclave following the death of John Paul II, when I had a contract with CNN, but in Spanish that time—and it's chaos. No one knows what time I am supposed to go on air, nor do I know the producer who called me and asked me to come—he hadn't given me his name. The "Roman" correspondents Ben Wedeman and Barbie Latza Nadeau apologize for the chaos. Elise Allen, the wife of John Allen of Crux, who was also hired as a contributor, arrives with her sister who is visiting Rome. The best part, though, is that amid the confusion, my son Juampy arrives. He is in his first year of university studies in PPE (Politics, Philosophy and Economics), speaks perfect Italian, Spanish, and English and when Chris Lamb told us a few months ago that they were looking for someone to do an internship, we introduced Juan Pablo.... And he just started working with them a week ago. How crazy to think that twenty years ago, during the 2005 conclave, I was pregnant with him!

I decide to head to the Vatican, where the news is coming and where I'll meet with Gerry. I take another taxi there, and the driver reflects the mood of mourning that has suddenly taken over Rome. "Francis fought for everything there was to fight for; I'm sorry he's gone," he comments. He drops me off near Via della Conciliazione, where they have already put up fences and increased police presence

---

3. Elisabetta Piqué, "Murió el papa Francisco, informó el Vaticano," *La Nación*, April 21, 2025.

because many people, on hearing the sad news, want to come to pray, to be there, to show their grief for the passing of this man who had been so close to them, who had come from the end of the earth.

The most impressive thing is the ringing of the six immense bells of St. Peter's Basilica, signaling the pope's death. I make a video and tweet. What has begun is what is technically called the *sede vacante*, the power vacuum that opens in the Vatican when a pope dies or resigns. The cardinal *camerlengo* becomes a virtual technical director of the transition, marked by the general congregations, that is, the meetings of cardinals—which begins tomorrow—in which the next steps will be decided. Above all, the date of the conclave that will elect Francis's successor will be selected.

When I arrive at the Press Room, the atmosphere is one of mourning. Many colleagues come to embrace me. I don't break down with anyone. I tell everyone that Gerry and I had already realized on Sunday that Francis was in bad shape. And, in the end, it is better that he left like this, from one day to the next, after bidding farewell to his people in a grand manner from the popemobile and avoiding an end like that of John Paul II, who was in very poor health and evidently absent, managed by others, for several years.

Like John Paul II, Francis fought to the very end to be with his people. And he surely went "to the house of the Father" in peace, after having given everything for his flock during a Holy Week that represented a true tribulation.

According to various sources, Pope Francis had awakened at 6:00 AM "reasonably well."[4] But half an hour later, at 7:00, he had the stroke that caused his death thirty-five minutes later.

His physique, which had endured a hectic schedule in recent years, was no longer the same. He was completely weakened after his fourth and final stay at the Gemelli, the popes' hospital, which he had left on March 23 a different person. Although with that indomitable spirit of his he had given his thumbs up as if to say everything was fine, he was far from recovered, and perhaps he sensed that he was going to return to his home in Santa Marta to try to recover, yes, but also perhaps to die, if that was God's will.

---

4. Elisabetta Piqué, "Las ultimas horas del Papa Francisco: una Semana Santa que fue un calvario y su esfuerzo final," *La Nación*, April 21, 2025.

It is true that, thanks to his determination to move forward and with the respiratory and motor physiotherapy exercises that had been prescribed for him, he had made "slight" improvements in the last three weeks. He had, in fact, resumed some work activities in a limited way, but he wasn't the same. He wasn't well, as could be seen in the images of his recent outings from his home in Santa Marta to be present during Holy Week, a time when he wanted to give his all. He was thinner, but with a swollen, almost deformed face, a stiff chin that prevented him from smiling, though his mind was completely clear.

"How are you experiencing this Easter?" Italian journalist Cristiana Caricato (TV 2000) had asked him on April 17, Holy Thursday, as he left Regina Coeli prison where, although he couldn't perform the traditional foot washing, he had wanted to be with a group of inmates, to remind them that God forgives everything and that they were not alone. "I am living this Easter as best I can," Pope Francis, a Jesuit who evidently had begun to perceive that God would soon call him, replied with great effort and difficulty. It was becoming an impossible mission to communicate the Gospel, not only in words, but also in concrete form.

Although doctors had prescribed a convalescence of at least two months and absolute rest, Francis, who had grown a little more obedient in recent times, would not heed them. The pope of the people [*pueblo*] wanted his end to be with the people.

That is why on Sunday after a two-minute greeting with the vice president of the United States in Santa Marta—when it was clearly evident that the pope was not well, according to the images released from the meeting—he made his great final effort, his final exertion.

At noon, amidst an eerie silence in St. Peter's Square, he appeared for the last time, in his wheelchair, on that same central balcony of St. Peter's Square from which he had astonished the world on the evening of March 13, 2013. Then, his body and, above all, his face, appeared, again, as on the day of his discharge from the Gemelli Hospital, as a symbol of suffering. There was no smile. His face was stiff. He had the look of a man, we now know, who was making a final effort. It was clear he wasn't well, and a true reflection of this was that he had to read what will be remembered as his last public words: "Dear brothers and sisters, Happy Easter!" Francis, a pope we had known as a wizard of communication, had had to read that simple greeting. He was very ill. Despite this, after a collaborator read his Easter message —another call for peace in a world gone mad and in favor of the least and the discarded—he managed to impart, with enormous difficulty, the *Urbi et Orbi* blessing to the city and the world.

Determined to say goodbye and to give his all, he then surprised everyone by climbing into the popemobile, braving the drafts, and making that final, marked turn, once again, in what we all realized was his final farewell. The Vatican cameras filming that final ride among thirty-five thousand people cheering him, with their cell phones aloft, focused on him from behind to avoid seeing his suffering face. Those of us who managed to see him from the front, waving his hands, but without seeking eye contact and with a serious expression, began to understand that this was his farewell. A farewell that included a stop for the popemobile to bless a child, giving his all, until the very end. "He died with the smell of sheep," summed up a cardinal friend, like him a Jesuit.

THE VERTIGO DOESN'T SUBSIDE. Foreign ministries around the world send messages of condolence with unanimous praise for Pope Francis. It's difficult to concentrate and write in the Press Room, which is being stormed by hundreds of journalists who are starting to arrive from everywhere on the planet. Many interrupt me to say hello, give me a hug, or ask for a comment. I try to be kind to everyone. It's hot. I don't understand why they don't turn on the air conditioning.

I send a WhatsApp message to Isa—Isabella, my niece—to let her know, with immense sorrow, that we'll have to cancel our trip to attend her wedding. I explain that the funeral and the conclave are coming up, which of course we have to cover, and that we're deeply sorry, but it's fate.

In the midst of the turmoil, I also contact Ulderico Baldesi at the travel agency to see how I can change those tickets—purchased in August of last year for a fortune—and, as is often the case because the airlines are thieves, I will lose.

My lifelong friend, Irene Hernández, former correspondent for Spain's *El Mundo* and mother of one of Juan Pablo's best friends Manuel—the boys grew up together and went to the same kindergarten when we were learning to be mothers—has also arrived in Rome. She is now working for the online site *El Confidencial* and is staying with our mutual friend, Ernesto Pérez, who is a film critic and friend of Cristina Taquini, whose birthday is today.

Irene and I covered the 2013 conclave together. Since it's easier to request interviews together, the idea is to put the "dream team" back together, this time of course with Gerry, the one Vatican expert who understood last time that the big surprise was going to be Jorge Bergoglio.

I write for a newspaper, I do live broadcasts for CNN and LN+ until late at night, just as Gerry does with his media outlets. When I'm faced with personal questions, asking how I'm experiencing all this, I don't flinch. I reply that I'm wearing my armor, the same that I habitually wear during my wartime coverage.

THE HOLY SEE ANNOUNCES THIS EVENING the causes of death of Jorge Mario Bergoglio, born in Buenos Aires, Argentina, on December 17, 1936, a resident of Vatican City. He died of a cerebral stroke (cerebrovascular accident, CVA); coma; and irreversible cardiocirculatory collapse, according to a document signed by Professor Andrea Arcangeli, director of the Vatican's Directorate of Health and Hygiene. The document also certifies the deterioration of his physical condition. "He was already affected by several episodes of acute respiratory failure due to multi-microbial bilateral pneumonia; with multiple bronchiectasis; high blood pressure; and type II diabetes."

The Press Room publishes Pope Francis's final will and testament,[5] which confirms that he had long known his end was coming, and for which he had been meticulously preparing.

> In the name of the Most Holy Trinity. Amen. Feeling that the end of my earthly life is approaching, and with a lively hope for Eternal Life, I wish to set out my final wishes solely regarding the place of my burial.
>
> Throughout my life, and during my ministry as a priest and bishop, I have always entrusted my life and my priestly and episcopal ministry to the Mother of Our Lord, Mary Most Holy. Therefore, I ask that my mortal remains rest awaiting the day of resurrection in the Papal Basilica of Saint Mary Major.
>
> I wish that my last earthly journey conclude precisely in this ancient Marian shrine, where I came to pray at the beginning and end of each apostolic journey, to confidently entrust my intentions to the Immaculate Mother and thank her for her docile and maternal care. I ask that my tomb be prepared in the niche of the lateral aisle between the Pauline Chapel (Chapel of

---

5. Pope Fracis's Testament, www.vaticannews.va, April 21, 2025.

the Salus Populi Romani) and the Sforza Chapel of the aforementioned papal basilica, as indicated in the attached appendix.

The tomb should be in the earth; simple, without special decorations, and with the only inscription: Franciscus.

May the Lord give the deserved reward to those who have loved me and will continue to pray for me. I offer the suffering that has been present in the latter part of my life to the Lord for peace in the world and brotherhood among peoples.

> —Santa Marta, June 29, 2022, to express my testamentary wishes solely regarding the place of my burial.

ACCORDING TO THE APOSTOLIC CONSTITUTION *Universi Dominici Gregis*,[6] on the vacant See and the election of the Roman Pontiff, when the latter dies (or resigns), "the government of the Church is entrusted to the College of Cardinals solely for the conduct of ordinary or unavoidable affairs, and for the preparation of everything necessary for the election of the new pontiff."

During this same period, the provisional head of Vatican City State is cardinal *camerlengo*. According to the Constitution governing the Roman Curia, upon the death of the pope, all heads of the dicasteries of the Roman Curia automatically resign from their positions.

When the See is vacant, the secretaries, including the substitute of the Secretariat of State, are responsible for the ordinary government of the curial institutions, dealing solely with ordinary matters.

Within the framework of these norms, this morning the dean of the College of Cardinals, ninety-one year old Giovanni Battista Re, sends an email to all cardinals informing them of the pope's death and inviting them to the first meeting of the general congregations, that is, the plenary assembly of all cardinals, both electors (under age 80) and non-electors (over age 80), at 9:00 AM tomorrow, April 22.

A day later, Chinese Cardinal Joseph Zen, 93, archbishop emeritus of Hong Kong, harshly criticized this decision. "How are the elderly in the peripheries supposed to arrive on time?" But the truth is that Cardinal Farrell, the *camerlengo*, has complied with the Constitution by convening the first general congregation as soon as possible. There are many matters to be decided, including the date of the funeral.

---

6. Pope John Paul II, apostolic constitution *Universi Dominici Gregis*, www.vatican.va.

I HARDLY EAT ANYTHING all day. I have no time and no hunger. They announce that the Press Room closes at 10:30 PM, but I'm supposed to make one last connection at 10:10 PM. When I return to the Press Room after having left everything inside, it is already closed, and I panic because all my things—my wallet, my computer—are still inside. There's a homeless, long-bearded foreigner sitting on the entrance steps who advises me to ring the bell. I do, and luckily someone appears and lets me in. I retrieve my things. But my computer case and tripod case are missing.... I ask the *uscieri* (attendants), and no one finds anything. ...Fortunately, my wallet is intact.

Since Francis's accession to the throne of Peter, many homeless people have camped out at night in the Vatican, in front of the Press Room and under Bernini's Colonnade. Will this change for them now that Francis is dead?

I ask this question of the homeless man who advised me to ring the doorbell, but who now reacts badly. Furious, he tries to take my cell phone, my main work tool. Stunned, I struggle until I get it back. A Brazilian colleague who happens to be there and sees the scene tells me that this man isn't well, that it's best if we leave.

It is dark. No one else is around, and the silence is broken only by the squawking of seagulls. I walk home, needing to walk, to refresh my brain. There's Caro, who's been abandoned all day, and Gerry and Juampy, who've also returned.

Exhausted, with a great emptiness and many memories burning bright, we eat very late...after midnight. Juampy prepares *spaghetto "aglio olio peperoncino"*—a classic, very simple dish with olive oil, chopped garlic, and spicy red pepper—which we wash down with a much-needed bottle of white wine. We toast Pope Francis, as he would surely have wanted us to: "Onward! Let's not lose our sense of humor!" he would have said.

Exhausted, we go to sleep, saddened by the abrupt end of a period of twelve years and thirty-nine very intense days, during which we were privileged witnesses of history, friends of a revolutionary pope who always accompanied us and was always present until the very end. And with the adrenaline rush of knowing that days and weeks of enormous work await us, of even more vertigo, and of strong emotions and suspense: Who will be chosen as his successor?

APRIL 22 TUESDAY [BETTA] _____

*The Shell Breaks*

IRENE ARRIVES AT OUR HOME at 9:00 AM with the morning newspapers. The joy of our reunion is short-lived. We dive into work. I make coffee and we spread out the newspapers on the dining room table. Every edition has dozens of pages dedicated to Francis, "the people's pope."

There are also rivers of ink about the recently begun *sede vacante* and the upcoming conclave, which must begin between May 5 and May 10, since the secret ballot must take place between the fifteenth and twentieth day after the pope's death.[7] The Italian right-wing newspaper *Il Giornale*, like several others, says that Cardinal Pietro Parolin, secretary of state, is the leading candidate.[8]

All the papers agree that the conclave will be shaped by Jorge Bergoglio. In ten consistories, he appointed 80 percent of the cardinal electors—those under age 80—and revolutionized the conclave that will elect his successor, which has never been so international and diverse. There are seventy-one countries represented, many from the peripheries.

The newspapers are filled with praise for this pope from the end of the world, who, with his simple preaching and humility, touched everyone like never before, especially non-Catholics.

But there are also those who criticized his manner, his informality, his spontaneity, his relaxing the papacy which had previously been remote and aloof. Among those voices is that of the former editor of the Vatican official newspaper *L'Osservatore Romano*, Giovanni Maria Vian. Irene has inaugurated the work of our "dream team" by setting up our 10:00 AM interview with him. Editor-in-chief of one of the world's most famous and influential newspapers from 2007 to 2018, Vian surprises us by calling Francis an "absolutist pope" who generated "obvious contradictions"[9] for twelve years. He asserts that the

---

7. *Universi Dominici Gregis*, 37.

8. Stefano Zurlo, "Al via un conclave senza fretta. Tutti i favoriti (dietro a Parolin)," *Il Giornale*, April 22, 2025.

9. Elisabetta Piqué, "El vaticanista Giovanni Maria Vian anticipa un cónclave polarizado y un futuro papa europeo que no será 'Francisco II,'" *La Nación*, April 22, 2025.

upcoming conclave will reflect the polarization of the Church, which he says grew during Francis's pontificate, and which he and the entire Catholic right harshly criticizes for having created confusion.

Although 80 percent of the cardinal electors were appointed by Francis, Vian believes that does not mean his successor will be a "Bergoglian." "The new pope will somehow have to distance himself from Francis if he wants to survive the confrontation, which will be relentless," he affirms, noting that in the media, Francis currently appears to be at the apex of his approval ratings, just as John Paul II was upon his death twenty years ago (April 2, 2005).

A 73-year-old professor of ancient Christian literature at the prestigious La Sapienza University, the retired journalist and author does not hide his doubts when asked about the two most talked-about candidates —Cardinal Pietro Parolin and the Filipino Cardinal Luis Antonio Tagle, both mentioned by Italian newspapers since Francis's confinement in the Gemelli Hospital. "These are two candidates who are indeed very likely," he states, "but it's a prediction that could also be refuted. Tagle, in fact, has been significantly affected by administrative issues, by how he has managed his congregation [the Dicastery for the Evangelization of Peoples]. The Italian candidates most likely to be considered are Parolin, Zuppi [Matteo, archbishop of Bologna and president of the Episcopal Conference], and Pizzaballa [Pierbattista, Latin patriarch of Jerusalem]. But there are two other European cardinals who I think have a chance: Cardinal Arborelius [Anders, Bishop of Stockholm], who has an extraordinary profile, and the Hungarian Cardinal Primate Péter Erdő. What I believe is that with the next pope, we will return to Europe, that Francis's successor will be European."

Asked about an assessment of Francis's pontificate, Vian speaks of an "important" papacy, one that has reached places many did not think were possible, but with "both highs and lows." He acknowledges that "Francis, in an age of very basic communication, has managed to handle it in an extraordinary way. But at the same time, he has been a contradictory pope, because he often improvised and sometimes said very different things." For example, regarding his possible resignation, "at first, he said he was glad that Pope Benedict XVI had opened a path and said there would be many emeritus popes. But then he evolved, saying that he would never resign. I personally have always been convinced that Francis would never have resigned."

Vian also criticizes Francis for canonizing John Paul II too quickly, given the entire sexual abuse issue. "Canonizing him seemed unwise to me, because in the end, his policies are also canonized. I believe that's precisely why popes shouldn't be canonized. Francis was the only pope to canonize three of his predecessors; he canonized the papacy, in a way, and he took papal absolutism to its extreme. Now it is urgent that the papacy reform itself and return to the collegiality outlined by the Second Vatican Council."

How, I ask, can we speak of papal absolutism with Francis, a pontiff who launched the Synod on Synodality, a process of global listening that included lay people and women, which, in theory, he left in motion?

"The Synod on Synodality is a good example of this: it was an excellent method of consultation, but without any results. At the Synod on the Amazon, Pope Francis didn't even approve the *viri probati*, the ordination of married men in remote areas. And let's not even talk about the female diaconate: two commissions were created, with their members carefully chosen so that there was a 50 percent vote in favor and 50 percent against, which is fine, because both sides must be heard. But afterward, the pope didn't make any decision; rather, it seems he wasn't in favor of the female diaconate. And so on.... The contradictions of Francis's pontificate are very evident. But, despite everything, we must bow our heads before this pope who took his pontificate to an extreme. I confess that I was very moved Monday morning when I learned of his death, because only twenty hours earlier, and until his last breath, the pope wanted to be with the faithful and give his most solemn blessing, *Urbi et Orbi*, to the city and to the world."

IRENE AND I TAKE A TAXI to the Vatican's Press Office, where a formidable line of journalists is trying to get accreditation.

The Press Office publishes the first images of the lying in state that began last night in the chapel of Santa Marta, Francis's residence inside the Vatican. His personal nurse, Massimiliano Strappetti, provides these details of his final moments to Vatican News:[10]

"Thank you for bringing me back to the Piazza," Bergoglio had told him. On Sunday, evidently aware of his increasing frailty before making that final farewell ride in the popemobile, he had asked him, "Do you think I can do it?" Strappetti, who in recent years had become Francis's most trusted person regarding health issues, also recounted

---

10. Salvatore Cernuzio, "Sus últimas horas: sereno y agradecido por volver a la Plaza," **www.www.vaticannews.va,** April 22, 2025.

that after that last ride in the popemobile on Sunday, his final effort, the pope had eaten dinner in the afternoon and then rested "peacefully."

Around 5:30 AM, Strappetti said, the first symptoms of a stroke and subsequent heart failure appeared, prompting immediate intervention by the pope's medical assistants. More than an hour later, after reaching out from his sickbed to touch Strappetti, who was at his side, the pope fell into a coma.

When those closest to him realized this, Francis received the anointing of the sick from the Argentine priest Juan Cruz Villalón—another of the "guardian angels" who cared for the former archbishop of Buenos Aires until the end. "He didn't suffer; everything happened quickly," said those who were at his side in those final moments.

"It was a discreet, almost sudden death, without long waits or too much fuss for a pope who has always kept his state of health a secret. A death that occurred the day after Easter, the day after he blessed the city and the world, the day after he embraced the people again after a lengthy absence. That people to whom, from the first moments of his election on March 13, 2013, he had promised a journey 'together,'" a source concludes.

THERE'S MORE NEWS. At General Congregation #1, the cardinals present decide that Pope Francis's solemn funeral—which will be much simpler than those of his predecessors, by his own choice—will be next Saturday, April 26. The faithful will be able to bid him their final farewell starting Wednesday at 9:00 AM in St. Peter's Basilica in a three-day lying in state that will end on Friday afternoon. Fifty cardinals participate in the meeting. Gerry learns that there are no interpreters, a problem for cardinals who do not speak Italian.

Gerry, a Vaticanist expert on Asia, notes that China was one of the last governments to express its condolences for the death of Pope Francis. It did so when, at a press conference in Beijing, the Spanish newspaper *ABC* asked for a comment on his legacy and its significance for Vatican-China relations, as well as for the Catholic community in China. Guo Jiakun, spokesperson for the Chinese Ministry of Foreign Affairs, stated: "China expresses its condolences for the death of Pope Francis. In recent years, China and the Vatican have maintained constructive collaboration and fruitful exchanges. China is willing to work with the Vatican to further improve China-Vatican relations." When asked by Bloomberg whether the Chinese government planned to send a representative to the Pope's funeral, Guo Jiakun replied: "I have no information to share at this time."[11]

There had been speculation that Beijing might send a Catholic bishop to the funeral, given the provisional agreement with the Vatican on the nomination of bishops. However, as will later be revealed, despite Francis's efforts to build bridges with China and avoid criticism of what is happening there, Beijing will decide not to send an official representative to the funeral, likely because the Holy See is one of only ten states that still maintain diplomatic relations with Taiwan, which, for its part, will have a representative at the funeral.

Meanwhile, as I am writing up these items in coordination with my newspaper editor and friend Juli Nassau, Spain's *ABC*'s Javier Martínez Brocal informs us via WhatsApp that he has just been to Francis's funeral chapel, which has been open since last night in the chapel of the Santa Marta residence. He says it's open on a limited basis to those who knew Pope Francis and to his collaborators, and advises us to go. I immediately call Gerry.

Emilce Cuda—an Argentine theologian and secretary of the Pontifical Commission for Latin America—and her husband, Patrick Dunbar, who have become our very close friends, have been in the chapel since it opened. Emilce tells me the room is freezing cold and asks me to bring her a sweater.

We arrive around 2:00 PM. There is no line at Santa Marta. It is indeed cold in the Santa Marta chapel; the air conditioning is on, as it is in any funeral chapel. The silence is total. There are people sitting in chairs, praying. Those arriving are approaching to pay tribute to Jorge Bergoglio, who lies in a simple wooden coffin, as he wished, in front of the altar. The coffin is lined with a burgundy cloth. Although Pope Francis would have truly preferred that the coffin be placed on the ground, so that it would be easily visible, the coffin is placed on two very simple platforms, completely different from the old papal catafalques worthy of monarchs, which he made known he did not want. Nor did he want the triple coffin of wood, zinc, and oak: he didn't want privileges, but rather to be buried "with dignity, like any Christian," he had told Javi Brocal.[12] Just as he lived in an austere and

---

11. Foreign Ministry Spokesperson Guo Jiakun's Regular Press Conference on April 22, 2025, Ministry of Foreign Affairs, People's Republic of China.

12. Elisabetta Piqué, "Me dolió que se usara a Benedicto: el papa Fran-

ordinary manner, he wanted a simple, austere repose. The lower platform is of plain wood; the upper one, smaller, is covered with the same burgundy fabric that lines the coffin. Both platforms rest on a rectangular carpet that stands out from the gray and yellow marble of the floor of the modern chapel of Santa Marta.

The burgundy is in keeping with the red chasuble in which the pope is dressed, wearing his white papal miter and with his hands clasped around a rosary with black wooden beads. He wears his silver archbishop's ring—which he always preferred to the Fisherman's Ring, which he wore only in the most solemn ceremonies—and, in that scandal of normality that was his papacy, his black leather orthopedic shoes with laces, which are so surprising at first because their soles are worn. His face is very different from the one the world saw on the night of March 13, 2013, when Francis appeared with an informal *"Buonasera!"* His complexion is waxy and deflated. He has a bruise near his left eye, the result of the stroke that caused his death. His eyes are closed, his expression serene.

When Gerry and I reach the coffin, I cannot see all those details. In fact, I cannot see anything because I cannot bear to see Father Jorge like this. And when I remember that there, in that same place, on the afternoon of March 15, 2014, Father Jorge, then more vital than ever, had married Gerry and me, in a ceremony with our children as altar servers. Juampy was 8, Caro 5.

What happens next completely astounds me. That steely facade I boasted about crumbles. I burst into unstoppable tears, sobbing like never before in my life, not even when my parents died. Gerry hugs me, gives me a handkerchief, and immediately helps me sit in a beige velvet chair in the front row, on the right, where I continue to cry, not recognizing myself. It's a cathartic cry, breaking the sepulchral silence of Santa Marta and even disturbing—I imagine—the two young Swiss Guards keeping watch over Francis's coffin with their halberds and striped suits.

I can't stop crying. I have never cried like this. I recall that my father, who was no longer in good health but happy, and Ana, his wife, were also present at that unforgettable wedding. (*It was also my birthday, and what a birthday gift I was receiving!*) *No one else.* Juampy, in addition to being an altar boy alongside Caro, had had to be the photographer, using one of our cell phones. And Pope Francis, loving

---

cisco reveló detalles de la convivencia entre dos papas y lanzó dardos contra su secretario," *La Nación*, April 2, 2024.

toward them and all of us present, had celebrated a simple ceremony, full of love, empathy, and humor, in which not only Gerry and I had been protagonists, but also Juampy and Caro.

For Father Jorge, that marriage had been a real achievement. He knew that, unlike Gerry, I really didn't care at all about getting married. As I had once told him, marriage was to me a mere formality, because I felt that, in the eyes of God, up above, Gerry and I were already married.

"Please don't appear in jeans, okay?" he had said, laughing, a few days earlier when I had asked him on the phone, "But what should I wear to the wedding?" And when Gerry, in another conversation, mentioned that I had bought a dress—obviously not white, but blue, very cool and simple, from Gap that he thought was too short, Father Jorge had taken my side: "Let her be free [to choose]."

I also remember the phone call that Father Jorge had made to me from the hospital, on February 19, despite the fact that he had difficulty speaking and in which he tried to de-dramatize his pneumonia: "I'm getting better," he told me, so that we wouldn't worry.

And the last call, on April 9, in which, again, despite the fact that he did not have to speak because it was difficult for him, he sent good vibes. "Thank you very much for the *Milanese*!" was his last phrase, surely said with effort, but with that same positive attitude, full of joy, strength, hope. He was referring to the *Milanese*—(breaded meat, what the Germans call *schnitzel*)—we had left for him in Santa Marta that day so that he could celebrate with his Argentine secretaries his improvement for that surprise public appearance of the previous Sunday. That day, when Gerry and I brought him the Milanese (packaged anonymously), he had just received a visit from King Charles and Queen Camilla, something that earned us a "scoop."[13]

Speaking of *milanesas*, I also remember a lunch we had with him in Santa Marta one Sunday in the summer of 2019. Then, to entertain the children—he was always into the details—he asked the cooks to make a different menu for them: *milanesas* with fries, to the happiness of Juan Pablo and Carolina! That time Gerry's son Edwin had also been there. And Caro, then 11 years old, had prepared for him, the previous afternoon, a *chocotorta* (typical Argentinian cold cake made

---

13. Elisabetta Piqué, "El Vaticano difundió la foto del encuentro del papa Francisco con el rey Carlos III y la reina Camila," *La Nación*, April 10, 2025; Gerard O'Connell, "Breaking: Pope Francis meets with King Charles III at the Vatican," *America*, April 9, 2025.

with Chocolinas, sweet chocolate cookies dipped in milk, cream cheese and *dulce de leche*), which we ate for dessert. Then Father Jorge chatted a lot with the kids, asking them about school. With Caro, always shy, he talked about classical music and told her that he hoped one day to hear her play the piano.

Amidst those memories and sobs, Emilce and Patrick come over to give me an unforgettable hug. They also are devastated. I take the opportunity to give Emilce my sweater, because it truly is very cold.

I calm down. We stay there in silence, praying and observing, for at least half an hour. We cannot stay longer because we must keep working.

I grab my notebook. To the left of the coffin there is a candle on an antique candelabra. The gendarmes control the flow of people: with gestures, they indicate who should advance in line to approach the coffin and say goodbye, and who should stop and wait in silence. At the entrance, they warn that taking photos or videos is strictly prohibited. But no one is interested in that; what matters is the saying goodbye.

Some leave bouquets of flowers: two large yellow sunflowers are visible, although most are white roses, the ones beloved by Pope Francis, a devotee of Saint Therese of Lisieux. "When I have a problem, I ask the saint not to solve it for me, but to take it in her hands and help me accept it. And as a sign, I always receive a white rose," he used to explain.

Among the people entering, there are some in suits and ties, very elegant, but also many in jeans and sneakers, dressed in work clothes or uniforms. There are ushers, gardeners, workers, priests, nuns from various congregations, an Orthodox bishop, a person on crutches, and families arriving with children in their arms.

In the back rows, almost blending in with other people, because he always kept a low profile, the Argentine priest Juan Cruz Villalón is praying silently. We go to give him a hug and to thank him for the immense love, the tenderness with which he cared for Francis until the very last moment. For many, the image of Juan Cruz adjusting the nasal cannulas with infinite affection during the pope's first public appearance in St. Peter's Square after his hospitalization, at the end of the Jubilee Mass for the Sick, as well as his speaking in Francis's ear during his final ride in the popemobile, his farewell last Sunday, will remain unforgettable.

Juan Cruz, also devastated but serene, consoles us: he tells us that Francis read the last email message we sent him on Easter Sunday night, the 20th, and that he was happy to have received it. "He loved you very much."

I WRITE A CATHARTIC ARTICLE, I send a video requested by my paper, I do more live broadcasts for LN+, and CNN sends me an Uber to do a live interview from their office terrace on Via di Col di Lana.

Gerry, working like crazy, is also doing live standups for various television channels in Canada and the United Kingdom.

We finish very late again. Thank goodness Irene stopped by the supermarket. Pasta with zucchini, prosciutto, mozzarella, red wine. We are grateful for the provisions, although the grief of the moment subdues any joy.

APRIL 23, WEDNESDAY [GERRY]
*The Goodbye Begins*

WE SLEPT LITTLE. At 8:30 AM Betta and I were already at the Vatican. The area was fenced off, filled with police with metal detectors controlling access. Today begins the grand farewell to Pope Francis, and a crush of people throng to bid him farewell during the three-day lying-in-state in St. Peter's Basilica.

With the scenography, theatricality, and solemnity that only the millennial Catholic Church possesses, the great bells of St. Peter's Basilica toll the papal death sequence of mourning, with Il Campanone, the largest and most famous of bell of all, sounding a deep, slow, sorrow-laden knell of bronze. The giant screens in St. Peter's Square show that, after a moment of prayer in Latin presided over by the American Cardinal Camerlengo Kevin Farrell, and accompanied by the Sistine Choir, Pope Francis's coffin slowly began to be carried from his home in Santa Marta to St. Peter's Basilica.

It is an unprecedented ceremony. Never before has a pope decided to break with all protocols to live in a place like Santa Marta, an austere hotel for ecclesiastics, instead of in the sumptuous Apostolic Palace. It would have caused him "psychiatric problems" to have lived in the papal apartment, a virtual gilded cage, as Jorge Bergoglio always explained, this pope from the end of the world who broke all conventions and decided to live in community and without supervision in Santa

Marta. From this building, constructed in 1996 during the pontificate of John Paul II as a residence for cardinals during a conclave or for other ecclesiastics passing through the Vatican, began the first of the solemn ceremonies to bid farewell to Pope Francis with full honors. At nine o'clock sharp, a procession of eighty cardinals dressed in their scarlet ceremonial robes and caps begins. Many of them are newly arrived in Rome from around the world to participate in the conclave that will elect Francis's successor, their faces sad, grief stricken.

On a sunny April morning, to the somber cadence of the sorrowful bell strokes, Francis's coffin advances slowly behind them. Made of simple wood and covered in a red cloth, it is carried on the shoulders of fourteen *sediaries* (chair bearers) wearing white gloves, escorted by eight halberdiers of the papal Swiss Guard in their striped suits and fourteen penitentiaries with red stoles and torches. Behind them are members of the papal family and those who cared for the pope with absolute dedication and fidelity until the end. There are his personal secretaries—the Argentine priests Juan Cruz Villalón and Daniel Pellizón and the Italian priest Fabio Salerno—his nurses, Massimiliano Strappetti and Andrea Rinaldi, and his valet Piergiorgio Zanetti. Also present are a number of distant Bergoglio relatives who reside in Italy. And others too.

The "translation," as the funeral procession is called, accompanied by psalms and antiphons, after passing through the Square of the Protomartyrs (the place where Peter was crucified upside down, and many other Christians were executed), then under the Arch of the Bells adjacent to the basilica, reaches St. Peter's Square. When the coffin enters the Vatican basilica through the central door, a spontaneous, almost liberating applause, full of affection, breaks out among the thousands of people watching this first ceremony from the giant screens in St. Peter's Square. While the choirs intone the litanies of the saints, the procession moves slowly to the Altar of Confession, under the shadow of Bernini's majestic Baldachin. Francis's coffin is placed on a carpet, then cordoned off. It is without a catafalque, as he, the pope of simplicity, wanted, but on a simple wooden platform, the same one that had been used in the chapel of Santa Marta.

Cardinal Farrell, who was very close to the deceased Pope, sprinkles holy water and incenses his body—dressed in a white miter and red chasuble—beginning a Liturgy of the Word in Latin, in which prayers are said "for the deceased Francis, that the Prince of Shepherds, who always lives to intercede for us, may graciously receive him into his kingdom of light and peace."

In addition, prayers are recited for "the holy Church of God, that, faithful to her mandate, she may be the leaven of a renewal in Christ of the human family." "For the peoples of all nations, that, in respect for justice, they may form one family in peace and be united by fraternal feelings." And finally, "for all of us who are gathered here in prayer, that we may one day be reunited together in the kingdom of heaven."

Cardinals, bishops, priests, deacons, and other ecclesiastics, lay members of the Roman Curia, mourners, and others then proceed to bid farewell, bowing and crossing themselves before the pope's coffin. Then, only one person does not advance, but remains standing beside the coffin, weeping. It is Sister Geneviève Jeanningros, a nun of the Congregation of the Little Sisters of Jesus and niece of Léonie Duquet, one of the two French nuns who disappeared during the Argentine dictatorship (1976–1983). Sister Jeanningros, 82 years old, wearing her simple light blue habit and backpack, has lived for five decades in a mobile home next to an amusement park in Ostia, on the outskirts of Rome, where she does pastoral work with people in need from that community, trans women, and others. She had become a close friend of Pope Francis. Although some deacons initially tried to push her away, telling her she couldn't be there, that it wasn't her turn, that she had to come at another time, some of the gendarmes recognize her. They lead her to the coffin and allow her to stay there as long as she wishes. These images—which confirm the belief that the last shall be first—go viral.

Among those who also say goodbye is Luis Liberman, one of Jorge Bergoglio's many Argentine Jewish friends, rector of the University Institute of Water and Sanitation and founder of the Institute for Global Dialogue and the Culture of Encounter. "It's very strange, this is not him, this is not Jorge," Luis, who is our friend, will later tell us sadly. "Today my soul aches, but here we are, those of us who love the pope from the end of the world. I came to say goodbye to an inspiring leader who, until his last breath, sowed goodness, beauty, and hope, who did not remain silent in the face of injustice, war, or inequalities. A fighter for the human cause of the future: our common home," he says, still shaken and having just landed from Buenos Aires. "I come with the voices of my comrades who asked me to offer their prayers," adds Luis, another friend from Buenos Aires who had quietly come to Rome to chat with Bergoglio about his initiatives for access to drinking water for all. "I come because I believe that after so many years of joy and fraternal communion, I do not give up, nor do we renounce, our shared history."

AT NOON, with Betta, Irene, and many of the four thousand journalists who have landed in Rome and managed to get accreditation, we go to the first media pool organized by the Press Room to enter St. Peter's Basilica without having to wait in the increasingly long line that slowly moves up the Via della Conciliazione to say goodbye to the beloved Argentine pope.

"Pray for me," Francis always asked when saying goodbye to someone. And the thousands of people waiting in line—for at least five hours, under the sun during the day, or in the damp cold at night—do not disappoint him.[14]

You see people of all generations and nationalities. It's an impressive sight, although you don't see the human rivers that formed twenty years ago, after the death of John Paul II, when people queued for seventeen hours from Castel Sant'Angelo to pay their final respects to the Polish pope. And yet the fervor is similar.

"I missed the World Cup, and I wasn't going to miss this," says Agustín, a 42-year-old Argentine living in Germany who traveled a thousand kilometers to pay tribute to Francis. Betta makes short videos of all the interviewees.

"I took a 6:00 AM flight from Freiburg, but I left my home in the Black Forest at 2:00 AM because I wanted to be here. I couldn't pass up this opportunity because it's something that will never happen again, and I came to represent my entire family and Argentina, all those who might want to be here wholeheartedly at this moment," says this Buenos Aires native who works in tourism, draped in a blue and white flag and deeply moved after being able to stop and pray before Francis's simple coffin. Thanks to the flag he met Josefina, a 29-year-old journalist from San Nicolás de los Arroyos "in tourist mode," with whom he joined the long queue. "I've always been very Catholic since I was a child. At first, I had mixed feelings because I saw a Church that didn't provide many answers, but then with Pope Francis, I felt very, very welcomed for my life choices as well. I felt that he could not only understand situations much more, but also the world of today, the world that is changing and what is happening today," Agustín says.

Josefina agrees, having been present at Pope Francis's last appearance, on Easter Sunday. "I had him twenty meters away and I shouted at the top of my lungs, 'From Argentina, Francis, Argentina.' And he

---

14. Elisabetta Piqué, "Más de 61.000 fieles rindieron homenaje al Papa en la basílica de San Pedro," *La Nación*, April 24, 2025.

looked, heard my voice, and heard 'Argentina.' So that also makes me happy that he was able to say goodbye in the square where so many people were cheering his name, thanking him, and also praying for him, who had been saying 'pray for me' so much lately," she recounts. "I also feel very proud as an Argentine that the first Latin American Pope was Argentine and that he brought about this great change in the Catholic Church. Because we mustn't forget all the actions he took to open the Church—as he said, to everyone—that he raised the flag for the LGBT community, that he took a stand on several issues that perhaps the Church in other times ignored. So," she adds, "I am very proud of this pope who also spoke about social justice."

Norma Beatriz Santos, an Argentine nurse who has lived in San Benedetto del Tronto for thirty-two years, was one of the first to enter the basilica. She got up at dawn to do so. What did she feel when she saw the pope in his coffin? "Sadness. But hey, he did everything he could, even while suffering, and he didn't hide behind his fragility because he was the pope, and that's good for humanity. That's from Jesus," she says. "The only thing I criticize this pope for is that he didn't go to Argentina, that's the only thing. After all, he did everything he could, and I'm very proud," she says.

Gustavo and Cristal, a couple from Corrientes on vacation in Italy, say they were visiting St. Peter's Basilica last Monday and, as they left, learned of Francis's death because the bells began to ring. Gustavo, a 55-year-old doctor and poet, says, "What did he represent to us? Someone humble who changed the Church a little, who thought about the poor, who opened up to the gay community, who defended women, who fought against pedophilia, and who, I think, brought the Church to the people, and that makes Argentina proud."

"That's why they call him the People's Pope; he's our pride," adds Cristal, a 31-year-old businesswoman.

"These are completely mixed emotions," says Alonso Ortiz, a Mexican who works in the hotel industry. On the one hand, we feel proud to be here, very blessed, very fortunate. But at the same time, the event isn't something that makes us happy; it's very rare, but it's unique." When he planned this trip, he never imagined that he and his wife would be experiencing the first day of Pope Francis's funeral.

What did he mean to them? His wife Ana Paula, a 41-year-old psychologist, replies: "A revolutionary pope, a different kind of pope, who turned the screw, did things differently, with great courage. He's a great example of life for modern times. We believe in this religion, and today we believe that leaders are needed to revive these values of brotherhood and humanism, and we believe he did a great job in that regard."

"He was a great man, an excellent human being. I have no words to describe him. He's a saint," says Cecilia de Suza, a retired teacher originally from India but living in Rome, dressed in her country's traditional dress.

Of course, Italians are in the majority. "Being here is a great emotion, it's indescribable," says Marinella Ascaloni, with tears in her eyes. Like many others, she had traveled to Rome with her family from Friuli, a region in the northeast, to spend the long weekend that combined Easter Monday—the day of Francis's death—and April 25th, the holiday commemorating the Liberation of Italy from Nazi-fascism.

Rosanna Morabito, also visiting with her husband and two children from Turin, tells us, "We got up early to come, we waited in line for two hours, and it was an immense emotion, it was a beautiful thing. We stopped to pray for him. . . . Pope Francis was a charismatic person, who tried to unite the good with the bad. Poor thing, in the end he couldn't achieve his greatest desire, peace, but he certainly left a mark."

Her husband adds, "What kind of pope am I expecting? It's a good question, I don't know. I hope that whoever is elected will somehow remember everything Pope Francis did and will somehow continue in this direction of peace, of serenity, which is what we need."

"He was a very good person," agrees Pietro, a baker from the town of Bracciano on the outskirts of Rome, who starts waiting in line past noon with his wife and two-year-old baby. Summarizing the feelings of many, Pietro chooses a definition given by the popular Neapolitan singer, Gigi D'Alessio, to explain what Jorge Bergoglio meant to him: "Francis was a man dressed as a pope."

AFTER TWO DAYS OF BEING BLOCKED, unable to write anything, paralyzed by the death of Francis, I finally manage to find some catharsis and write "A Final Goodbye to My Friend, Pope Francis,"[15] a much-praised endnote in which I summarize these last few days of sadness and the immense emotion I felt when Betta and I were at the funeral chapel in Santa Marta, where we had been so many times.

---

15. Gerard O'Connell, "A Final Goodbye to My Friend, Pope Francis," *America*, April 23, 2025.

Some memories go back farther. Among them, when then-Cardinal Bergoglio came to our home for dinner on the evening of February 28, 2013, when together we watched on television the historic moment when the gates of Castel Gandolfo closed and the Swiss Guard withdrew, marking the end of Pope Benedict XVI's papacy.[16] Or the end of 2012 when he called me during a time when Elisabetta was covering one of the many wars in Gaza to ask how I was and to tell me that he was praying for God's protection for her. "We lost a friend on earth, but now we have a friend in heaven," I summarize.

THE ATMOSPHERE OF MOURNING and sadness is interspersed with the vertigo of the inexorably approaching conclave. Due to the Translation ceremony this morning, the second general congregation of cardinals today is to be held in the afternoon. These initial meetings discuss procedural issues, such as next Saturday's funeral, which will become a world summit of leaders, as many have already confirmed their presence.

Although Pope Francis clearly expressed that he wanted the ceremony to be as simple and austere as possible, there are some who would like to return to the pomp of yesteryear. But American Cardinal Kevin Farrell, who was chosen as *camerlengo* by Francis precisely because he trusted him, does not budge. Everything will be done as he intended.

Cardinals begin to arrive from all continents. Some lodge at their national colleges, such as the North American College for the United States, and various pontifical colleges for the other countries, such as the Philippines, Mexico, France, England. Jesuits stay at the Jesuit General Curia, while Augustinians, Dominicans, Franciscans, Salesians and others stay at the headquarters of their religious orders. Still others stay in the Vatican's guesthouses for ecclesiastics, namely, on Via Traspontina, Via della Scrofa—which is where Jorge Bergoglio stayed before his election —or in Santa Marta. There, as the cardinal electors will be numerous, a number never before seen, renovation work has already begun. And since all the rooms are required, Francis's private secretaries have already begun packing and boxing up all the belongings he didn't want destroyed, which are in rooms adjacent to his second-floor suite. All of this will be moved to a room in the papal apartment of the

---

16. Gerard O'Connell, *The Election of Pope Francis: An Inside Account of the Conclave that Changed History* (Orbis Books, 2019), 85.

Apostolic Palace. There are 252 cardinals from ninety-six countries, 135 of them electors (under 80 years of age), but it has been reported that two electors have withdrawn for health reasons.

Many complain about the absence of translators, which makes work difficult for the cardinal electors who represent seventy-one countries around the world. Several don't speak Italian—a necessary requirement for election—nor Latin, English, or French. It seems that Cardinal Farrell, the person ultimately responsible for this period of power vacuum, has sent for translators. He has also ordered identification tags because—and this is the big problem—the cardinals don't know each other.

APRIL 24, THURSDAY [GERRY]

*A Loose Cannon*

THE AIR IS ELECTRIC. While the massive farewell to Francisco in St. Peter's Basilica continues, Rome prepares for Saturday's funeral which 130 national delegations as well as some fifty heads of state and ten kings and queens are expected to attend, according to the Vatican Press Office, which has been flooded by accreditation requests from all over the world.

The countdown to the final farewell to Jorge Bergoglio has begun, as has the exceptional security operation that will include more than eleven thousand people, including the Italian armed forces.

The Eternal City begins protection operations by erecting barricades while helicopters fly overhead. The Vatican has installed giant screens and chemical toilets for an influx of at least 250,000 people.

Romans who can take advantage of the April 25 Liberation holiday escape to avoid Saturday's chaos and follow the proceedings on television.

In the midst of a climate of mourning and farewell, with flags at half-mast and electronic billboards bearing the image of Pope Francis and just one word "Grazie!" ("Thank you!"), the novelty is that the powerful will not be the only ones with a prominent view of the funeral on Saturday. In addition to simplicity, Francis wanted the poor to be at the center of the ceremony.

As a Vatican announcement states: "The poor have a privileged place in the heart of God. So, also, in the heart and teaching of the Holy Father, who had chosen the name Francis to never forget them. For this reason, a group of poor and persons in need will be present on the steps that lead to the Papal Basilica of Saint Mary Major (Santa Maria Maggiore) to pay the last tribute to Pope Francis before the burial of his coffin. "This does not please some cardinals who never accepted the notion of "a poor church for the poor," as stated by Jorge Bergoglio on March 16, 2013. They recoiled from the homeless who were welcome to camp at night around the Vatican, and where, thanks to Francis, they also had access to showers, a hairdresser, and even a home.

THE AUXILIARY BISHOP OF ROME, Monsignor Benoni Ambarus, director of the Diocesan Office for Prison Pastoral Care, explains that before Pope Francis died he donated 200,000 euros[17] as a final gift to a pasta factory in the juvenile prison in Casal del Marmo, a penitentiary where the pope washed the feet of prisoners on Holy Thursday in 2023. Ambarus, whom Francis nicknamed "Don Ben," told him that the pasta factory they had was under a heavy mortgage and that "if we managed to cover it we would lower pasta prices, we would sell more, and we could hire more workers." The pope, who gave cash to many people, replied: "I am almost out of money, but I still have something in my account."

Moved by his death, Romanian-born Ambarus also says that the pope invited him to accompany him to the Rebibbia prison on December 26, when he became the first pontiff to open a holy door in a penitentiary. "Don Ben, come with me," he would say. "I was always Don Ben for him. I don't think he knew my name or my surname," he adds. "The pope was extremely inspiring for the detainees," he says, evoking the Gospel of St. Matthew.

Since Monday, "Don Ben" has been receiving countless messages from detained people who say they feel orphaned. "Yesterday some detainees asked me to put a flower on Francisco's tomb," he said. "But

---

17. Elisabetta Piqué, "El último regalo de Francisco antes de morir: donó 200.000 euros a una cárcel de menores," *La Nación*, April 24, 2025.

I am really working so that his favorite children can be at the funeral. We will see what we can do," he concludes.

The Italian Penitentiary Administration Department (DAP) announces that, if a number of conditions are met, special permits will be granted to some prisoners to attend the funeral. In certain prisons the prisoners may be able to follow the live transmission of the final farewell.

"I ENTERED THE ROOM and the pope had his eyes open. I tried speaking to him, but he did not answer. I gave him a caress." These are the words of the Roman surgeon Sergio Alfieri, who told the newspapers *Corriere Della Sera*[18] and the *Repubblica*[19] about the dramatic moments[20] after he arrived at Santa Marta on Monday morning.

Alfieri, who knew Francisco well because he had twice performed colon surgery on him (in 2021 and 2023) and had accompanied him in these recent, difficult last months of his life, said that on Monday at about 5:30 AM the pope's personal nurse Massimiliano Strappetti had called him and said, "The Holy Father is in very bad shape; we must return him to the Gemelli Hospital."

Twenty minutes later Alfieri arrived at Santa Marta. What he found was that, although the pope's eyes were open and he had no respiratory problems, he was unresponsive—even to painful stimuli. "At that moment," Alfieri said, "I understood that there was nothing that could be done. He was in a coma."

"We would have run the risk of his dying during the transfer [to the Gemelli]," Alfieri explained, adding that a hospitalization would have been useless. Furthermore, like anyone else, the pope wanted to die at home. Strappetti knew this. "When we were in the hospital he always said it," he stated. "He died without suffering, and at home. When he was at the Gemelli, he didn't say 'I want to return to Santa Marta.' He said 'I want to go home.'"

---

18. Fiorenza Sarzanini, "Sergio Alfieri, il medico di Papa Francesco e gli ultimi minuti," *Corriere della Serra*, April 25, 2025.

19. Elena Dusi, "Alfieri: 'A noi medici papa Francesco chiese di non essere intubato,'" *La Repubblica*, April 24, 2025.

20. Elisabetta Piqué, "Los últimos minutos del Papa, según su médico personal: 'Tenía los ojos abiertos, pero no contestó; le di una caricia,'" *La Nación*, April 24, 2025.

After Francis's death, Alfieri stayed in his room at Santa Marta with Strappetti, the other personal nurse, Andrea Rinaldi, and the secretaries and other assistants. "Then everyone arrived and Cardinal Parolin asked us to pray and recite the rosary with him. I felt privileged, and now I can say that I was. That morning I gave him a caress as a last greeting," he says without hiding his emotion.

Alfieri, who, during Francisco's thirty-eight days of hospitalization for bilateral pneumonia, which marked the beginning of the end, became the exclusive medical spokesman for the updates on his condition—a conference at the beginning of the hospitalization and another at the end—tells of the last time they spoke, on the eve of Easter Sunday.

"I can say that he was doing well. He also told me he felt well. I brought him a cherry *crostata* [tart] that he liked and he told me 'I feel very well. I will resume my work and it will do me good.' He knew that the next day he was going to impart the *Urbi et Orbi* blessing and that we would meet again on Monday," he added. "He was happy to have been able to go to the Regina Coeli prison on Holy Thursday. He realized, however, that he was physically faltering and that he was having difficulty concentrating. He regretted not having been able to wash the feet of the detainees. 'This time I couldn't.' It was the last thing he said to me."

Alfieri confirms that, as many who knew the pope were aware, ever since the first colon operation in 2021 the pope had always asked doctors to avoid extraordinary therapeutic measures: "During the last hospitalization he expressly asked not to proceed in any case to intubation."

The doctor confesses that it did not seem wrong to him for the pope to disobey medical advice of taking at least sixty days of convalescence by resuming his work and making dangerous outings, first at the end of the Mass for the Jubilee of the Sick, and then to the Regina Coeli prison, to the Basilica of Saint Mary Major, and to other places.

"It was fine. He was the pope. It was as if, approaching the end, he had decided to do everything he had to do, as happened on Sunday when he accepted Strappetti's proposal to ride among the crowd in St. Peter's Square or as he did ten days ago, when he asked me to organize an encounter with all the people who had taken care of him during his hospitalization. When I told him that there were seventy people and that perhaps it would be better to do it after Easter and the end of his convalescence, he rebuked me—even though that audience would have been contrary to the recommendation that he avoid meeting with large groups. But Francisco's response was firm: 'I receive them on Wednesday,' he said, "Today," Alfieri concluded, "I have the feeling that he felt he had to do a series of things before he died."

AS ALWAYS, we go to the Vatican briefing by Matteo Bruni, the director of the Holy See Press Office, which usually takes place after the general congregation at 1:00 PM. Moreover, it is from the nearby Vatican Press Room that we make our television standups."

Although, due to the large number of journalists, the Vatican opens a second press room on the Dell'Ospedale Road a few blocks away, there is almost no space in the so-called John Paul II press hall. All seats are occupied.

Bruni says that the cardinals in General Congregation #3 discussed the challenges facing the Catholic Church. One hundred and thirteen Cardinals participated, fewer than half of them electors. We learn that now they have interpreters.

Since too few cardinals have yet arrived in Rome, they do not decide what everyone wants to know: the start date for the conclave to choose the 267th pontiff in the history of the Catholic Church.

The norms establish that the conclave should begin between fifteen and twenty days after the death of the pontiff, that is, between May 5 and 10.

"We still don't have a clear idea ourselves, so imagine if we are going to announce that to the world," joked a cardinal when leaving the pre-conclave meeting. All 252 cardinals are expected to arrive (135 electors and 117 non-voters). We think that the date of entry and confinement into the Sistine Chapel will be decided after Francisco's funeral.

Suddenly, a divisive issue erupts, unprecedented in the modern history of conclaves: the "Becciu case." It has to do with Italian cardinal Giovanni Angelo Becciu, who was one of Pope Francis's closest collaborators in the first years of his papacy, but who in 2020 fell into disgrace. He held the key position of substitute for General Affairs in the Secretariat of State [chief of staff], essentially the number-three man at the Vatican. He held that powerful position from 2011 to 2018, when Pope Francis appointed him prefect of the Congregation for the Causes of Saints. Francis disciplined him in September 2020 for a corruption scandal, forcing him to resign his position as prefect and his rights as a cardinal (including entry into a conclave), while still maintaining the title of cardinal. He was convicted in December 2023 of embezzlement and abuse of office in a highly public trial and sentenced to five and half years in prison, a sentence which he is currently appealing. Already before the death of Francis, Cardinal Becciu had launched a campaign to be readmitted to the College of Electors.

Challenging Pope Francis's sanction, he now claims that, in truth, he was pardoned by the pope and that for a cardinal to choose a pope is a duty, rather than a mere right.

His argument is backed by the conservative sectors. It has yet to be determined if the cardinals who participate in the general congregations have the power to reverse a decision of the pope.

Becciu participated in General Congregation #1 on Tuesday. "Everyone has been invited," Bruni said. But the truth is that, as the famous meals and gatherings where pre-conclave maneuvers begin to occur outside the public spotlight, the "Becciu case" is the one that is monopolizing the conversations.

And the big question is whether in history any cardinal's rights have ever been restored to anyone.

"The situation is very different from all past cases because, at the moment, there is no known papal document that specifies his status. We simply know of a statement from the Vatican Press Office indicating that Cardinal Becciu was losing his cardinal's rights. But what are a cardinal's rights?" asks Father Roberto Regoli, professor of church history at the Pontifical Gregorian University, in an interview with Elisabetta and Irene.

"There is no papal document that answers this question," he says and points out that "Professor Alberto Melloni, a renowned expert on the Second Vatican Council and the history of the Catholic Church, has commented that the election of a pope is not a right, but a duty of cardinals."

Could Cardinal Becciu then be correct? "The point is whether or not there is a document from Francis stating that he lost this rights and this duty," Regoli asserts.

Matteo Bruni reports that there were thirty-four interventions (formal speeches) at General Congregation #3. Some logistical issues were decided, such as that Argentine Cardinal Víctor Manuel "Tucho" Fernández, one of the pope's closest associates, will celebrate Mass on the sixth of the nine days of mourning for Pope Francis, instead of Cardinal Camerlengo Kevin Farrell. Also, Bruni said, "a shared reflection on the Church and the world began."

For Giacomo Galeazzi, a Vatican expert for the newspaper *La Stampa,* the Becciu case represents "a loose cannon."[21]

Beyond this issue, as is normal, the cardinals' meetings appear to be marked by a sharp division between progressives and conservatives.

Father Regoli warns that it is oversimplifying to speak of a struggle between reformers and conservatives, since someone can be a reformist on certain issues, but a conservative on others. "Furthermore, what does a reformer mean, a reformist?" he asks. He does confirm, however, that a climate of great division exists. "Obviously, the Church's urgent need now is to avoid polarization and internal conflicts and instead create a dynamic of unity among its pastors. There will always be differences, but it is not possible for everyone to be looking askance at one another," he insists, emphasizing that, in his view, "we need a candidate who is recognized as someone capable of uniting the various elements of the Catholic Church."

APRIL 25, FRIDAY [BETTA]

## *The* Cartonero *Returns*

TOMORROW IS POPE FRANCIS'S GRAND FUNERAL, and the approaching tsunami is in the air. For security reasons, everything will be closed off around the Vatican for the arrival of the more than 160 expected delegations. Irene is moving to our home because it is closer to the Vatican.

While we sip coffee and look through the newspapers spread out on the dining room table, Irene, after much insistence, finally gets me to relent: she interviews me as a biographer and friend of the pope for her newspaper.[22]

---

21. Giacomo Galeazzi, "Parolin, Zuppi e il conclave a trazione italiana," *La Stampa,* April 25, 2025.

22. Irene Hernández Velasco, entrevista a Elisabetta Piqué, "La gran amiga y biógrafa del Papa: 'El proceso que ha iniciado Francisco es irreversible,'" *El Confidencial,* April 26, 2025.

When she asks whether, as a woman, I am disappointed that Pope Francis did not open the door to the ordination of women deacons, I reply that Pope Francis always had enormous respect for women, a fact I experienced firsthand. When I was working as a war correspondent, my parents or my brothers often accused me of being crazy, of leaving my two young children in order to cover conflicts. Pope Francis never said that to me; he respected my work, my vocation, and never told me I had to stay home ironing shirts or taking care of my children. He always showed utmost respect for me as a woman and as a journalist. Regarding the female diaconate, I tell her that I believe the pope did not want to provoke a division in the Church with this, as with many other issues. Furthermore, the Church does not change overnight; it takes time. Pope Francis initiated processes, processes of transformation.

When Irene asks what some people did not understand about Francis—misunderstandings that occurred in Spain, Argentina, and many other countries—I answer that I think those who didn't understand him simply didn't want to understand him. His message was always very simple: to be with the least, to practice austerity in a world of superficiality and brands—a message that's the opposite of what we're witnessing, against the social injustice we see all over the world, where a minority lives in absolute luxury, compared to a vast, invisible majority of migrants, discarded people, detainees.... In fact, it's emblematic that Francis's last trip out of the Vatican was to visit prisoners in a jail, people accused of having committed crimes. But Francis's message is that God forgives everyone, God includes everyone, and the Church isn't there to condemn or to be perfect, but to welcome everyone.

What do I expect from the new pope? That he be someone capable of continuing the processes initiated by Francis. I hope, of course, that he's someone who thinks along the same lines and that he doesn't take any steps back. In reality, I believe the process Francis has initiated is quite irreversible, so I hope his successor will be a pope who is completely in line with him and his vision of a close to people, open, and young Church, as he was. Although he was 88 years old, I have never seen a person as open, as young in mind and spirit as he was.

WE HEAD TO THE VATICAN. There is a plot twist. By confirming the portrait of an intrigue-filled Vatican painted by fiction author Dan Brown, the great mystery threatening the pre-conclave meetings has been resolved on the eve of Pope Francis's solemn funeral: whether the controversial Italian Cardinal Giovanni Angelo Becciu can participate in the election of the next pontiff.[23]

And the answer will be "No." The pope left two letters in which he confirmed his will [resolve] to exclude Becciu from the conclave, the newspaper *Domani* reveals.[24] Cardinal Pietro Parolin would have shown these letters to Becciu to urge him to abandon his campaign.

Becciu was sentenced in December 2023 to five and a half years in prison by a Vatican court in the so-called "trial of the century," the first of its kind against such a high-ranking official in the Holy See.

Becciu, 77, always declared his innocence and even accused the Vatican justice system of being neither fair nor impartial, describing himself a scapegoat for shady operations hatched by his enemies.

And despite being deeply implicated in a shady plot—including a multimillion-dollar investment in London with secret funds from the Secretariat of State, as well as the transfer of unsolicited funds to his Sardinian relatives—he began, along with lawyers, a media campaign to clear his name. He surprised observers by suing *L'Espresso* magazine, which first revealed the scandal, and demanding enormous compensation for having lost his chance to become pope by being excluded from the conclave.

Determined to spin a narrative and defy Francis's sanction (evidenced by the fact that, according to the Vatican Press Office lists, Becciu, who is under 80, is not among the electors who will be allowed access to the Sistine Chapel), during the general congregations of these days he began an underground campaign to garner support for his right to participate in the conclave. Although in these preparatory meetings an oath is taken that no one should reveal what is discussed there, it is already an open secret that the issue arose during the General Congregation #1 on Tuesday.

Just as the pope had generously invited Becciu to participate in various ceremonies and liturgies in recent years, he was then also invited to these meetings. According to *Domani*, since there appeared to be no documents confirming the pope's intention to exclude him,

---

23. Elisabetta Piqué, "Revelan que Francisco dejó dos cartas que cerrarían el 'caso Becciu,' el escándalo que amenaza la elección del próximo papa," *La Nación*, April 26, 2025.

24. Giovanni Maria Vian, "Conclave, giallo su Becciu: spuntano le lettere del papa," *Domani*, April 25, 2025.

merely a press release, it seems that Cardinal Giovanni Battista Re, the 91-year-old dean of the College of Cardinals and the person in charge of this transition phase, initially told Becciu that he was in favor of his reinstatement on the list of electors.

Strongly disagreeing with this action, Cardinal Kevin Farrell, the *camerlengo* who manages the vacant seat, told Re that Pope Francis had clearly informed him that he did not want Becciu to enter the conclave. Two sources indicate that Re then reportedly told his Sardinian colleague Becciu to "step back," according to *Domani*, which noted that Becciu then returned to the fray, insisting that he would not renounce his duty to elect the next pope as there was no papal document on the matter.

The cardinal *camerlengo* reportedly remained silent. Amid an atmosphere not seen even in the film *Conclave*, the other cardinals "wisely" decide to address the matter later, when all the remaining cardinals have arrived.

And this is where the twist comes in the plot. "Last night, Cardinal Parolin reportedly showed Becciu two typewritten letters signed by the pontiff with an 'F' that would exclude him from the conclave: one from 2023 and the other from March 2025, when the pope was facing his latest and most serious illness," wrote *Domani*. "The Sardinian cardinal has taken note, but it's not clear whether he will step back or whether it will be up to the general congregations to decide," writes Giovanni Maria Vian, former director of *l'Osservatore Romano*, a journalist and historian, who is known to be close to Becciu.

WHEN ASKED AT THE DAILY BRIEFING about this bombshell news of the appearance of papal letters confirming an irrevocable papal decision, Press Office Director Matteo Bruni prefers not to comment on the subject. He simply informs dozens of journalists that General Congregation #4 took place this Friday with 149 cardinals in attendance. The new arrivals took the oath of secrecy, and he specifies that there were thirty-three interventions.

"They continued with the reading of the apostolic constitution *Universi Dominici Gregis*,"[25] he explains, referring to the procedural Vatican document drafted by John Paul II and amended by Benedict XVI, which details how the *sede vacante* and the election of the Roman pontiff is to work.

---

25. Apostolic constitution *Universi Dominici Gregis*, www.vatican.va.

The cardinals also made new logistical decisions, including that on Sunday, the day after Francis's funeral and burial, the cardinals will go to the Basilica of Saint Mary Major in the afternoon to recite Vespers at his tomb.

The Vatican yesterday released a photo of the projected tomb, which stands out for its striking simplicity. It is made of white marble from Liguria, the land of Jorge Bergoglio's ancestors; it has only a one-word Latin inscription that reads "Franciscus" and above it a reproduction of his silver pectoral cross with the image of the Good Shepherd. It will be noticed in a few days that there is an error in the engraving, a space that is too large between the letters F and R, something that will surely be fixed in the coming months.

"They also continued talking about the situation of the Church and the world," says Bruni, whose reports are always concise.

A true indicator of a growingly intense atmosphere, given that reports have begun to leak—as they always do—is the news that the cardinals are asked to be cautious and avoid giving interviews.

One such leak is another "bombshell" article that appears in the newspaper *Il Fatto Quotidiano*, which claims that at Thursday's general congregation the Italian Cardinal Claudio Gugerotti proposed establishing a commission of five cardinals—which would include Becciu—to decide whether to exclude him from the election of Francis's successor. Gugerotti, prefect of the Dicastery for the Eastern Churches and close to Parolin, nevertheless spoke out against the cardinal's eventual reinstatement. The Polish Cardinal Konrad Krajewski, papal almoner and prefect of the Dicastery for Charity, also spoke against it. On the other side, Italian Cardinals Lorenzo Baldisseri and Fernando Filoni spoke in support of Becciu's appeal.

As if this were not enough, in an ambience rather far from that of the Holy Spirit that is usually invoked to decide the election of a new pontiff, Becciu determines to go all out, persisting with his challenge. In statements to Reuters on Thursday night, he insists that he must be admitted as an elector because, according to him, the pope never intended to exclude him from the vote.[26] He even claims that in January, before his hospitalization, Francis told him that he had found "a solution" for his case. He also said he doesn't know whether the pope left instructions or not, and that "it will be my

---

26. Phillip Pullella, "Convicted Cardinal Wants to Vote for Pope, His Brother Prelates Must Decide," Reuters, April 24, 2025.

brother cardinals" who will come to a decision on the matter in the pre-conclave meetings.

Since tomorrow will be the day of the solemn funeral and subsequent six-kilometer procession from the Vatican to Saint Mary Major and, on Sunday, Cardinal Parolin will celebrate the second Mass of the *novemdiales*, the nine days of mourning scheduled for the Jubilee of Teenagers (had Francis not died, it would have been the canonization of Carlo Acutis), the next general congregation will be held on Monday April 28.

By then, more cardinals will surely have arrived. And many will have spoken among themselves about the Becciu issue, which, sadly, has monopolized the pre-conclave debate. This increasingly convoluted matter of intrigue, corruption, nepotism, and the typically "Roman" underground and press operations has many Vatican experts thinking it will reduce the chances of the next pope being Italian.

IN THIS RAREFIED BUT CAPTIVATING ENVIRONMENT, we write, make television appearances, talk to our sources.... Gerry also welcomes three colleagues from his team at *America* magazine who arrive from the United States. Sam Sawyer, SJ, editor in chief, arrives from New York; JD Long Garcia, senior editor, arrives from Phoenix, Arizona; and Colleen Dulle, associate editor and co-host with Gerry of the podcast "Inside the Vatican," arrives from New Orleans. Because Colleen arrived at the airport very early, she called Gerry to ask if she could leave her suitcase at our home until the apartment she's renting near the Vatican became available at noon. He agrees, and when she gets here, they have breakfast together, and Gerry tells her what has been happening at the Vatican and suggests what she can do.

An old acquaintance has also arrived in Rome: Sergio Sánchez, a *"cartonero"*[27] friend of Francis. Just as Jorge Bergoglio had wanted Sánchez to be by his side in the front row at the inaugural Mass of his pontificate on March 19, 2013, dressed in his work clothes and shoes, he expressly told his top collaborators that he wanted Sánchez

---

27. Cartoneros are people in Argentina who comb the streets or trash bins to gather recyclable materials in makeshift wagons for income. In some circles the term has a stigma, but in others it has become a symbol of resilience and solidarity.

to be there at his final farewell, alongside the most powerful people in the world. Sergio tells us that he arrived today just in time to enter Francis's lying in state in St. Peter's Basilica, minutes before it closed after 250,000 people had passed through. "I was there, just like when I came for the inauguration, two meters away from him, and always to his right. It brings back many memories of when I came to his inauguration, and I leave with a painful farewell on behalf of an organization that always fought for people's rights. As always, I hope I've left a good example of continuing to fight for Land, Housing, and Work, which are fundamental. All priests must continue to fight for that ideal, for a very important change for the world, not just for our country," the leader of the Unión por los Trabajadores Informales Populares (Trade Union for Informal and Self-Employed Workers) told us upon leaving the funeral chapel.[28]

"What did Jorge Bergoglio represent for me? A lot, and not just for me.... He was someone who always fought for the rights of the most vulnerable, and he was an extraordinary spiritual guide for us," he adds.

Sánchez was invited to travel to Rome by the Dicastery for Promoting Integral Human Development, the Vatican's social ministry, headed by Czech-Canadian Jesuit Cardinal Michael Czerny. Sánchez will return to Buenos Aires on Monday, in a lightning trip that reflects Pope Francis's fidelity to his friends and the consistency of his message to the very end. Gerry and I remember well when, in October 2015, Francis baptized one of Sergio's sons, Francisquito, in the chapel of Santa Marta. Also present at that ceremony were Juampy and Caro, and Michael Czerny (who was not yet a cardinal). Francisquito's godfather was the Argentine social leader Juan Grabois, also a member of the Dicastery for Promoting Human and Integral Development and a friend of the pope.

The *cartonero* tells us that he now hopes that the pope's successor will maintain Francis's commitment to the poor. "We hope that his legacy will be carried on by the person who will be elected as his successor. And that the next pope will be a pope for the poor, as Francis was, and that he will recognize, as Francis did, that in this world we must reach out and lift up those who have fallen," he tells us. Dressed in the blue jacket of the *cartoneros*, carters, and recyclers, the leader of the

---

28. Elisabetta Piqué, "La historia del cartonero amigo de Francisco que viajó a Roma para despedirlo," *La Nación*, April 25, 2025.

Movement of Excluded Workers (MTE) states that he traveled to represent all his colleagues and "to say that the social and popular movements are saddened, but that doesn't mean we're going to give up. We will continue trying to make the pope's voice be heard not only in Argentina but throughout the world," he says, "and to make it understood that we, the popular movements, the workers of the informal economy, who are present not only in Argentina, will continue working."

Pope Francis, who from the beginning of his pontificate denounced the current socioeconomic system as having "lost its human face," firmly supported the popular movements. He held meetings with them not only in Rome but also in different parts of the world—such as Santa Cruz de la Sierra,[29] Bolivia, and Temuco, Chile—and supported their main demands: land, shelter, and work, a universal basic wage, and a reduction of the workday. Such was their closeness that he even came to call them "social poets."

APRIL 26, SATURDAY [BETTA]
*The Farewell Popemobile*

WE WAKE AT DAWN. Juampy leaves first, at 5 AM—unheard for him. CNN asked him to be in position in the pen at St. Peter's Square at 5.30 AM. He had a hard time getting there because people were camping overnight near Piazza del Sant'Uffizio to get a good spot during the funeral.

Gerry, Irene, and I leave the house at 6 o'clock. Irene and I are quite exhausted because we had stayed up late chatting.

Incredibly, we find a taxi in Piazza di Pantaleo. Since everything is blocked off, Gerry gets out at the Vittorio Emanuele II Bridge to walk to the Augustinian House (Augustinianum) terrace for the CTV Canada broadcast. Between television standups, Gerry goes to the Braccio di Carlo Magno, a spectacular venue reserved for accredited press atop the left Bernini colonnade, where he meets Sam Sawyer.

---

29. Gerard O'Connell, "Pope in Bolivia Calls for 'Structural Changes' in World's Economy," *America*, July 9, 2015.

There, the Vatican has set up a special pen exclusively for accredited journalists traveling with Donald Trump.

Irene and I continue to Piazza del Risorgimento. At 7:30 AM I have to be there on a terrace rented by CNN. Torrents of faithful are arriving, as are black cars with diplomatic license plates. A street café is open — and being besieged — with the Red Cross, Civil Defense, and other personnel controlling access. We sit down to a much-needed cappuccino and *cornetto* and read the newspapers to kill time. Then we part ways. Irene goes to the Sala Stampa, and I go to the designated terrace, where I also meet Elise Allen. It will be nice to spend time together. It's chilly; thank goodness I brought a shawl. I have my first standup a few minutes after eight. We have chairs and a plastic table which I requested because I have to write for the newspaper. We also have a monitor to follow the live Vatican broadcast. Luisa Corradini, *La Nación*'s correspondent in Paris, will be in charge of providing color coverage from St. Peter's Square. As happened at the 2013 conclave, she brings reinforcement for the paper's coverage of the funeral.

ALTHOUGH THE POPE WANTED a simplified ceremony with less pomp, choosing a single, simple wooden coffin instead of the traditional three coffins of zinc, oak, and cypress, the funeral is nonetheless solemn, like those of his predecessors, and is marked by precise, age-old rites. Among the more than 170 delegations from around the world, there is an imposing presence of presidents — among whom are Argentina's Javier Milei, in a privileged position as the president of the deceased pontiff's country; the American Donald Trump (his predecessor, Joe Biden, also traveled privately); France's Emmanuel Macron; and the Ukrainian Volodymyr Zelensky. Many heads of government, and members of royal families including King Felipe VI and Queen Letizia of Spain, are here. In addition, representatives of other Christian churches are present. Notable among them are the ecumenical patriarch of Constantinople Bartholomew I and the number-two of the Patriarchate of Moscow, Metropolitan Anthony,[30] along with 220

---

30. When Metropolitan Anthony met Francis for the last time on July 12, 2024, he wore the Marian icon Salus Populi Romani as he does today at the funeral. In an interview with *La Repubblica* on July 24, 2025, he recalled that "When Pope Francis saw it during our last meeting, before his illness, he told

cardinals, 750 bishops, hundreds of priests, and leading representatives of Judaism, Islam, and the other world religions.

The funeral begins with a procession of *sediari*—traditional carriers of the (*sedia*) chair of the pope—who now, wearing white gloves and amid applause, carry the coffin to the sanctuary in St. Peter's Square a few minutes before 10:00 AM. The open Book of the Gospels is placed on the coffin by the Vatican's master of ceremonies. The cardinals arriving in procession from the basilica to the sound of the beautiful choirs of the Sistine Chapel bow before the coffin. In a Mass celebrated in Latin, the readings and prayers are in various languages—English, French, Arabic, Spanish, Portuguese, Polish, German, and Chinese—following the spirit of the Catholic Church, that is, the "universal" spirit.

Cardinal Re's homily, which summarizes Francis's life and legacy, first highlights how "the massive outpouring of affection and participation we have seen in these days, following his passing from this earth to eternity, shows us how deeply the intense pontificate of Pope Francis has touched minds and hearts." He is referring to the more than 250,000 people who lined up for three days to say their farewells at the funeral chapel set up in St. Peter's Basilica. Cardinal Re, 91, who has the delicate task of leading the pre-conclave meetings, recalls that Jorge Bergoglio, elected on March 13, 2013, at the age of 76, with the experience of having served for twenty-one years first as auxiliary bishop and then archbishop of Buenos Aires, previously held various positions of responsibility in the Society of Jesus.

Cardinal Re continues his homily by noting that "the decision to take the name Francis immediately seemed the pastoral plan and style choice on which he wanted to base his pontificate, seeking inspiration from the spirit of Saint Francis of Assisi.... He maintained his temperament and form of pastoral leadership, and from the beginning left the imprint of his strong personality on the governance of the Church, establishing direct contact with people and communities, eager to be close to everyone, with special attention to those in difficulty, giving himself without measure, especially to the marginalized, the least among us....

"He was a pope among the people with a heart open to everyone. Furthermore, he was a pope attentive to the signs of the times and what the Holy Spirit was awakening in the Church."

---

me that, in a short time, when I go to invoke the Mother of God at the Basilica of Saint Mary Major, I could also pray in front of his tomb. So it was."

Then, highlighting the revolution Francis set in motion with his totally different way of being, he adds: "With his characteristic vocabulary and language, rich in imagery and metaphors, he always sought to illuminate the problems of our time with the wisdom of the Gospel. He did so by offering a response guided by the light of faith and encouraging us to live as Christians amid the challenges and contradictions of recent years, which he loved to describe as an 'epochal change.'

"He had great spontaneity and an informal way of addressing everyone, even those far from the Church. Full of human warmth and deeply sensitive to current challenges, Pope Francis truly shared the anxieties, sufferings, and hopes of this time of globalization, seeking to console and encourage with a message capable of reaching people's hearts in a direct and immediate way.... His charisma of welcome and listening, combined with a way of acting appropriate to today's sensitivities, touched hearts, seeking to awaken moral and spiritual sensibilities. The primacy of evangelization was the guiding principle of his pontificate. With clear missionary vision, he spread the joy of the Gospel, which was the title of his first apostolic exhortation, *Evangelii gaudium.*"

Cardinal Re also emphasizes that the guiding thread of the pope's mission was "the conviction that the Church is a home for all, a house with its doors always open." He recalls that Francis often used the image of the Church as a "field hospital" after a battle, to care for the wounded. "A Church determined and willing to take on the problems of people and the great anxieties that tear apart the contemporary world; a Church capable of bending down to every human being, regardless of their creed or condition, to heal their wounds. Countless were his gestures and exhortations on behalf of refugees and displaced persons. His insistence on working on behalf of the poor was constant," Re adds, recalling his Francis's trip to Lampedusa, "an island that symbolizes the tragedy of emigration, with thousands of people drowning at sea," a statement that draws applause. He also recalls Francis's trips to the island of Lesbos, to the border between Mexico and the United States, and to Iraq in 2021, a journey "made in defiance of all risks. That difficult apostolic visit was a balm for the open wounds of the Iraqi people, who had suffered so much from the inhuman actions of the Islamic State. It was also an important trip for interreligious dialogue, another significant dimension of his pastoral work."

The cardinal points out that "with the 2024 apostolic visit to four countries in Asia-Oceania, the pope reached 'the most peripheral periphery of the world.' Pope Francis always placed the Gospel of mercy at the center, repeatedly emphasizing that God never tires of forgiving us. He always forgives, whatever the situation might be of the person who asks for forgiveness and seeks to return to the right path."

He also notes that "mercy and the joy of the Gospel were two key words for Pope Francis. In contrast to what he defined as 'the throwaway culture,' he spoke of a culture of encounter and solidarity. The theme of fraternity ran throughout his pontificate in vibrant tones."

Cardinal Re then mentions Francis's most significant writings, such as the encyclical *Fratelli Tutti*, the document on "Human Fraternity for World Peace and Living Together" signed in Abu Dhabi, and the encyclical *Laudato Si'*, dedicated to the care of our common home.

In front of an audience of people in power—among them Ukrainian President Zelensky, who was applauded when he arrived at the square—Cardinal Re emphasizes Pope Francis's constant call for peace. "Faced with the outbreak of so many wars in recent years, with inhuman horrors and countless deaths and destruction, Pope Francis incessantly raised his voice, imploring peace and calling for common sense and honest negotiation to find possible solutions, because war is nothing more than the death of people, the destruction of homes, hospitals, and schools. War always leaves the world 'Build bridges, not walls' is an exhortation Pope Francis repeated many times, and his service to the faith as the successor of the Apostle Peter was always linked to service to humanity in all its dimensions."

With a voice growing in intensity, drawing renewed applause, he concludes, "In spiritual union with all of Christendom, we are here in great numbers to pray for Pope Francis, that God may welcome him into the immensity of his love. Pope Francis used to conclude his speeches and meetings by saying: 'Do not forget to pray for me.' Dear Pope Francis, now we ask you to pray for us and from heaven to bless the Church, to bless Rome, to bless the whole world, as you did last Sunday from the balcony of this basilica in a final embrace with all the People of God, but also with all humanity that seeks the truth with a sincere heart and holds high the torch of hope."

His final words unleash a torrent of applause and profound emotion from the crowd.

AS THE HOURS PASS, in a deeply meditative atmosphere and under the gradually intensifying heat of the sun, some people protect themselves with umbrellas. After reciting the Lord's Prayer in Latin, at the moment of exchanging the sign of peace, world leaders shake hands.[31] Trump is then seen turning to shake hands with Macron and other leaders nearby. During the ceremony, Macron and his wife, Brigitte, appear to share deep feelings. Brazilian President Lula, an admirer of the pope, is visibly moved.

Some four hundred priests distribute Communion to the crowd, largely composed of young people from various countries.

As the silence is broken by the squawks of the seagulls that often hover in the area, the rite of the final recommendation begins. The enormous bells of St. Peter's begin to ring. The litany of the saints is intoned, followed by the rite of Valediction and the final farewell, pronounced in Latin by the Cardinal Vicar of Rome, Baldo Reina.

The finale is a beautiful ancient supplication intoned by the patriarchs of the Eastern Churches, based on the Byzantine liturgy for the deceased.

During the final response, Cardinal Re sprinkles holy water on the coffin, incenses it, and prays that the pope's soul be commended "to the mercy of God." At that moment, a light breeze rises, stirring some pages of the Book of Gospels. A striking image, also seen at the end of the funeral of John Paul II, another pontiff who gave his all to the very end and who died in April 2005, like Francis, after Easter. When, at the conclusion of the ceremony, the coffin is carried back into the basilica, the crowd—which not only packs the square but also extends out in front of dozens of giant screens along Via della Conciliazione and in Piazza del Risorgimento and Castel Sant'Angelo—erupts into sustained applause.

Moments later, a sort of final "miracle" from Pope Francis occurs: an unexpected face-to-face meeting between Donald Trump and Volodymyr Zelensky. In an image published by the Ukrainian president on his social media, which has become the source for breaking news, the two appear face to face, conversing confidently, almost in a confessional tone, sitting on two simple chairs inside St. Peter's Basilica.

---

31. Elisabetta Piqué, "Una emotiva homilía, 400.000 personas y su último 'milagro': así fue la despedida a Francisco en el Vaticano," *La Nación*, April 27, 2025.

Weeks earlier, in the Oval Office of the White House, Trump and his vice president had humiliated Zelensky live and in person.

ELISE AND I ARE STILL on the terrace in Piazza del Risorgimento, and it is now quite hot. We have been listening to CNN's live broadcast. I am called on live just as the historic procession transporting Pope Francis's body from the Vatican to the Basilica of Saint Mary Major begins. Suddenly I'm stunned by Pope Francis's final big surprise: the transfer is not in a classic, gloomy, and sad black hearse. No! The transfer is in a white popemobile, the same one he used in his 2016 visit to Mexico and which Mexico later gave to the Vatican in 2017 for the twenty-fifth anniversary of diplomatic relations. A cardinal will later confirm to Gerry and me that Francis had decided down to the last detail how he wanted his final farewell to be.

I'm on air, speaking with CNN's Anderson Cooper, and I am so amazed by this brilliant move by Francis that it comes from my heart to say just that: we are seeing Francis's last great surprise. Cooper asks me if it was Francis's decision to use the popemobile and, without hesitation, I reply: "Of course!" The choice of that vehicle transforms the atmosphere. It is not the classic atmosphere of mourning that existed, for example, during the transfer of Queen Elizabeth II's coffin from Westminster Abbey to Windsor Castle. In the streets of Rome, one can see a very different atmosphere, almost one of joy, just as Francis would have wanted. Why? Because with the unexpected white popemobile, no one thinks about death, but rather about life—and about all those occasions over the past twelve years when Pope Francis used the popemobile on his forty-seven international trips, carrying his Gospel message with passion and determination.

I think back to his trip to Rio de Janeiro at the beginning of his pontificate—July 2013—when, full of energy, he encouraged thousands of young people who filled Copacabana with soccer metaphors to always play forward, to not be afraid. And he called on young people to "stir things up," although, in the end, he did that himself too, revolutionizing the Church to be a field hospital, healing today's wounded, open to all. In the six kilometers between the Vatican and Saint Mary Major, the popemobile carrying the coffin of the Argentine pope recalls a living Francis. The applause that accompanies this incredible procession is full of gratitude, emotion, and recognition for a pontiff who came from the end of the world, an outsider, who loosened the papacy. With his authentic, simple, sincere, and direct way of communicating, he reached everyone with his message of peace, hope, and support for the marginalized and the discarded.

So many people crowd the sidewalks of Rome to greet Pope Francis that when Carolina, who is at home, goes to Corso Vittorio Emanuele II to say goodbye to Father Jorge, she can see only the convoy of cars from afar. "There are too many people!" she laments in a message she sends me via WhatsApp.

When the popemobile, after a half-hour procession, arrives at the Basilica of Saint Mary Major, one of Rome's oldest churches, its bells ring out in celebration. His "favorites" are waiting for him there: forty people, representatives of the forgotten, the vulnerable, the weak, holding white roses—his favorite flower. There are migrants, detainees with special permission to be there, trans people, marginalized people, and the homeless—the group he always placed at the center of his concerns, the ones he always defended and supported, until the very end.

After speaking on CNN, speaking of all these things from the heart, I quickly write another article and send it to editor Juli Nassau in Buenos Aires who had woken up early to follow the dramatic farewell.[32]

At 1 PM the coffin is carried into the Basilica of Saint Mary Major, where in 1538 Ignatius Loyola celebrated his first Mass. Amid Latin chants, children carry their white roses to the chapel that holds the Byzantine icon of the Madonna Salus Populi Romani, venerated for centuries by the Jesuits. The funeral procession pauses for a few moments before the entrance to this chapel and then moves to the burial niche next to it. Francis is laid to rest, as was his wish, in a simple tomb near the icon before which he had so often prayed.

The Vatican ends the live broadcast because the burial is to be private. This final rite, which lasts half an hour, is carried out according to the prescriptions of the *Ordo Exsequiarum Romani Pontificis*, the document on papal obsequies that Francis modified to simplify his funeral and allow him to be buried next to the icon of Our Lady of Salus Populi Romani, his "favorite" Virgin. This ceremony is presided over

---

32. Elisabetta Piqué, "La elección de su clásico vehículo blanco en lugar de un coche fúnebre cambió el tono con el que saludaron al pontífice durante la procesión hasta la basílica Santa María la Mayor," *La Nación*, April 26, 2025.

by Cardinal Camerlengo Kevin Farrell before a few high-ranking prelates, Jorge Bergoglio's family members—between fifty and sixty people, including his nephews and great-nephews—and his "pontifical family" of private secretaries and personal nurses who cared for him until the end.

I FINISH EVERYTHING and head to St. Peter's Square, now half-empty, where Juampy is still guarding the CNN cameras. He has been chatting with some of his bosses, and they congratulate me on how polite, quick, and kind he is.

I call Gerry, who's still on his terrace, and I walk home. After so much emotion, it's always good to cool off a bit. When we meet up with Irene, she tells us she disliked Cardinal Re's sermon: "It sounded like something from Wikipedia!"

GERRY WRITES HIS ARTICLE FOR *America* magazine on the funeral.[33] He also does television interviews that afternoon for Canada and the UK.

In the evening, after having worked all day, I write another article, do a television program and then make an "indecent" proposal to my friend Cristina Taquini, a veteran ANSA journalist, foster mother, and neighbor: that she please go to the supermarket near her house, which often has Argentine steaks. If there are any, I ask that she buy them and bring them home and then come eat with us no earlier than 9 PM. Cristina, delighted, immediately accepts the mission. She's eager to see us and to hear details about the historic moment we are experiencing.

---

33. Gerard O'Connell, "The Three Surprises of Pope Francis's Funeral," *America*, April 26, 2025.

PART II

THE QUEST FOR A NEW POPE

APRIL 27, SUNDAY [GERRY]
*A New Pilgrim Site*

I WAKE UP EARLY AS ALWAYS. I let Elisabetta sleep a little. We have breakfast with Irene, read the newspapers, and start watching on TV the teeming crowd assembled for the Mass presided over by Cardinal Pietro Parolin in St. Peter's Square for the Jubilee of Adolescents. It had originally been planned to coincide with the canonization of the Italian teenager Carlo Acutis, the first millennial saint. However, the Council of Cardinals decided to postpone the canonization because there was no pope who could declare him a saint.

Some two hundred thousand young people, Italians, and pilgrims from every continent attended Mass under a blue sky and radiant sunshine. They arrived early in the morning for this great event that Pope Francis—who is now buried in the Basilica of Saint Mary Major—was eager to preside over. The spotlight is on Cardinal Parolin, considered by many to be the leading Italian candidate to become Francis's successor, so the Mass could be a grand dress rehearsal for his eventual papacy. After the Gospel reading, all eyes turn to the secretary of state who begins his homily in Italian, reading from the text prepared for the occasion. He speaks in a firm, monotone voice, but at no point does he deviate from the text or attempt to connect directly with the young people, who applaud loudly when he mentions Pope Francis. But otherwise, they listen in silence. Parolin fails to connect with them or arouse their enthusiasm. "He simply lacks charisma," a European cardinal tells us afterward.

"All the cardinal electors, attentive to his performance, were shocked by Parolin's lack of connection with young people, his lack of empathy, his lack of charisma," confides another cardinal. "That Mass was a killer for his candidacy; it was like the final nail in the coffin," he adds.

THE OTHER NEWS THIS SUNDAY is how that humble, simple white marble tomb of Pope Francis has suddenly become the destination of pilgrimage for thousands of people who want to pay tribute to him.[1]

Even before the doors of the Basilica of Saint Mary Major open at 7 AM, countless people are already there, lining up to enter and pay homage to the pope of the people.

At noon, when the sun was beginning to beat down, members of the civil protection forces asked those in line if they had eaten or drunk water, because the wait times to enter could be at least two hours.

Given the number of people—of all ages and nationalities—the ushers inside urge people to hurry up and move quickly. Some arrive with flags—from Poland, Portugal, and other countries.... The teenagers who arrived en masse in Rome for the Jubilee as well as the disabled are allowed in through a special line. Everyone must nevertheless go through airport-style security checks, complete with metal detectors.

Singing can be heard, and people can be seen carrying bouquets of flowers to leave on the tomb, which is striking for its simplicity and plainness.

Pope Francis was responsible for designing it to reflect his papacy, marked by gestures of humility and austerity and his predilection for the poor: he chose white marble from Liguria, the land of his grandparents, a single inscription, "Franciscus," and a reproduction of his silver pectoral cross with the image of the Good Shepherd carrying the sheep on his shoulders.

For the lesser-known Esquilino neighborhood, it is believed that the placement of Francis's tomb there will mark a transformation for the better, an "upgrade." "It will make the whole area grow," said Francesco Rutelli, former mayor of Rome and former minister of culture, who emphasized to the Italian press that few people know that the basilica's bell tower, which is 75 meters high, is the tallest in Rome.

Pope Francis is not the first pontiff not to be buried in the Vatican, where most of his predecessors are buried (147 out of 266), but he is the first in 122 years to have made the decision to leave the Vatican. The last was Leo XIII in 1903, who rests in the Basilica of St. John Lat-

---

1. Elisabetta Piqué, "El mundo incesante desfile de fieles ante la humilde y austera tumba del papa Francisco en la basilica," *La Nación*, April 27, 2025; J. D. Long García, "Pilgrims from Around the World Visit Pope Francis's Tomb to Thank God for His Pontificate," *America*, April 29, 2025.

eran; he, too, was carried there in procession from the Vatican. The Basilica of Saint Mary Major—where seven other pontiffs, the artist Gian Lorenzo Bernini, and Pauline Bonaparte, Napoleon's sister, are buried—in a way closes the circle of Francis's pontificate.

The day after his election, on March 13, 2013, Jorge Bergoglio surprised the world by leaving the Vatican to venerate the Madonna Salus Populi Romani, the ancient Marian icon in the basilica to which he was always devoted and which he also used to visit as archbishop of Buenos Aires whenever he traveled to Rome. After leaving a bouquet of flowers, that day, the pope surprised everyone even more by stopping at the guesthouse for clergy on Via della Scrofa, where he often stayed, to pay his bill. Before and after each international trip, Pope Francis would stop by to greet his favorite "Madonna," something he did again, even though he was very ill, on March 23, the day he was discharged from the Gemelli Hospital after thirty-eight days of hospitalization, during which he was twice close to death and which marked the beginning of his end.

And he returned again on Saturday, April 12, the eve of Holy Week, when he unexpectedly appeared there wearing a nasal cannula and accompanied by his guardian angels, his nurse Massimiliano Strappetti, and the Argentine priest Juan Cruz Villalón, one of his private secretaries.

Although few imagined it, in addition to going to pray one last time before the Madonna Salus Populi Romani, near whom he now rests, he had also gone to check on his tomb, Lithuanian Cardinal Rolandas Makrickas, archpriest of the basilica, revealed to the media.

As Elisabetta saw with her own eyes, having managed to access the small group of journalists organized by the Press Room, Makrickas presided over Vespers prayer today when more than a hundred cardinals prayed before the Madonna Salus Populi Romani and for the first time paid homage to the simple and austere tomb of Pope Francis. Elisabetta could see that they too had to pass through fairly quickly, and without privileges, so as not to delay the line of faithful surrounding the basilica, which did not diminish even when it began to rain. Nor did the flow of people stop during Vespers, which they prayed "for Pope Francis, that the Risen Lord may welcome him into his house of light and peace."

Because of the crowd's size, the basilica, which has suddenly become the center of the world where everyone wants to be, remains open exceptionally late, until 10 PM.

Among the thousands of people who entered to venerate the tomb of the first Argentine pope, there were, of course, many of his fellow countrymen. "I was in line from 11:35 when I arrived, until 1:38, because I looked at my watch, so it was two hours.... And it was impressive," says Anita, an Argentine who traveled from Barcelona not to miss this historic moment. What did Pope Francis mean to her? "Life itself, an example of life, an example of a human being, a good man. I read somewhere on social media that it was like the farewell of the last good man.... May God grant that he is not the last good man and that we all follow his example, especially young people," she adds.

ELISABETTA DOES A STAND-UP for LN+ from Saint Mary Major which we watch on television. It is an informal Sunday program, and we have a good laugh when the host, Robertino Funes Ugarte, suddenly praises her and calls her "the Meryl Streep of journalists"!

Elisabetta also meets with our journalist friend Nelson Castro—who has her appear live on the Argentine news channel TN—and also with our dear friend Paloma García Ovejero—the first female spokesperson for a pope, and former correspondent for Radio Cope—who just happens to greet Austrian Cardinal Christoph Schönborn, archbishop emeritus of Vienna. A refined theologian, Schönborn—who some Vatican experts initially called a follower of Ratzinger and later became one of the "most disciplined of the Bergoglians" by supporting all of his reformist measures—will not participate in the conclave because he turned 80 in January.

When Schönborn leaves the basilica he is "assaulted" by journalists seeking statements. Over the following days, such a scene will be repeated with other cardinals also.

When asked about the conclave that will elect Pope Francis's successor, Schönborn says, "Will we commit to following the advances of Pope Francis's pontificate over the past twelve years? It depends on what we mean by advances. What Pope Francis has achieved is to show the Christian world and the entire world that we are one human family, that we are all children of God, and that God has shown us a path through Jesus, through the Gospel. This is the path he has shown us: to follow the Gospel, the joy of the Gospel." In response to a question about yesterday's "miraculous" meeting between US President Donald Trump and Ukrainian President Volodymyr Zelensky in St. Peter's Basilica before Pope Francis's funeral, Schönborn said: "I had a vision of Pope Francis extending his hands toward both of them and blessing them with the profound conviction that good is stronger than evil. I was deeply moved by this image."[2]

IT IS RAINING. Elisabetta takes a taxi from Saint Mary Major to pick up Irene. In another feat of the "dream team," they have just secured an interview with a Spanish cardinal.[3] Upon entering the general congregations, the cardinals swore to keep the proceedings confidential. Some interpret this oath to mean they should not speak to the press; many others, however, grant interviews, on the condition that they will not discuss matters inherent to these closed-door discussions.

Born near Almería, Spain, López Romero, 72, also holds Paraguayan nationality, a country where he lived from the ages of 32 to 50. A graduate in information sciences and journalism from Barcelona, he was appointed archbishop of Rabat by Pope Francis in 2017. Two years later, in October 2019, the pontiff created him cardinal soon after visiting Morocco, a Muslim-majority country, to mark the eighth centenary of the historic meeting between Saint Francis of Assisi and Sultan al-Malik al-Kamil.

López Romero's name appears on the lists of papal candidates, but he laughs it off. "It's better to be listed than lost," he jokes using a Spanish pun. "But seriously, I don't like my name appearing on those lists—it's something that completely overwhelms me," he says during the interview over cappuccino in a bar near the Porta Santa Ana in the Vatican.

Bearded and with a strong sense of humor reminiscent of Pope Francis, López Romero says that in the pre-conclave meetings "there's an atmosphere of curiosity and interest in getting to know one another, because we don't know each other very well.

"The problem is that to get to know each other, you have to talk, and in an amphitheater where you see the person speaking on a screen, and where one person speaks and then the other, it's difficult."

When Betta and Irene ask him if it's true that polarization in the Church has increased during Francis's pontificate, the cardinal answers

---

2. "Papa Francesco, Cardinale Schönborn: 'L'ho visto stendere le sue mani su Trump e Zelensky,'" *Il Sole 24 Ore*, April 27, 2025.

3. Elisabetta Piqué, "Cristóbal López Romero: 'No me gusta que salga mi nombre en las listas de papabiles,'" *La Nación*, May 1, 2025.

by saying that "polarization is something we have to combat. We have to build unity, which is not the same as uniformity. We have to accept that we are different and know that these differences are not an obstacle but an enrichment, and that we have to listen to and accept one another." He points out that the world is very polarized, and warns, "the danger is that the Church will become similar to the political world."

"Obviously, we are different," he admits. "There are cardinals who, for example, see the synod as a disastrous and useless thing, and others like me who are enthusiastic about synodality. But these differences shouldn't prevent us from living unity, because every day we celebrate the Eucharist together, we give each other [the sign of] peace, and we partake of the same body of Christ."

What should the profile of the next pope be? "I think we need a pope who is capable of building unity among all; that is, a pope who is inclusive, who does not exclude anything or anyone. A pope who encourages us to walk, because the Church is the people of God who walk, who march, not who settle and remain fixed. We are pilgrims and we must march, but march together. He also has to be a pope who connects us to Christ from the roots, from the source, and who allows us to drink from the spring. And, finally, I think we need a pope who embraces all of humanity."

ANOTHER SPANISH CARDINAL, José Cobo, the archbishop of Madrid, told Cristina Cabrejas, correspondent for the Spanish news agency EFE two days ago[4] that he would like a Spanish-speaking pope to be elected. "Of course, I would like it. Francis has been very good for all of us and I think he has made interrelations with all of Latin America, with Spain, very easy. But here among the cardinals, Spanish is heard a lot. There are many who speak it."

At the same time, he wants "a courageous pope who guides the Church." Noting that not all the cardinals have arrived yet, he explains that this is a time to get to know one another. "We come from all over the world. Some were recently created cardinals. I think we need a little time to talk, to get to know each other, to lay the foundation together."

---

4. Cristina Cabrejas, "El cardenal Cobo: 'Necesitamos un papa valiente,'" Swissinfo.ch, April 25, 2025.

Cobo, 59, who was created a cardinal by Pope Francis during the Consistory of September 30, 2023, explains that "the profile" of the pontiff that the Church will need is also being studied and the atmosphere during these first meetings "is very pleasant, " in addition to the fact that "the universality of the Church is made visible there in a small room. "

And although "there is a certain sense of orphanhood" since "the pope isn't there," he says, among the cardinals there is also "a sense of hope and urgency, that is, a desire to give the Church the pope it needs right now." Cardinal Cobo states that he is looking for a pope who "is on the one hand someone who welcomes everything that has been sown previously, who also welcomes the mission that Pope Francis has had, and someone courageous who guides the Church toward the great challenges of the future, toward the great problems and challenges that come from this immense change of era that we have ahead of us. But he has to be brave," he insists.

So, who will be elected? Cobo responds with a smile to this question that everyone asks him. "I am very calm, because God already knows. I think it's better to ask him, rather than us. There is a group of cardinals who are very well qualified. And whoever it is, we'll come to find out, but, whoever it is, it will be the one God has in mind." ... So these will be days of prayer," he concludes. "This morning I prayed for a while before of the body of Francis and I believe that these are also moments of listening to God."

I MEET FOR DINNER with my old friend, 93-year-old Chinese Cardinal Joseph Zen Ze-kiun, SDB, whom I've known since 1996. Zen is technically out on bail following his arrest in 2022 on suspicion of collusion with foreign forces under the national security law, a charge he is appealing. However, the Hong Kong court temporarily returned his passport to allow him to travel to Rome for ten days to attend Pope Francis's funeral and participate in the general congregations. Nevertheless, he has to return to Hong Kong on Saturday, May 3.

We dine at a Japanese restaurant near the Pontifical Salesian University, where Zen is staying—north of Rome—along with Father Carlos from Hong Kong, who now studies here and was the cardinal's secretary for many years, and Deacon John, also from Hong Kong, who also studies here.

During the two-hour dinner, the cardinal talks about Pope Francis, the general congregations he is attending, and the upcoming conclave, which, like the one in 2013, he cannot participate in because he is over 80. He also gives me a preview of some of the topics he will cover in his speech, which he will give in a few days, on April 30, as I learn later. Although speakers are required to respect the (fairly flexible) five-minute time limit, many, especially those over 80, do not. Cardinal Re, who leads the meetings, allows Zen to speak for fifteen minutes, but then asks him to end his talk. His text is published later.[5]

"I have come for the funeral of the Holy Father, who has departed to heaven, and I gladly join the choir that surrounds us singing 'hosanna' to the august deceased pastor (almost a cry of *'Santo subito'*)," Zen, born in Shanghai, tells the other cardinals as he begins. He shares some of the many "joyful memories" of his "jovial friendship" with Pope Francis, including his last private meeting with him on January 6, 2023, after the funeral of Benedict XVI.[6]

Zen clarifies that he cannot speak about "certain matters" related to China, as this could bring him into trouble with the law. Immediately afterward, in what will be the main part of his speech, Zen emphasizes that he traveled to Rome to participate in the general congregations "because the Church is at a crucial moment of confusion and division, and our brother cardinals in the upcoming conclave now have a great responsibility: to give us a pope who, with the help of the Holy Spirit, can guide us back to harmony and peace." The cardinal then launches into a harsh critique of the Synod on Synodality and its final magisterial directive for the development of a synodal church, which he considers "an approach that risks bringing us closer to Anglican practice."

"How will the unity of the Catholic Church be preserved?" he asks. "The electors of the next pope must be aware that he will have the responsibility to continue this synodal process or to decisively halt it, something that is a matter of life or death for the Church founded by Jesus," he warns.

---

5. "Cardinal Zen: Reform Needed 'because we are sinners,'" *The Pillar*, May 4, 2025.

6. Gerard O'Connell, "Pope Francis Meets with Hong Kong's Cardinal Zen the Day after Benedict XVI's Funeral," *America*, January 6, 2023.

FILIPINO CARDINAL PABLO VIRGILIO DAVID thinks differently. I manage to interview him via email after his visit to pay tribute to Pope Francis at the Basilica of Saint Mary Major. At 66, he is one of three Filipino cardinals who will enter the Sistine Chapel, along with Luis Antonio Tagle, 67—a leading papal candidate—and José Advíncula, OP, 73, archbishop of Manila.

Cardinal David is currently serving his second term as president of the Catholic Bishops' Conference of the Philippines, the country with the third largest number of Catholics in the world, after Brazil and Mexico. He is also vice-president of the Federation of Asian Bishops' Conferences. He was elected to the post-synodal council at the second session of the Synod on Synodality, which will be held at the Vatican in October 2025, and is a great enthusiast for this process.

Cardinal Ambo, as he is popularly known in the Philippines ("Ambo" is a term of endearment for Pablo), is a biblical scholar who studied in Leuven, Belgium, and in Jerusalem. He is also a polyglot who, in addition to Filipino and English, speaks eight other ancient and modern languages and is brushing up on his Italian.

He received several death threats for helping victims of the war on drugs and their families waged by Rodrigo Duterte, former president of the Philippines, as he told me in an interview I conducted with him for *America* after he received his cardinal's hat on December 7, 2024.[7] Duterte was arrested in March 2025 on orders from the International Criminal Court and is now in prison in The Hague, Netherlands.

When I ask about the dangers he sees in the Church's current direction, the cardinal warns that "we cannot expect our faithful to deepen their understanding of their shared identity as participants in the life and mission of the Church, the body of Christ, if we do not address clericalism, reinforced by a theology of ordained ministry that is not adequately grounded in the common priesthood of the faithful."[8]

He believes that evangelization, in today's world, "must be a task of the entire Church, not just of the ordained or religious, a task that truly, effectively, and profoundly impacts society, the world, and all of creation." He emphasizes that "for Asians, a fourfold ecclesial conver-

---

7. Gerard O'Connell, "Interview: Why Cardinal 'Ambo' David Received 'a lot of Death Threats' in Duterte's Philippines," *America*, January 15, 2025.

8. Gerard O'Connell, "Cardinal 'Ambo' David on the Greatest Need of the Church Today," *America*, May 3, 2025.

sion is required, involving a synodal encounter with neighboring religions, with neighboring cultures, with the poor, and with creation."

For him, the next pope "should have extensive experience of service as a bishop of a local church. Like Francis, he should uphold the spirit of the Second Vatican Council, promote a missionary synodal Church that listens, is welcoming and participatory, and fosters co-responsibility in mission." And he goes further: "At a time when the globalized economic and political order is crumbling—especially exposed during the Trump era and its aftermath—the Church may well be one of the last stubborn institutions that still retains a truly global character. This unique position imposes a serious responsibility on the Church: not to take refuge in self-preservation or nostalgic idealism, but to connect with the world by offering credible witness to a renewed model of humanity.

"The Church must relate to the world not with fear or condescension, but with a humble but bold presence that takes seriously the realities of the world: its wounds, its aspirations, its complexity. We are called to propose—with words and witness—a vision of human fraternity, dignity, justice, and ecological responsibility, demonstrating that faith can foster a future worthy of the entire human family," he affirms, very much in line with Francis.

I ARRIVE HOME AFTER 11 PM. Betta is eating pizza with Carolina, watching a very funny Argentine series on Netflix called *Envidiosa*. She says she needs to get away from the conclave for a bit, "relax and get some fresh air."

APRIL 28, MONDAY [GERRY]
*We Have a Date*

BETTA AND I GO TO THE BRIEFING by Holy See Press Office director Matteo Bruni at 1 PM. Before it even begins, the news of the day has already leaked. The conclave will begin on Wednesday, May 7, as decided this Monday by the cardinals present in Rome—both those over and under 80—during the General Congregation #5. Bruni makes it official.

He specifies that 180 of the 252 members of the College of Cardinals participated in the meeting in which this crucial decision was taken, of whom "about a hundred" were under 80 years of age.

Voting to elect Francis's successor will begin on the afternoon of Wednesday, May 7.

In accordance with the norms of the apostolic constitution *Universi Dominici Gregis*, a single ballot will be held on that day. In the morning, the "Mass for the Election of the Pope"—*Missa Pro Eligendo Pontifice*—will take place in St. Peter's Basilica, a rite prior to the most secret and mysterious vote that captures the attention of the entire world. Afterwards, the cardinals will process to the Sistine Chapel, where they will listen to a meditation by the former preacher of the papal household, Capuchin Cardinal Raniero Cantalamessa, before closing themselves *"cum clave"* to vote until the 267th pope of the Church is elected. The Vatican also announced that the Benedictine abbot of the Basilica of St. Paul Outside the Walls, Dom Donato Ogliari, will give the first of two meditations to the cardinals, as prescribed by the Constitution for the election of the pope.

The Mass for the Election of the Pope will be presided over by Cardinal Giovanni Battista Re, who also officiated at Pope Francis's funeral last Sunday. However, because he is 91 years of age, he will not participate in the conclave. Instead, Cardinal Pietro Parolin, former secretary of state of the Holy See and a strong favorite to be pope, will preside in the election process.

The College of Cardinals currently has 252 members from ninety-six countries, but only 135 of them, from seventy-one countries, are electors, that is, cardinals under the age of 80 with the right to vote in the conclave.

An analysis of the 135 cardinal electors shows that 53 are from Europe, 23 from Asia, 23 from Latin America, 14 from North America (10 from the US, 4 from Canada), and 4 from Oceania. There are 17 Italians among the 53 Europeans, but there are also two Italians not included in the European bloc: one in the Holy Land (Cardinal Pierbattista Pizzaballa) and the other in Mongolia (Cardinal Giorgio Marengo).

NOW THAT THE DATE—which had been the big question mark of recent days—is known, logistical operations are under way, preparing not only the Sistine Chapel, adorned by the impressive frescoes by Michelangelo and other Renaissance masters, but also the space where the cardinal electors will be confined.

"No one will be left on the street," Bruni assures jokingly. He does not specify whether the final number of electors will be 135 or fewer, even though there are rumors that two cardinals, one Spanish and one Bosnian, will not be able to travel to Rome because of health problems. He clarifies that, in addition to the Santa Marta residence, some cardinal electors will be able staying in what is known as the "old" Santa Marta.

The Santa Marta guesthouse, where Francis lived, was established in 1996 by Pope John Paul II with the aim of providing the cardinals with a more comfortable and modern space. However, given that the number of cardinals exceeds the 120 decreed by Paul VI, not all of the electors will be able to stay in the new Santa Marta. Therefore, the old Santa Marta, which houses some offices of the Pontifical Commission for the Protection of Minors, will be refurbished and 16 electors will reside here.

Bruni confirmed that work will begin on the famous stoves that will allow the black smoke (if no pope is elected) or white smoke (if *Habemus Papam* will be proclaimed) to issue forth from the Sistine Chapel.

He also stated that during this morning's meeting of cardinals, twenty interventions were made, in which "the future of the Church" was discussed, as well as "its challenges in today's world, its challenges in evangelization, its relationship with other faiths, and the issue of abuse." In addition, they discussed the "qualities that the new pontiff must possess to be able to respond to these challenges," Bruni stated, without going into detail on the specifics of the challenges. General congregations are held in the utmost secrecy, and the cardinals swear an oath of confidentiality at the outset. However, there are always leaks.

Bruni announced that the following cardinals had been chosen by lottery to assist Cardinal Camerlengo Kevin Farrell for the next three days: Filipino Cardinal Luis Antonio Tagle (a frontrunner), German Reinhard Marx (a progressive figure) and the Corsican-French Dominique Mamberti, prefect of the Supreme Tribunal of the Apostolic Signatura, one of the three main judicial bodies of the Holy See. As he is also the cardinal protodeacon (the senior cardinal deacon), Mamberti will have the highly visible role of shouting *"Annuntio vobis gaudium magnum: Habemus Papam!"* ("I announce to you great joy: we have a pope!") He will be the first to speak from the central balcony of St. Peter's Basilica to announce to the world the new name of the new pontiff. There had been speculation that the conclave would begin on May 5 or 6. We hear that the Italian cardinals were pushing for the election to begin quickly in order to favor the Italian frontrunner, Parolin. Evidently those who requested more time prevailed.[9]

There isn't a cardinal who doesn't informally complain that the big problem is that the electors from seventy-one countries do not know each other. And, in this turbulent climate, twenty-four or forty-eight hours more time to meet and devise strategies could be crucial. Therefore, today's decision gives them just eight days to overcome this lack of knowledge and conscientiously discern who among them is the most qualified and best suited to govern the Catholic Church and guide its 1.4 billion members into the next phase of its history.

In response to a question, Bruni acknowledges that the "Becciu case"—concerning the Italian cardinal sanctioned by Pope Francis, who is seeking readmission to the conclave—was discussed. "There was no resolution" on the matter, he states. Asked if the circulating version that Becciu had taken a step back on his own is true, Bruni answers that he has "no indications" on the matter.

The College of Cardinals is expected to cut to the chase and inform Cardinal Becciu that he must renounce his claim, which many consider "unpleasant."

"We wasted precious time, we lost three days," an English-speaking cardinal confides to me.

WE LEARNED TODAY that in one of the early sessions of the general congregations, Cardinal Re drew attention to the fact that among those attending is the Nigerian cardinal Francis Arinze, 92, who is the only member of the College of Cardinal to have attended the

---

9. Elisabetta Piqué, "El Vaticano anuncia que el cónclave para elegir al próximo papa será el 7 de mayo," *La Nación*, April 28, 2025; Gerard O'Connell, "How the College of Cardinals Chose the Date for the Next Conclave," *America*, April 28, 2025.

Second Vatican Council.[10] He was ordained bishop at the age of 32 and attended the final session of the council in 1965. He was then the youngest bishop in the world and was listed among the papabile in the 2005 conclave. Today he is one of the cardinal bishops. The cardinals applauded warmly. He responded with a big smile.

AFTER WRITING AND SENDING OUR ARTICLES to our respective media outlets and television stations, Betta and I go to a bar on Via della Conciliazione. We eat a *tramezzino* and have Coca-Colas. Betta makes use of the opportunity to take a silk shirt to Remo's dry cleaners in Borgo Santo Spirito.

We then go to the Jesuit General Curia—just a few hundred meters from the Vatican—where, in a room on the ground floor, we interview Chinese Cardinal Stephen Chow Sau-yan, bishop of Hong Kong, whom I've known for a long time. He is one of the twenty-three Asians in the College of Electors and the only one from China who will enter the Sistine Chapel to elect Pope Francis's successor.

A Jesuit like Francis, Cardinal Chow is 65 years old, a psychologist with a degree in philosophy and theology, a master's in organizational development from Loyola University Chicago, and a doctorate in human development and psychology from Harvard. In the interview he defends Pope Francis's legacy.[11] He especially supports the synodal process that Francis launched, which aims for greater listening and participation of all the baptized in the Church.[12]

Furthermore, he believes it is unfair to say that the polarization of the Church increased during the recently concluded papacy, as the conservative wing often claims.

He prefers not to mention China, a communist giant with which the Vatican does not have diplomatic relations, but with whom, at the behest of the Argentine pope, a controversial secret provisional agree-

---

10. *God's Invisible Hand: The Life and Work of Cardinal Francis Arinze, An Interview with Gerard O'Connell*, Paulines Publications, Africa, 2003, Ignatius Press, 2006.

11. Gerard O'Connell, "Hong Kong's Jesuit Cardinal Chow on the Conclave, the Next Pope and Francis's Legacy," *America*, May 2, 2025.

12. Elisabetta Piqué, "Stephen Chow, el único cardenal chino del cónclave, defiende a Francisco: 'No creo que la Iglesia esté ahora más polarizada!," *La Nación*, May 4, 2025.

ment was signed in September 2018 on the delicate issue of the appointment of bishops.

When asked about criticism of the *Fiducia Supplicans* document on the blessing of persons in same-sex unions, Cardinal Chow laments that many people criticize this text without having read it. "But I think when people read it honestly, they clearly see that we are not blessing the union. We are blessing the people," he clarifies. "To those who often criticize the document, I frequently say: If people come to me for a blessing after Mass or here on the street, should I ask them if they're gay? If they're divorced? I simply bless the person who asks. And the document says that we can actually bless those who ask," he explains.

Commenting on Francis's document on Human Fraternity, which was poorly received by the conservative wing for its approach to Islam, Chow points out that there are six religions in Hong Kong, and that Islam is one of them. "We meet regularly and talk with them; we are friends; we share values. Francis has allowed us to grow closer; he has brought us closer together. In fact, he has facilitated dialogue, mutual trust, and respect. There are always fanatics and fundamentalists in every religion, as Francis said, and it can be difficult to dialogue with them, but most are not like that. Francis broke the ice—so much so that after his death I received letters of condolence from all the religious leaders [in Hong Kong], and this is explained only by the fact that he managed to reach everyone," he emphasizes.

I ask, how do you feel about the responsibility of having to enter the conclave to elect your successor? "To be honest, I wish I didn't have to vote, because I wish Francis were still alive. But it's a fact that he's left us. So this is something we have to face. And I'm really praying. I know that each person has a different understanding of the conclave and says, 'Oh, the Holy Spirit doesn't choose. The Holy Spirit just gives us the freedom and the space to respond, to make our decision.' But I think if we go into discernment, we need to go back to our hearts, to the inspiration of the Holy Spirit in our hearts. Because that's where the Holy Spirit communicates, and he will give us some kind of indication.... We will have greater peace and certainty in choosing one option over the other. But," he acknowledges, "this isn't going to be easy."

Does he think it will be a long or a short conclave? "I hope it won't be too long. But it's a big responsibility. People are asking us to please elect a pope who is good for us, for the Church, and good for the world. Although, personally, I'm calm: I don't speak Italian and I'm a Jesuit," he answers with a laugh.

Another Asian cardinal elector, Charles Maung Bo, SDB, 76, archbishop of Yangon and president of the Bishops' Conference of Myanmar, whom we have known for many years (and who organized Pope Francis's trip to that country in November 2017, when he also went to Bangladesh), outlines the profile of what the next pope should be like.

"We find ourselves at a historic crossroads. Across the torn plains of Gaza, the devastated cities of Ukraine, the silent cries of Myanmar, and the arid fields of Africa, the world yearns for peace. This is no time to waver: a true tribute to the late Pope Francis is to tirelessly pursue peace," Bo asserts, in a reflection he shares with me and a few other journalists that will be very similar to his address at the general congregations.

"We remember with profound reverence how Pope Francis, frail yet determined, knelt before the leaders of South Sudan, pleading for peace with the urgency of a father for his wounded children. That moment became a sermon stronger than any words, a proclamation that true leadership springs from humility, not domination. His voice was not a political calculation, but a cry from the heart of Christ," adds the cardinal, who is a friend of Burmese leader Aung San Suu Kyi, a Nobel Peace Prize winner now either in prison or under house-arrest. "Yet the storms rage with greater intensity. Today, six major wars and more than twenty smaller conflicts continue to kill thousands and displace millions. It is a vale of tears in many nations. No one can escape the machinery of hatred. At this very moment, more than thirteen thousand nuclear weapons remain armed and ready to destroy human civilization several times over. A single moment of madness, a single spark of hatred could unleash a nuclear holocaust, turning cities to ash, rivers to poison, and the sky to darkness.

"Meanwhile, global warming ravages our common home. Crops wither, rivers dry up, glaciers melt, and the earth itself groans in anguish. Scientists warn that tomorrow's wars may not be fought for oil, but for water, the very blood of life.

"We need a voice! A voice that evangelizes the hardened hearts of those who threaten the very survival of humanity and nature. A voice that calls humanity back from the brink of destruction! Indeed, the next pope will nourish the Catholic faith and guide the Church toward a deeper encounter with Jesus and his Trinitarian mission of love on earth. But the Incarnation cries out today: we must renew and strengthen the instruments of peace: the United Nations, international courts, and humanitarian agreements. However, these structures are lifeless without the breath of moral authority. Religions must unite in a common cause to save humanity. The world urgently needs a new breath of hope: a synodal path that chooses life over death, hope over despair. The next pope must be that breath!" exclaims the cardinal who served as president of the Federation of Asian Bishops' Conferences for six years, until last January.

BEYOND THE NEWS OF THE CONCLAVE DATE—which was at the center of a bidding war among the cardinals—media attention on what's happening in the Vatican this Monday is actually significantly reduced—at least for non-Vaticanists—because Spain and Portugal suffered a massive power outage that left tens of millions of homes, hospitals, and businesses without electricity, causing hours of chaos and uncertainty. The LN+ team sent to Rome for the conclave even decides to travel to Spain to cover this. Betta tells me her television interview was also canceled for the same reason.

Our friend Paloma García Ovejero, one of the many people who traveled to Rome to attend Francis's solemn funeral and who was due to return to Madrid tonight, does not know whether her plane will be able to take off. When she drops off her suitcase at our home because the flight is at night and she has to meet people downtown, Betta and Irene interview her on the fly.[13] Paloma, who rose to fame in July 2016 as the first woman papal spokesperson, makes no secret of the fact that her three years at the male-dominated Vatican were not easy. Her resignation, submitted along with that of her boss, American Greg Burke, on December 31, 2018, was interpreted at the time as a true earthquake in the field of Vatican communications and a setback for Francis himself. Having worked as a correspondent for

---

13. Elisabetta Piqué, "Entrevista a Paloma García Ovejero: ser mujer en el Vaticano, el cónclave que viene y cómo era trabajar con un 'workaholic' como Francisco," *La Nación*, April 29, 2025.

Cope radio in London and Brussels, Paloma, who is now the international press officer for Mary's Meals—an organization that provides daily meals to millions of children in some of the world's poorest communities—emphasizes how hard it was to work with a workaholic like Francisco. "My job was extremely difficult. I gave everything: my time, my energy, my ability... everything, however much or little I could contribute, I gave it all; I held nothing back. But after almost three years of working twenty-four hours a day, seven days a week, I was exhausted, I was *"esaurita,"* an Italian word that I think best describes it. I couldn't get anything out of myself anymore. I had nothing left. My job required an extremely high level of performance, because the pope is a head of state, a spiritual leader, and the vicar of Christ on earth. And on top of all that, Francis was a *stakhanovite*, a workaholic, and you had to work at a very fast pace, an exhausting pace, to keep up with him. I gave it my all. And when the time came, I decided it was best to leave and make way for others. But I don't regret a single moment of those three years," she says, as she speaks for the first time about that period.

Asked whether the next pope will be a candidate for continuity with Francis's pontificate or a candidate for a break, Paloma answers ironically. "I'm going to give you an exclusive scoop: the next pope will be Catholic and his axis will be the doctrine of the Church. Joking aside, I think there are processes that are already irreversible. It's clear that Pope Francis didn't have enough time to complete these processes of change. It will take three or four pontificates to complete these reforms. What Francis has done is open a door, and that door can no longer be closed. It's like those emergency doors that, once opened, can no longer be closed from the outside: that's how the reform processes that Francis has set in motion are," she asserts.

For her, the most important change that Bergoglio introduced was that he has reminded Catholics and the rest of the world of the joy of the Gospel, of how beautiful it is to be Catholic. "Francis has reminded us that being Catholic isn't about having a face like a pickled cucumber, as he used to say; being Catholic isn't about being bitter. Being Catholic is about having the joy of the risen Christ in your heart, about being certain that there is someone who loves you unconditionally just as you are and without asking anything in return," she explains, full of enthusiasm.

Asked for her two favorites to succeed Francis as pope, Paloma doesn't hide her admiration for Pietro Parolin, whom she has come to know very well. "I can only speak highly of Cardinal Parolin; I can only speak of him with admiration and gratitude. He is a great man; he has been a great servant of Francis in silence, in the background."

When Elisabetta reminds her that on their trip to the Philippines in 2016, the two had the impression that Francis was pointing to Cardinal Luis Antonio Tagle as a likely successor, Paloma expresses her doubts. "Cardinal Tagle is a magnificent pastor. I will never forget the Mass that Pope Francis and Cardinal Tagle celebrated in Manila, attended by seven million people. I will never forget all the Filipinos in the streets shouting '*Lolo kiko, Lolo kiko*,' which means 'Grandpa Francis.' Tagle is a great pastor, and Pope Francis saw this. But nearly ten years have passed since then, and new faces have arrived at the conclave," she says, and then adds, "Besides, the Holy Spirit laughs at human plans."

FINALLY, PALOMA'S FLIGHT TAKES OFF from Fiumicino without problems and later lands safely in Spain. We finish writing late. Carolina cooks a delicious *spaghetto al sugo* (a simple tomato sauce). For the second day in a row, together with Betta, who insists she needs to relax, they watch another episode of the series *Envidiosa* and crack up laughing.

APRIL 29, TUESDAY [BETTA]
*Not the Favorite*

I WAKE UP EARLY. I write up the interview we did with Paloma. I go to the Vatican with Clarabella, the name the kids christened my old yellow bike.

The Press Room is packed to the rafters. Before Matteo Bruni arrives, the news that has already leaked to the Italian media is that the Becciu case, which poisoned the pre-conclave atmosphere with Dan Brown–style intrigue, has been resolved.

As various Italian media outlets anticipated yesterday, Becciu—ousted by Francis in September 2020 after being implicated in a corruption scandal, but who had been clamoring to be reinstated for the election—finally stepped aside, pressured by the evidence.[14]

"Having at heart the good of the Church, which I have served and will continue to serve with fidelity and love, as well as contributing to the communion and serenity of the conclave, I have decided to obey, as I always have, Pope Francis's will that I not enter the conclave, remaining convinced of my innocence," Becciu announces in a statement released minutes before 10 AM local time.

According to *Corriere della Sera*, the cardinal had renounced his obsession with entering the Sistine Chapel after Secretary of State Cardinal Pietro Parolin showed him a text signed by Francis with a simple "F" that clearly states Becciu cannot participate in the conclave, as the *Domani* newspaper had anticipated.[15] It was then that Becciu reportedly gave up, understanding that his demand to enter at all costs meant going against the will of the deceased pontiff.

The only fellow-cardinal who came out to defend Becciu—whose case monopolized pre-conclave talks and sparked outrage among non-Italians because it involved stereotypical Roman intrigues—was 81-year-old Italian Cardinal Giuseppe Versaldi.

"Cardinal Becciu is a much-esteemed person. There has been a trial, there will be an appeal, and you know that until there is a final verdict, one is innocent," Versaldi, prefect emeritus of the Congregation for Catholic Education, told a group of reporters who intercepted him upon entering the General Congregation #5, according to ANSA. "We'll check," he added, recalling, when asked whether an excommunicated cardinal could vote in a conclave, that "Clement V issued this rule, but it's a bit far-fetched. We'll see."

According to ANSA, which cited sources present at the general congregations, Becciu reportedly took the floor during the pre-conclave meeting to insist that it was his "right and duty" to enter the conclave. But in the end, he backed down.[16]

---

14. Elisabetta Piqué, "Becciu desistió de participar en el cónclave, pero la aparición de un cardenal del Opus Dei sancionado detonó otra bomba," *La Nación*, April 28, 2025.

15. Erica Dellapasqua, "Becciu rinuncia al Conclave: 'Obbedisco a Francesco, per il bene della Chiesa, ma resto convinto della mia innocenza,'" *Corriere della Sera*, April 29, 2025.

16. "Versaldi, Becciu persona stimabile, verificheremo se può votare," ANSA, April 28, 2025.

THE BECCIU CHAOS is not the only controversy polluting the atmosphere. The mere presence at the general congregations of Peruvian Cardinal Juan Luis Cipriani, 81-year-old archbishop emeritus of Lima and the first Opus Dei cardinal, is also causing a scandal, tension, and bad humor.

Although it became known at the end of January that, following accusations of abuse, he had been sanctioned by Francis with disciplinary restrictions that include exile from his native country and a ban on wearing cardinal symbols and on making public statements, he is currently in Rome.

I saw him with my own eyes on Sunday in the Basilica of Saint Mary Major, when some one hundred cardinals prayed Vespers at Francis's tomb. The cardinals were leaving the basilica in procession, and seeing him dressed in his cardinal's robes like the others, I said hello to him. He politely turned around, greeted me, and walked on.

I remember Cipriani very well from a distant 1997, when for months as a special envoy for *La Nación* I covered the crisis surrounding the attack on the Japanese ambassador's residence in Lima by the Túpac Amaru Revolutionary Movement (MRTA). Then archbishop of Ayacucho, Cipriani was a member of a commission of guarantors that was supposed to peacefully resolve that crisis, which ended on April 22 in a bloodbath perpetrated by order of then-president Alberto Fujimori, an order based on a plan that counted on the support of the influential prelate.

When Matteo Bruni announced the date of the conclave yesterday, I asked him how Cipriani could be present at the basilica and at the general congregations, given the Vatican sanctions. "We don't give out specific information about cardinals," Bruni responded.

A late January exposé by our friend Iñigo Domínguez in *El País* uncovered the papal punishment. Bruni confirmed that Cipriani had been sanctioned at the behest of Pope Francis but did not provide details of the accusations.

In a statement, Bruni confirmed that "after accepting his resignation as archbishop of Lima," a penal precept and certain disciplinary measures related to his public activity, place of residence, and use of insignia were imposed on him. "The measures in question were signed and accepted" by Cipriani. Bruni added that, "according to Vatican News, the Vatican website, although on specific occasions certain permissions were granted to address requests due to the cardinal's age and family situation, the penal precept remains in force today." He indicated that the sanctions were imposed after Cipriani had stepped down as head of the Peruvian church in 2019 "as a result of the accusations against him," suggesting there was more than one allegation.

The sanctions are similar to those imposed on other high-ranking prelates accused of sexual abuse. The former archbishop of Agaña (Guam), Anthony Apuron, and the Nobel Peace Prize–winning bishop and former bishop of East Timor, Carlos Ximenes Belo, were also forced to leave their home countries and limit their public ministries following abuse allegations.

AFTER A FEW PHONE CALLS with my sources, I learn that Cipriani was officially summoned to the pre-conclave meetings by Cardinal Re, the dean of the College of Cardinals. I immediately call the German Jesuit priest, Hans Zollner, one of the Vatican's top experts on sexual abuse, to ask him how he could be disobeying a punishment imposed by Pope Francis. "For me, if there are sanctions against Cipriani, the cardinals have to intervene," Zollner comments.[17]

Without hiding his perplexity at this situation, he reiterates that Cardinal Camerlengo Kevin Farrell, who plays a key role in this *"sede vacante,"* and the three cardinals who have been chosen to assist him during the first three days (Filipino Luis Antonio Tagle, German Reinhard Marx, and Corsican-French Dominique Mamberti) should take action.

"I don't know what the sanctions are, but if they exist and he is disobeying them, I insist that the cardinals must intervene, because it means there is a problem with the application of the sanctions and the credibility of the sanctions," warns Zollner, who helped Francis create the Pontifical Commission for the Protection of Minors—which he left two years ago—and has directed the Institute for the Protection of Minors at the Pontifical Gregorian University for thirteen years.

Zollner, a theologian, psychologist, and consultant to the diocese of Rome, warns that it is crucial that Francis's successor be very clear about the scandal of abuse—sexual, of conscience, and of power—

---

17. Elisabetta Piqué, "Escándalo: el pedido de un experto en abusos ante la presencia de un cardenal del Opus Dei sancionado antes del cónclave," *La Nación*, April 29, 2025.

which has damaged the Church's credibility like never before, and the steps taken in recent years to confront it.

He states that "it is necessary for the papal candidates to be very clear about how they acted regarding abuse in the past and how they will act in the future, because this is an important issue for the pontificate, regardless of who becomes pope."

According to Zollner, Pope Francis has done three very positive things in his twelve-year pontificate regarding this issue. "The first is that he met with many victims. After his death, in recent days, I have received numerous messages from victims who had personal contact with the pope, who had the opportunity to meet with him, and who felt deeply moved and grateful to Francis for his way of listening to them. Francis listened to the victims with empathy, sharing the pain of those wounded. I have seen this with my own eyes because I have been present at some of these meetings, when the pope has received victims of abuse committed by members of the Church," he says.

He adds that "Francis was obviously not able to meet with all the victims. I say this because these days I am seeing news of people complaining that he did not do everything possible and did not meet with them to listen. This is especially the case in Latin America, where, probably due to cultural and linguistic proximity, many victims thought they would have greater access to the pope."

The second point Zollner highlights is the anti-abuse summit in February 2019, when Francis convened all the presidents of the world's episcopal conferences. "This allowed for discussion of the structural dimension of the abuse problem, the institutional and systemic dimension of the problem. Pope Francis allowed us to spend three days not just repeating what we all already know: that we must listen to the victims, that we must confront the abusers, etc. Francis also allowed for a questioning of the role of the Church as an institution in regard to abuse, the role of a Church that for decades has not only allowed cases of abuse and therefore has a collective responsibility in this regard. Cases of abuse have been repeated everywhere, very often following the same pattern. That is why it is very important that at that summit, the co-responsibility of bishops and the need to hold them accountable were discussed for the first time.

"Before that, there was no awareness about it; there was no need to hold bishops accountable for their behavior in cases of abuse. It was Francis who introduced it, although obviously you can't expect to change a culture overnight, or even over a period of five or ten years. It's a long process that began with Pope Benedict XVI and that Francis has continued, expanded, and deepened. This is like a marathon, and although we've covered a significant amount of ground, we must continue the race, and there's still a long way to go."

Pope Francis's third achievement, in Zollner's opinion, was to change various laws regarding this scourge, including the motu proprio *Vos estis lux mundi*.[18] "The problem is that, unfortunately, we don't know if these laws are being applied consistently throughout the world," he warns.

"In *Vos estis lux mundi*, it is said for the first time that bishops have responsibility and are obliged to be accountable. That motu proprio also speaks for the first time about the responsibility of clergy, as well as lay people, and it also speaks of abuse not only as sexual but also spiritual, physical, and emotional. And," he adds, "for the first time, it speaks of vulnerable adults."

What should the next pope do regarding abuse? Zolner answers that "he must continue along the same path and must find ways of verifying that things are really changing. If we truly want things to change regarding abuse, we need to develop a different sensitivity and reach the conviction that all of us, all Catholics, all members of the Church, are co-responsible and therefore all have the capacity to initiate proceedings, not only against priests but also against lay people and against superiors, such as bishops or provincials. We all have the obligation to denounce someone who is not acting as they should," he answers.

When I ask him if Francis's successor might take steps back on the issue of sexual abuse and pedophilia, Zollner is blunt: "The Church has begun a process that must continue and that I hope will expand, intensify, and become increasingly consistent."

IN THIS HEATED, COUNTDOWN-LIKE ATMOSPHERE, Bruni says at the daily 1 PM briefing that General Congregation #6 opened this morning at 9 AM with a moment of prayer, followed by a meditation led by Dom Donato Ogliari, abbot of Saint Paul Outside the Walls, which continued until 9:40 AM.

---

18. Pope Francis, motu proprio *Vos estis lux mundi*, May 9, 2019.

The session was attended by 183 cardinals, of whom more than 120 are electors, indicating that almost all of them have arrived. This is important because rumors circulate that a tense atmosphere has prevailed during the first few days. "Some conservatives have already spoken and seem better prepared and organized. But the conversations opened up more when those who did not reside in Rome began to arrive, as they speak more freely, express their thoughts, and are not tactical," one participant tells *Le Monde*.[19]

Bruni reports there were approximately twenty interventions. Reflections focused on the role of the Church in today's world and the challenges it faces. The cardinals shared different perspectives, enriched by the experiences and contexts of different continents, and wondered what response the Church should offer in these times.

During yesterday's general congregation, the college sent a message of gratitude to the world for participation in the recent events and the support received in the days following the death of Pope Francis, in a message made public this morning.

Bruni confirms that, ultimately, 133 cardinal electors will enter the conclave. Two are unable to participate for health reasons: Antonio Cañizares, emeritus of Valencia, Spain, and John Njue, of Kenya. Thus, the next pope will need 89 votes (two-thirds) to be elected.

Furthermore, he confirms that the conclave will begin on May 7 at 4:30 PM, when the 133 cardinals will enter the Sistine Chapel for the pre-election oath as provided for in the *Ordo Rituum Conclavis*, after praying in the Pauline Chapel. That morning, Cardinal Re, dean of the College of Cardinals, will preside with the 133 cardinal electors at the *Pro Eligendo Pontifex* Mass in St. Peter's Basilica.

If the trend of the last two conclaves, which lasted just two days, is repeated, there could be a new pope the following day, May 8.

I RETURN HOME TO HAVE LUNCH.

I talk to some of my deep throats at the Vatican to see what they're saying. Suddenly, I get a phone call from a journalist colleague who has worked for a few years at a Vatican dicastery. She tells me of an Italian prelate who was very close to Francis and is very concerned about

---

19. Sarah Belouezzane and Benoît Vitkine, "Major Maneuvers for Pope Francis's Succession Begin," *Le Monde*, April 29, 2025.

what is happening and would like to talk to me, but off the record. While at first my reaction is that, with all the work I have, I don't want to waste time, my journalistic instinct tells me it might be worth hearing what this is all about. And my instinct doesn't fail me. I speak at length with this new deep throat, who finally identifies himself: he is a young Italian bishop who was very close to Francis until the very end and who is desperate because he fears that, given the intense campaign under way in the Italian media, Cardinal Parolin will end up being elected as his successor, and that Parolin is someone whom, in recent years and as is widely known, Jorge Bergoglio no longer trusted.

After that call, which I immediately discuss with Gerry, I feel like I'm in a movie thriller called *Conclave*. I decide to write an article I have had in mind for several days, which Gerry and Irene and I had been discussing for some time, but which seemed inelegant to publish so close to the death of our beloved Father Jorge. The odds-on favorite Cardinal Parolin has an Achilles' heel: Pope Francis made it very clear before leaving for the "Father's house" that he did not want him to be his successor.

With Father Jorge in mind, I feel like I must write the article. Coming from me, I know it will have repercussions. It is important to put into black and white something that is common knowledge among Italian Vatican experts, but that everyone keeps quiet about, perhaps because of undue pressure. I speak with Juan, one of my bosses at the newspaper, and he happily gives me the green light. Juli, whom I also told that I felt like I was in a movie, asked me, "When is the book coming out?"

I begin to write the article, opening it with a vital fact: leading up to the 2013 conclave, Milan archbishop Angelo Scola was the odds-on favorite, but this cardinal who entered the conclave as pope left as a cardinal. The little-known archbishop of Buenos Aires, who chose to call himself Francis, was elected.[20]

With one week and one day to go, the Italian newspapers have no doubt that the grand papabile is an Italian: Cardinal Parolin, secretary of state, Francis' number two. But he could suffer the same fate as Scola.

---

20. Elisabetta Piqué, "Los puntos débiles de Parolin, el favorito a ser el próximo papa, y el secreto a voces de su relación con Francisco," *La Nación*, April 29, 2025.

Pressure prevails in the Italian media for an Italian pope after a forty-seven-year absence. The last Italian pope was John Paul I (Albino Luciani), the pope of thirty-three days, in 1978, followed by the Polish John Paul II (1978–2005), the German Benedict XVI (2005–2013), and the Argentine Francis (2013–2025).

The article underlines Parolin's many strengths: he is a very amiable and moderate cardinal—whom we have known for some time and whom we like very much—a skilled diplomat, whom many believe would calm the situation after a papacy that inside the Church stirred the waters and was considered by some to be too open, informal, and disruptive.

All analysts agree that the cardinal from the Veneto region will enter the election with a privileged position and a solid package of votes. Seventy years old, with a curial style that's the polar opposite of his recently deceased boss, he is the best-known candidate among a college of cardinal electors that has never been so international (71 countries represented), numerous, and diverse (how many people know where the archipelago-kingdom of Tonga is located in Oceania?).

During his term, Parolin—who, it is said, played Mass as a child and stated that he wanted to be pope when he grew up—traveled all over the world, making him the most well-known among cardinal electors who lament having rarely seen each other.

In addition, following the procedures of *Universi Dominici Gregis*, the apostolic constitution that is the "bible" of the conclave, Parolin will preside over the conclave, since he is most senior elector from the order of cardinal bishops. Both the dean of the College of Cardinals, Re, and the vice dean Leonardo Sandri, outrank Parolin in the order but are ruled out of entering the Sistine Chapel because of age.

Parolin is positioned as a candidate for continuity in the eyes of many electors, having been Francis's second-in-command. But those who truly understand reality question this interpretation.

Among his weaknesses is his lack of pastoral experience. He lived in a parish for only a couple of years. As was the case with Scola in 2013, he does not have the support of the nineteen Italian cardinals who will participate in the vote. They are not a united bloc. Parolin faces two other candidates considered *papabili*. The first is Cardinal Matteo Zuppi, 69, archbishop of Bologna and president of the Italian Episcopal Conference, and associated with the Community of Sant'

Egidio. He is closely aligned with Pope Francis. The third Italian possibility is Latin Patriarch of Jerusalem Pierbattista Pizzaballa, 60, supported by a conservative wing.

The Italians' division also has to do with something that the Italian newspapers barely hint at, but that is an open secret. Although Parolin was brought by Francis to Rome from Venezuela where he was nuncio (Vatican ambassador) to become the pope's second-in-command in August 2013, many know that they have grown apart over the years. "Although Francis appointed him as secretary of state, over time he realized he no longer trusted him. Everyone knows that," my new deep throat told me. He fears that Parolin, if elected, could put a stop to the "reflourishing of the Church" brought about by the Argentine pope. "I can't believe there are Italian newspapers that keep quiet about this and say Parolin is the favorite 'because he was Bergoglio's strongman,' because that is not true," he laments.

The truth is that in his final months of life the pope himself made it clear that Parolin was not his choice to be his successor. In February, shortly before being admitted to the Gemelli Hospital and considering his succession, Francis decided to extend ninety-one-year-old Cardinal Re's completed five-year term as dean of the College of Cardinals.[21]

At the time, he offered no explanation for his decision. But it was obvious to Vatican insiders that, since the dean of the College of Cardinals plays a fundamental role in the *sede vacante*, he preferred to leave that position to Re, who cannot enter the conclave. Observers recall that in the 2005 conclave following the death of John Paul II, the dean of the College of Cardinals was Joseph Ratzinger, and it was he then who presided over the general congregations, the funeral, the Mass for the election of the pontiff, and the conclave, key moments that allowed him to have high visibility and consolidate his candidacy.

If Francis had not renewed Re's mandate as dean of the College of Cardinals, it is very likely that the twelve cardinal-bishops charged with electing a new dean to fill that position would have opted for Pietro Parolin. This would have given Parolin tremendous visibility, boosting his chances in the papal election.

---

21. Elisabetta Piqué, "Una decisión del papa Francisco con impacto en el cónclave abre especulaciones sobre su sucesión," *La Nación*, February 7, 2025.

Furthermore, Francis also refused to give Parolin any significant role in the events of last Holy Week, when Bergoglio was convalescing. Many also remember that, during his final stay at the Gemelli Hospital, he preferred to receive Italian Prime Minister Giorgia Meloni in his sickbed before Parolin, whom he never received alone, but together with his substitute, Venezuelan Archbishop Edgar Peña Parra. "He trusted the substitute, but not Parolin," the same prelate states.

"The Italian cardinals who are diplomats or members of the Curia want to make Parolin pope by any means necessary, to keep their positions and because they hope he will centralize everything again in the Secretariat of State, from which Francis took away not only power but also funding, which would be a step backward," another Vatican insider tells me. This source tells me that tomorrow, at General Congregation #7, the topic will be the economy.

I INTERRUPT WRITING the sensitive article on Parolin's weaknesses to join Gerry for Mass at the nearby Chiesa Nuova, celebrated by Luxembourg Cardinal Jean-Claude Hollerich, whom we know well. Hollerich, former president of the Commission of Bishops' Conferences of the European Union countries, is a Jesuit like Francis and one of the most progressive and outspoken cardinals in the College of Cardinals. I first interviewed him in October 2019, after he had been created cardinal. He had no problem stating, in black and white, that women should become cardinals. A polyglot who lived for many years in Japan, a country he adores, Hollerich was the general rapporteur for the Synod on Synodality. During the Mass at the Chiesa Nuova (where Juampy and Caro took their catechism classes and received First Communion), while he highlights the homily Cardinal Re gave last Saturday during Francis's solemn funeral, he also points out that Re forgot to touch on two key points in the late pope's legacy. "He failed to speak about the Holy Spirit and the Synod," Hollerich notes. It marked a before and after, in which women participated with voting rights for the first time and where everyone, including the pope, sat at large round tables, all on the same level. Hollerich, who, as a Jesuit, is not considered by many to be "papabile" (two consecutive Jesuits seems impossible), makes it clear in an informal meeting he held afterward with the two of us and some other journalists that Francis's candidate to follow the synodal path is Maltese Cardinal Mario Grech, who served as his right-hand man as secretary general of the Synod. At 68, Grech is not considered as open-minded as Hollerich; he is more moderate, and his figure could bring a cross-section of votes. Thanks to their role as orchestra conductors of the Synod, which was attended by some sixty cardinal electors, both are quite well-known, and their names also appear on the lists of papal candidates.

We return home, I finish the fateful Parolin article. Gerry reads it carefully, suggests I soften certain points, and is worried. He has known Parolin for many years and considers him a very good person. He is aware that this article, although it does not invent anything but rather reports true things, could damage his candidacy.

APRIL 30, WEDNESDAY [GERRY]

*Betrayal*

IN THE MIDDLE OF ANOTHER HECTIC DAY, I learn some bombshell news, which I immediately share with Betta and which will be our scoop of the day. A cardinal I've known for a long time, who is participating in the general congregations and who, of course, asks to remain anonymous (everyone has been sworn to secrecy), tells me something this Wednesday that evokes dismay: Italian Cardinal Beniamino Stella has disconcerted the cardinals by openly attacking Pope Francis "for ignoring the deep-rooted tradition of the Church that linked the power of government with holy orders."[22]

Pope Francis, according to Cardinal Stella, "imposed his own ideas," by opening positions of governance in the Roman Curia and the Church to men and women who are not in holy orders.

Cardinal Stella, former prefect of the Dicastery for the Clergy, is 83 years old and therefore cannot vote in the conclave.

---

22. Gerard O'Connell, "Backer of Cardinal Parolin Attacks Pope Francis's Push for Lay Involvement in Church Governance," *America*, April 30, 2025.

Pope Francis introduced this important change in *Praedicate Evangelium* ("Preach the Gospel"), the Constitution for the Reform of the Roman Curia, promulgated on March 19, 2022. There, he separated the power of governance in the Church from that of the orders, thus allowing the participation of non-bishops, lay people, men and women, in the governance and responsibility of the Church. Even before then, Francis had already appointed a layman for the first time as prefect of the Vatican Dicastery for Communication (Paolo Ruffini in 2018[23]) and, for the first time in five hundred years, in January 2025 he appointed a woman, the Italian nun Simona Brambilla, MC, as prefect of the Dicastery for Institutes of Consecrated Life and Societies of Apostolic Life.[24] Then, in another absolute novelty which shocked everyone in the Vatican, Brambilla became the superior of a cardinal: Francis had appointed Spanish Cardinal Ángel Fernández Artime, the former superior of the Salesians, as her second-in-command and, therefore, as "pro-prefect" of the same dicastery.

"We have heard many complaints against Francis's papacy in recent days, but Cardinal Stella's speech was by far the worst," this cardinal tells me. He also reveals that the ultra-conservative American Cardinal Raymond Burke, who addressed the assembly yesterday, made the same argument as Stella against reforming the Curia, but focusing on aspects of canon law. Cardinal Burke, a former head of the Apostolic Signatura, is known to have long been one of the most vocal critics of Pope Francis's policies and writings.

Cardinal Stella's speech was particularly troubling to several of the 181 participants, including very many of the 124 cardinal electors present today, for various reasons, the main one being the fact that he was one of Francis's closest confidants. Second, because he is perceived as the organizer of the campaign to have Cardinal Parolin elected as the next pope.

A second cardinal, who also requested anonymity, told me that Cardinal Stella "has been pressuring cardinals to vote for Cardinal Parolin in the conclave" that begins on May 7, claiming that Parolin already has forty votes pledged. The same is maintained by the Italian

---

23. Gerard O'Connell, "Pope Francis Appoints First Layperson as Head of Vatican Communications," *America*, July 5, 2018.

24. Gerard O'Connell, "Historic First: Pope Francis Appoints Woman as Prefect of Vatican Dicastery," *America*, January 6, 2025.

press, which, like the English bookmakers, has been describing Parolin as the favorite to be elected the 267th successor to St. Peter.

Cardinal Stella's reasoning is that, after Francis's papacy, which generated disorder and confusion, a diplomatic, moderate, institutional figure like Parolin is needed to restore order.

CARDINAL STELLA DEDICATED MUCH OF HIS LIFE to the diplomatic service of the Holy See. After being ordained a priest in 1966, he entered the Pontifical Ecclesiastical Academy, where diplomats of the Holy See are trained. Subsequently, after earning a doctorate in canon law, he joined the diplomatic service of the Holy See in 1970 and served first in its diplomatic missions in the Dominican Republic and Zaire (now the Democratic Republic of the Congo), before being recalled to the Vatican Secretariat of State from 1976 to 1978 and from 1983 to 1987. Pope John Paul II ordained him archbishop and appointed him pro-nuncio in the Republic of the Congo and Chad in 1987. The pope sent him as nuncio to Cuba in 1992 and as nuncio to Colombia in 1999. Pope Benedict XVI appointed him director of the Pontifical Ecclesiastical Academy in 2007. Francis, who knew and trusted Stella before being elected pope in March 2013, appointed him prefect of the then Congregation for the Clergy in September 2013 and created him a cardinal in 2014. Cardinal Stella remained prefect of the congregation until 2021.

"Stella's speech made me angry, and it damaged Parolin because some cardinal electors who were not pro-Francis reacted very negatively to it and turned away from Parolin," one elector told me. "Stella's talk went down badly, especially among the younger cardinals," another elector said.

Cardinal Re, dean of the College of Cardinals and presider over the general congregations, also actively supports Cardinal Parolin's candidacy, according to several of his fellow cardinals.

Unlike Chinese Cardinal Joseph Zen Ze-kyun, who addressed the assembly on Wednesday, apologizing for "not speaking about certain matters" (namely, the secret Provisional Agreement on the Appointment of Bishops signed by the Holy See and the People's Republic of China in Beijing on September 22, 2018, which he always opposed), other cardinals speak about this controversial topic during the general congregations.

I learn that at least two cardinals have spoken out strongly against this agreement: the Italian, Fernando Filoni and the American Raymond Burke. However, it is known that several others have serious reservations about it and believe the Vatican should take a firmer stance with Beijing.

Cardinal Filoni, 79, is considered an expert on China, having served in Hong Kong between 1992 and 2000, where he inaugurated the Holy See's study mission on China and monitored developments of the situation. He was John Paul II's bridge with the bishops of the ecclesiastical communities, both official and clandestine, in mainland China. Benedict XVI sent him as nuncio to the Philippines in 2006, but then recalled him to Rome as a "substitute," or chief of staff, at the Secretariat of State in 2007. Four years later, he appointed him prefect of the Congregation for the Evangelization of Peoples, a position he held until 2019, and created him a cardinal in 2012. At the general congregations, Filoni spoke out strongly against the provisional agreement, about which he had already expressed serious reservations in 2019.

Cardinal Burke, 76, former archbishop of St. Louis (2002–2008) and former prefect of the Supreme Tribunal of the Apostolic Signatura (the Vatican's Supreme Court) (2008–2014), became a leading traditionalist voice in the Church and a spearhead of the opposition to Pope Francis. "Burke spoke out against the interim agreement with China, and it seemed as if Zen had written his speech," one cardinal confided to me.

We have learned that several other cardinals from Asia, Eastern Europe, and the United States share the reservations expressed by Filoni and Burke regarding the Holy See's Provisional Agreement with China on the appointment of bishops. This bodes ill for Cardinal Parolin in the conclave, since he is considered the architect of the agreement.

IN THE DAILY BRIEFING WITH JOURNALISTS in the Press Office—in which Betta again asks why the sanctioned Cardinal Cipriani participates in the general congregations, but receives no response—Bruni reports that the meeting on Wednesday focused primarily on the economic and financial situation of the Holy See. He details that German Cardinal Reinhard Marx, coordinator of the Council for the Economy, presented an updated overview of existing challenges and critical issues, offering proposals aimed at sustainability and reiterating the importance of economic structures continuing to stably support the mission of the papacy.

American Cardinal Kevin Farrell, a confidant of Francis who, in addition to being the *camerlengo*, is president of the Investment Committee, spoke about the role and activities of that body. In turn, Austrian Cardinal Christoph Schönborn, president of the Cardinals' Commission for the Supervision of the Institute for Works of Religion (IOR), offered a reflection on the current situation of the Institute. Spanish Cardinal Fernando Vérgez Alzaga (another confidant of Bergoglio, who was for years private secretary to Argentine Cardinal Eduardo Pironio), president emeritus of the Governorate of Vatican City State (succeeded by decision of Francis by the Italian nun, Sr. Raffaella Petrini[25]), then explained some details relating to the Governorate, also referring to some renovation works on state buildings and the support provided to the Holy See. Finally, the Polish Cardinal Konrad Krajewski, papal almoner, spoke, illustrating the dicastery's commitment to the Service of Charity, according to Bruni. Although Sister Petrini and Mr. Caballero Ledo[26] are respectively the current heads of the Governorate of the Vatican City State and the Secretariat for the Economy, they are not cardinals and were therefore not invited to speak.

The cardinals discussed the Holy See's deficit and disastrous economic outlook. "The deficit will be a very serious problem for the next pope, whoever that may be," a cardinal who requested anonymity told *La Repubblica*.[27] "It would take a miracle," he added, pointing to the problem of declining donations and the enormous burden on the pension system.

After addressing the complex and worrying topic of finances, the cardinals heard fourteen interventions in the Synod Hall. They discussed the issue of vocations, the polarization in the Church and the division in society, and the value of synodality, Bruni says. Several in-

---

25. Gerard O'Connell, "Pope Francis Appoints an Italian Nun as the First Woman Governor of Vatican City," *America*, February 15, 2025.

26. Gerard O'Connell, "Pope Francis Accepts Resignation of Top Vatican Economy Official, Appoints Lay Man to Role for First Time," *America*, November 30, 2022.

27. Andrea Gualtieri, "Vaticano, il bilancio in rosso irrompe nel Conclave. 'Un miracolo per salvarci,'" *La Repubblica*, May 1, 2025.

terventions made explicit reference to the documents of the Second Vatican Council, particularly the apostolic constitutions *Lumen Gentium* and *Gaudium et Spes*. Another topic, he adds, was evangelization, emphasizing "the necessary coherence between the proclamation of the Gospel and the concrete witness of Christian life."

Bruni seems to be unaware that his official statement will be overshadowed by Cardinal Stella's unexpected critique/attack on Pope Francis, which two nuncio friends described to us as nothing less than "a betrayal."

"Stella's attack was offensive; it left most of us 'Francis's' cardinals [created by Francis] horrified…. With the pope's body still warm and when just days before Stella had been speaking wonders of him, we were all dumbfounded by such hypocrisy," one shocked cardinal confides, convinced that this venomous intervention will ultimately backfire on the pro-Parolin campaign.

Bruni announces that tomorrow, Thursday, May 1st, Labor Day in Italy, there will be no general congregation. They will resume on Friday at 9 AM. This means that tomorrow the various *cordate* (groupings of cardinals around a given candidate) will have twenty-four hours free to carry on with lunches, dinners, and private meetings to continue the discussions and maneuvers in view of an increasingly imminent and unpredictable conclave.

Despite the ongoing maneuvers, the College of Cardinals, through the Press Office, issues a statement stating that "aware of the responsibility to which we are called, we perceive the need to be sustained by the prayers of all the faithful" and inviting the "People of God to experience this ecclesial event as a moment of grace and spiritual discernment, listening to the will of God."[28]

BETTA AND I EAT AT A BAR ON VIA DELLA CONCILIAZIONE and then interview the Czech-born Canadian Cardinal Michael Czerny with Irene. He's one of the five Jesuits who will participate in the conclave and is among those "cool" cardinals who believe it's important, beyond the oath of maximum secrecy, without, of course giving details, to speak to the media at this moment in history.

---

28. "Bolletino," Comunicato della Santa Sede, Sala Stampa della Santa Sede, April 30, 2025.

"How am I preparing for the election? By doing what I'm doing right now. For me, it's very important to have a dialogue with the media; it's part of my preparation. Otherwise, I pray, and I try to eat and rest well. It's a big responsibility," he says.[29]

Czerny, 78, doesn't hide his irritation with those on the conservative side who denounce Pope Francis, saying that he caused confusion during his papacy. "We live in a confusing world, and the Church, to fulfill its vocation, must generate confusion. Jesus generated a lot of confusion, a lot," he says, as he warmly welcomes us into his apartment next to the General Curia of the Society of Jesus. "Of course, there should be more order, there should be more unity, and there should also be more creativity. And more ways to reach the peripheries, the black holes that the Gospel doesn't reach or penetrate," he adds.

Born in what was then Czechoslovakia, Czerny had to leave his homeland at age two with his family and immigrate to Canada. He studied in the United States and, after the murder of the Jesuits at the Universidad Centroamericana (UCA) in El Salvador in 1989, served as vice-rector there. He lived in Africa for ten years, where he founded and directed the African Jesuit Network on AIDS. He served as an advisor to Cardinal Peter Turkson, president of the Pontifical Council for Justice and Peace, and in recent years was one of the Argentine pope's closest collaborators, helping him draft and launch his encyclical *Laudato Si'*, on the care of our common home. He was ordained a bishop and created cardinal in 2019, and appointed prefect of the Dicastery for Promoting Human Integral Development in 2022.

Cardinal Czerny tells us that, in the midst of a world and society "on fire," he is looking for a pope who is close to those who suffer, open to dialogue, creative, and forward thinking. "A pope should not think of going backwards; honestly, I think it makes no sense. A pope should think about the challenge of bringing the Gospel to the whole world by 2025," he asserts. Unlike the other cardinals, Czerny's pectoral cross is neither silver nor gold: it is made from the discolored wood of a barge carrying migrants who drowned in the Mediterranean; it sends quite a message.

When we ask him what he considers the great challenges in this burning world, the cardinal responds insightfully. "What I learned

---

29. Gerard O'Connell, "Interview: Cardinal Czerny on Why It Shouldn't Matter Where the Next Pope Is From," *America*, May 5, 2025.

from Francis is that you can't answer that question if you don't know from where it's being asked. When you view the world from a satellite, it all seems one, but it isn't. The answer to the question you posed is different if you ask it from Bolivia, Johannesburg, or Hong Kong. If you want to know what the important problems are, ask the UN, not us. We're not interested in problems in general, but in specific problems, real problems. For example, it seems rather silly to me when people ask me about migration in general. I don't talk about migration, I talk about migrants."...He reminds us that "Francis's approach was pastoral; it began with people."

On the other hand, he downplays the concept of the Church's polarization. "The most significant thing I can say about polarization is that it's an issue the media likes," he states. "I'm not saying all of them do, but some do. I really only hear about polarization in the Church in the media. Those of us who are old enough remember that even in the time of Paul VI, people talked about polarization, although that word wasn't used back then. What was said then was that there were different visions of how to be Catholic."

Does he have the feeling that the next pontiff could be Italian, as the ongoing media campaign suggests? "I think it's speculation, especially from the Italian press. I can understand and even sympathize with that speculation. But I can't imagine it will have any effect on the vote of the cardinal electors; it's impossible. Place of origin is a category of no importance when it comes to choosing the pope. When I hear people say that the time has come for an American pope, an Italian pope, an African pope, a pope from the East, it strikes me as utter stupidity," he says. And he bids us farewell by confessing that, for him, the next pope will surely speak English.

BETTA AND I AGREED TO PUBLISH OUR BOMBSHELL ARTICLE about the disconcerting attack on Pope Francis by Stella, the strategist behind Cardinal Parolin's candidacy, simultaneously in the respective digital editions of *America* and *La Nación*. The feeling is that of being part of a puzzle that is slowly coming together. In fact, Betta has received several messages from people involved congratulating her for her "courage" in writing and publishing the article about Parolin's weaknesses. It's an article currently circulating among several "Bergoglian" Latin American cardinal electors who had been convinced that Parolin would have been Francis's choice to succeed him. But now, having been alerted that this isn't the case at all, they are considering another, more daring option.

MAY 1, THURSDAY [BETTA] ─────────────────────
*An Exhausting Labor Day*

ST. PETER'S SQUARE IS EMPTY, desolate, and shrouded in gloomy, black clouds. A storm is about to break; the wind begins to blow, and it captures the moment, I start filming a video. Suddenly, a wind gust hits. It is so powerful and violent that it almost rips my cell phone out of my hand. Like someone in an apocalyptic movie, I desperately start running toward the Holy See Press Office at 54 Via della Conciliazione to try to save myself. . . . But I can't, and I start screaming.

This is the nightmare I wake up to, startled, after a night of poor sleep. At five in the morning, I had already woken up to see if Caro had returned. I usually hear the doorbell when she returns from her outings with her friends, but this time I haven't heard anything. I get up and go to her room, where she's sleeping. I go back to bed and fall into a deep sleep, until that terrible nightmare.

Could it have something to do with the day I have ahead of me? Today is the Labor Day holiday in Italy and the Vatican; the cardinals don't have general congregations, and we have three interviews scheduled!

At 8:40 we meet Irene at the taxi stand in Piazza San Pantaleo. The "dream team" strikes again: Irene has secured an interview with German Cardinal Gerhard Müller.[30]

Müller, spearhead of the conservative opposition, is waiting for us at 9 AM in his apartment in Piazza della Città Leonina, the same book-filled apartment where Joseph Ratzinger lived for twenty years.

─────────────
30. Elisabetta Piqué, "'Francisco ha creado confusión y hay que poner orden,' dice el cardenal alemán Gerhard Müller," *La Nación*, May 3, 2025.

We arrive early, so there is time to have a quick cappuccino in a bar where the topic of conversation is my nightmare....

Müller, created a cardinal by Francis in 2014, has remained in Rome with no relevant role other than to write books, give lectures, and travel around the world to ensure that a successor from the conservative wing emerges. His candidate is believed to be Hungarian Cardinal Péter Erdő.

A tall, powerfully built 77-year-old theologian and elector, Müller is extremely amiable during the forty-minute interview, in which he clearly states that he hopes the next pope will be different from the Argentine one and will undo many of his reforms (for example, that of the Curia). For him, "an orthodox pope" is needed because Francis "has created confusion and order must be restored."[31]

When asked if the next pope could reverse Francis's decision to incorporate lay people and women into Vatican dicasteries, the cardinal makes no secret of his anxious hope. "In everything that relates to ecclesiastical law, the pope can make changes; what he cannot change is divine law," he affirms.

On the other hand, he does not hide his sharp criticism of the synod, something that he claims has created confusion. "All the cardinals agree that the concepts need to be clarified. The term 'synod' is a vague concept. What is a synod? A synod of bishops only?" he asks.

Like many others, he acknowledges that one of the great difficulties of pre-conclave meetings is that many cardinals do not know each other.

"That's right, and it is a big problem, because it's not just about knowing a person's name, but about knowing their personality, about being able to form an image of them. Choosing a pope is a great responsibility; we must find the right person, and in that sense, we are instruments of the Holy Spirit, but we are intelligent instruments," he maintains.

Like most of Jorge Bergoglio's opponents, he accuses Pope Francis of having created confusion and believes the time has come to restore order.

When Gerry, who has covered the Vatican for more than forty years, reminds him that Saint John Paul II had also been accused of

---

31. Gerard O'Connell, "Interview: Cardinal Müller on if Pope Francis Was a Heretic and What He Wants in the Next Pope," *America*, May 3, 2025.

creating confusion after an interfaith meeting in Assisi in 1986, which even Cardinal Ratzinger had refused to attend, and asks him if this accusation, now applied to Francis, is unfair, Müller replies: "The same thing happened with Paul VI. There was great confusion in the Church at that time. But, ultimately, it always depends a bit on style. The pope is not the commander of an army."

"I think Francis has sometimes created confusion and that order must be established, yes, the relationship between doctrine and pastoral care must be made very clear.... When Francis improvised or, for example, spoke on board an airplane, the things he said were not presentations of the Church's magisterium. They were simply his private opinions," he adds, alluding to when, on the return flight from his trip to Brazil at the beginning of his pontificate, Francis uttered that famous phrase: 'Who am I to judge [a gay man]?' It was very clear to me that the pope was referring to a specific case, but some have misinterpreted it. Combining doctrine for all and application to individuals is always a bit tricky," Müller says.

Asked if Francis could have committed heresy, Müller recalls when, during a visit to a parish in Rome, a boy, in tears, asked him if his father, who had died and was an atheist (but had had all his children baptized), had gone to hell. And Francis, embracing and comforting him, assured him that no, his father was in heaven. For Müller, this caused confusion.

And what should he have said? "The right thing would have been to tell that boy that we hoped his father was in heaven, that we had that hope."

GERRY AND I TAKE A TAXI directly to the Seminary Palace, adjacent to the Archbasilica of St. John Lateran, to interview Italian Cardinal Baldassare Reina, vicar of Rome, who is expecting us at 10 AM. It's not easy to arrive on time because the area is blocked by the *concertone*, the classic popular May Day recital in the iconic Piazza San Giovanni in Laterano.

Reina, 54, is not on the list of papal candidates because he is too young. Francis, who evidently had his eye on him, appointed him auxiliary bishop of Rome in May 2022; in January 2023, he named him vicegerent (number two) of the diocese; and in October of the same year, he appointed him cardinal vicar, archbishop, and archpriest of the Basilica of St. John Lateran. A Sicilian, Reina met the pope from

Argentina in July 2013, when Francis made his first and historic trip to the island of Lampedusa, a symbol of the migrant plight. Since Reina is from Agrigento, he was among the group of priests who welcomed the pope. He was struck by his sermon, in which he wept for those who died at sea fleeing war and misery and by his denunciation of the "globalization of indifference."

Shy and humble, Cardinal Reina recounts that he last saw Francis on April 10—eleven days before his death—convalescing at Santa Marta. Reina brought his right-hand man, Auxiliary Bishop Renato Tarantelli, to give the pope the embrace of Rome. "The pope spoke slowly, but he was very lucid. He asked us a few things about the life of the diocese, we told him a little about what we were doing, and he remembered everything very well. And we found him in good shape, with his usual sense of humor. At one point I said to him, 'But your face has a nice color!' And—with his usual humor—he told me the illness wasn't in his face."[32]

With a very different vision of the Church than Müller's, Reina is convinced that Francis's successor, whoever that may be, must continue his reformist impulse.[33] He rejects the mantra that his pontificate has been too disruptive and that now someone is needed to restore order.

"Pope Francis always described the scene of Pentecost. He said that the Holy Spirit came to stir things up, creating great confusion even among the apostles. And then we must listen to the Spirit in order to discern. Discernment has been a key word in Pope Francis's teaching, and I don't see that as confusion at all. Pope Francis was always in line with the doctrine, with the teaching, with the wealth of the Church's tradition. I repeat, he had the courage to confront and measure himself against what men and women today experience, starting, for example, with the situations of the divorced and remarried. And always evangelically, he said that reality is more important than the idea, and reality is what we see before our eyes every day. To pretend that reality doesn't exist would be truly foolish," he says. "So I don't at all share this idea of a pontificate that has created disorder. I

---

32. Gerard O'Connell, "Cardinal Reina: The Next Pope Must Continue the Reform Francis Began," *America,* May 5, 2025. La *Nación,*

33. Elisabetta Piqué, "Cardenal Baldassare Reina: 'Francisco era consciente de las resistencias, pero siguió adelante con sencillez y determnación,'" *La Nación,* May 5, 2025.

see it rather as one that has embraced the concerns of many people and has attempted to respond to those concerns with the Gospel of Jesus Christ. In Pope Francis, many people have recognized pages of the Gospel. Since his burial in Saint Mary Major, the lines there have been endless. The crowd that was there on the day of the funeral was a multitude of convinced people, who had traveled thousands of kilometers to pay homage to a person who, within his limitations, of course, knew how to translate the Gospel today."

What should be the profile of Francis's successor? "Francis was, in my opinion, a great interpreter of the Second Vatican Council. Dialogue with the world has identified one of the characteristics of the emergencies the Church now faces. Today the Church must engage in dialogue. Whoever comes after Francis must reap the legacy of Vatican II."

Reina was in the spotlight a few days ago because in his homily at one of the *novemdialis* Masses he alluded to the risk of taking a step backward. We asked him if he fears that this could really happen. "There has been resistance to Pope Francis's teaching over the past ten years, not that it's just now becoming evident in the pre-conclave meetings. It's always been there, in varying degrees. Let's remember what happened after *Amoris Laetitia*; let's also remember the reactions to the Synod on Synodality. And Pope Francis was aware of this, but he moved forward with great simplicity, and also with great determination," Reina says, adding, "I am not afraid. Just as twelve years ago the Holy Spirit raised up in the Church Pope Francis, who was a great prophet, I am convinced that today he will ... find a man who has the prophetic spirit of Francis and will continue the process of reform he began."

Reina expresses his absolute support for the commitment to a synodal Church. "The Spirit speaks through everyone, and Pope Francis, through the principle of synodality, reminded pastors that the Spirit is also present in the faithful by virtue of their baptism and that we have a duty to listen to the Spirit who acts in everyone and through everyone. It's an exercise we weren't used to. Pope Francis reminded us of this duty to listen to the lay faithful. Some very interesting things came out of it. The bishops who activated synodal teams in their dioceses experienced the liveliness of the Spirit because they are the faithful who live real life and bring you their experience of faith and help you see a point of view that you, as a pastor, probably hadn't considered," he explains. "I hope there's no going back. It's a style. Pope Francis has said several times: 'Synodality is not a document to be produced, but a style to be acquired.' And I think this style definitely needs to be strengthened."

FROM THE SEMINARY PALACE, we return to the Vatican. We honor Labor Day by working and...we have another interview. This third interview of the day is with another young cardinal, Canadian Frank Leo, whom Gerry has known since June 2023.[34] He awaits us at the Casa del Clero on Via Traspontina—a hotel for clergymen a few blocks from St. Peter's Basilica—where other cardinals are also staying. First, we go to a nearby bar for lunch—a *tramezzino* with mozzarella and tomato—and for the interview, we return to a quieter, small room on the ground floor of the clergy residence on Via Traspontina.

The archbishop of Toronto, just 53 years old and considered rather conservative by the media in his country, seems very engaged. He has us understand that this interview is exceptional, explaining that on this "free day" he prefers to avoid meeting with other cardinals; he also doesn't want to watch the news or be concerned with the media, social media, or his cell phone. He wants to be free from external influences, but focused, praying in preparation for the conclave.[35]

The son of working-class Italian immigrants, with a degree in philosophy and a doctorate in theology, Cardinal Leo, affable, speaks several languages and, after pastoral experience, studied at the Pontifical Ecclesiastical Academy in Rome (2006–2008) before serving in prestigious diplomatic service of the Holy See for six years, including posts in Australia and the Holy See's Study Mission in Hong Kong. But he decided to leave the diplomatic service when he realized he preferred being among the people as a pastor.

In 2012, he returned to Montreal, where he began a meteoric career. After teaching in the major seminary, he served as secretary of the Canadian Bishops' Conference from 2015 to 2021, when he was appointed first vicar general and in July 2022, auxiliary bishop of Montreal. In February 2023 he was named archbishop of Toronto,

---

34. Gerard O'Connell, "Exclusive Interview with Archbishop Frank Leo, Pope Francis's Ally in Toronto," *America*, July 5, 2023.

35. Elisabetta Piqué, "Cardenal Frank Leo: 'Francisco no era un comunista y el próximo papa tiene que ser un hombre de unidad,'" *La Nación*, May 6, 2025.

and in Pope Francis's last Consistory, in December of last year, he was created a cardinal.

"I believe we live in a broken world. Our world is broken, wounded, and polarized. And the Church is not of the world, but is in the world. We are not of the world, as Jesus said, but we are in the world, and that's why these divisions and the polarizing mentality of our presence in the world are also present in the Church," he says.[36]

What qualities should the next pope possess? "Number one: a great capacity to listen, first to God—he must be a man of prayer, of hope, of faith—to listen to the Church, to the People of God, to the laity, to the ordained, to the consecrated; and to listen to the world, to human suffering, to aspirations, with a Marian attitude of meditation in his heart. Listening also means consulting.

"On the other hand, in the broken and polarized world we are talking about, the next pope must be a man of unity, a man of peace, a man of communion, of reconciliation. It is imperative that he be a man of profound faith, of profound prayer, and of profound spirituality. This is the only thing that will keep him grounded and not susceptible to the winds of change or the trends of what is popular today, rooted in that spirituality and in his relationship with God. Then, he will be a credible witness and will speak to the world, to the heart of the world," he adds, emphasizing the importance of knowing how to speak to the world. He must be "a clear communicator of the faith" because "we must give people a word of hope, of a brighter future, so they can dream of a better life, and I'm not talking about positive thinking, but about the Gospel of God. And," he concludes, "it is not an esoteric message."

WE RETURN HOME. It is a day without general congregations, but the cardinals participate this afternoon in the sixth Mass of *novemdiales* in prayer for the soul of Pope Francis, on a day that coincides with the feast of St. Joseph the Worker, especially dear to him. The service, which we follow on the Vatican channel, is presided over by Argentine Cardinal Víctor Manuel "Tucho" Fernández. In his sermon, he recalls not only that Jorge Bergoglio was "a worker" who never took vacations, completely dedicated to his mission, but also reaffirmed his

---

36. Gerard O'Connell, "Interview: What Toronto's Cardinal Leo, One of the Youngest in the Conclave, Wants in a New Pope," *America*, May 6, 2025.

constant defense of workers and the value of the dignity of work.

Prefect of the Dicastery for the Doctrine of the Faith and a close friend of Pope Francis, Fernández takes the opportunity to lament how "some dishonest people" misinterpreted Francis's message on these issues in Argentina.

"I remember a video he sent a while back to a meeting of Argentine business leaders. He told them: 'I will never tire of talking about the dignity of work. Some people say that I advocate a life without effort, or that I despise the culture of work.' In fact, some dishonest people said that Pope Francis defended the indolent, the idle, the delinquent, the lazy.

"But the pope continued: 'Imagine if this can be said of me, a descendant of the Piedmontese, who came to this country not with the desire to be supported but with a great desire to roll up their sleeves and build a future for their families.' It seems he had had enough," Fernández adds.

In his sermon, delivered before about one hundred cardinals, employees of the Roman Curia, and faithful in St. Peter's Basilica, Fernández recalls that Francis used to emphasize that "work is the greatest help for a poor person" and that "there is no poverty worse than that which deprives him of work and the dignity of work."

Fernández also reiterates Francis's warnings about "false discourses about meritocracy," saying: "Let's look at the case of a person who was born into a good family and managed to increase his wealth, lead a good life with a nice house, a car, and vacations abroad. That's fine. He was fortunate enough to grow up in the right conditions and performed meritorious deeds. Thus, with skill and time, he built a very comfortable life for himself and his children. At the same time, someone who works with his hands, with equal or greater merit for the effort and time invested, has nothing. He wasn't fortunate enough to be born in the same conditions as the other man, and no matter how much he sweats, he barely manages to survive," Fernández continues.

He then shares a personal anecdote about an experience he had with a cardboard and bottle collector whom he used to cross paths with every day, morning and night, in Buenos Aires. "He would be working when I went to university in the morning. Then I would come back at night and find him still working. Once I asked him, 'How many hours do you work?' And he replied, 'Between twelve and fifteen hours a day, because I have several children to support and I want them to have a better future than mine.' So I asked him,

'But when are you with them?' And he answered, 'I have to choose: either I am with them or I bring them food.' Despite this, a well-dressed passerby snarled at him, 'Get a job, you lazy bum!' This is often heard in Argentina, and it helps us understand certain insistences of Pope Francis," he adds with his voice trembling, deviating from his prepared sermon.

"'Get a job, you lazy bum!' Those words struck me as horrendously cruel and vain. But those words are also hidden behind more elegant speeches," he declares. He goes on to point out that "Pope Francis launched a prophetic cry against this false notion, and in various conversations, he made me realize: look, we are led to believe that most of the poor are poor because they have no 'merit.' It seems that someone who inherited many possessions is more worthy than someone who did hard work all his life without saving anything or even buying a small house," he says, alluding again to the Argentine situation.

Fernández, the only Argentine prelate the pope brought to the Roman Curia for such an important post and his best interpreter, then emphasizes that Francis was "a hard worker," something he displayed until his final days. "It was a mystery to me how he could endure such a demanding work schedule, even as such an elderly man and suffering from various illnesses. He not only worked in the morning, with various meetings, audiences, celebrations, and encounters, but also all afternoon," he recalls. "And I thought it was truly heroic that with the very little strength he had in his final days, he found the strength to visit a prison." Moved by that memory, he recalls that Bergoglio never took vacations and that, in Buenos Aires during the summer, "if you couldn't find a priest, you would surely find him," and that "his daily work was his response to God's love. It was the expression of his concern for the good of others." Fernández mentions Francis's devotion to Saint Joseph, "that strong and humble worker, that carpenter from a small, forgotten town, who with his work cared for Mary and Jesus."

He concludes by saying, "And let us also remember that when Pope Francis had a serious problem, he would place a small piece of paper with a prayer under the image of Saint Joseph. So let us ask Saint Joseph to give our beloved Pope Francis a big hug in heaven."

I QUICKLY WRITE AN ARTICLE about this homily for the newspaper. We get in the car and rush to the Filipino College on Via Aurelia. We have been invited to attend Mass there by Filipino Cardinal Pablo Virgilio

"Ambo" David, whom we met last December when he was created a cardinal by Francis. Gerry, who interviewed him at the time,[37] became a friend, as per usual. The Mass is celebrated in Filipino, with some interventions in English and Italian. We are seated in the front row, like distinguished guests. I'm so tired that at first my eyes close. But I quickly wake up because there's an excellent choir, an orchestra, and a very lively, joyful, spiritual atmosphere, totally different from the Masses we attend in the center of Rome, which seem like funerals. ... Although the most striking thing is the large number of Filipino migrant workers present who later join the cardinal and the other priests for a meal. There are some 200,000 Filipino migrant workers in Rome and 250,000 in Milan, and they are considered modern-day missionaries here in Italy, as in many other countries around the world, as we saw on various papal trips.

In this conclave, for the first time in history, the Philippine Church has three cardinal electors: in addition to David, Cardinals Advincula and papal candidate Tagle, whom we did not meet that evening.

Dinner at the Filipino college was delicious: several dishes were served, including *kare-kare* (beef tripe) in peanut sauce with *bagoong* (shrimp paste); pork stew; chicken adobo in sugarcane vinegar and soy sauce; fried *lumpia* (spring rolls) with sweet and sour sauce; *lechon de cerdo* (whole roasted pig) with liver sauce; coconut dessert with *pandan* and *leche flan*. All delicious....

MAY 2, FRIDAY [GERRY]
*Outside Interferences*

ANOTHER DAY BEGINS without respite, marked by the classic—albeit increasingly less subtle—interference from lobbies or power groups seeking to influence the approaching conclave from the outside. The

---

37. Gerard O'Connell, "Cardinal 'Ambo' David: 'We're Not Catholic if We Believe that God Wants to Save only Catholics,'" *America*, January 16, 2025.

Vatican has begun installing the traditional chimney on the roof of the Sistine Chapel from which, starting on the afternoon of May 7, the emblematic smoke will begin to rise: black if a pope is not elected, white if a cardinal reaches the necessary 89 votes, equivalent to two-thirds of the 133 electors.

As in the previous conclave, a US-based advocacy group for abuse victims, Bishop Accountability, is calling a press conference to launch a media bombshell.

I cannot attend because I have to do a podcast, but Betta and Irene do. Luckily, they arrive early at the appointed place, a very small ground-floor room in the Orange Hotel on Via Crescenzio near the Vatican. There the organization's director Anne Barrett Doyle warns that the two leading favorites to succeed Pope Francis—Italian Cardinal Pietro Parolin, former secretary of state, and Filipino Cardinal Luis Antonio Tagle—would not be good choices to lead the Church because of their questionable records in handling sexual abuse cases.

"We cannot have another pope who does not take action against the cover-up,"[38] warns Doyle, who emphasizes that "little has been said about Parolin's involvement in abuse cases due to his profile as a diplomat, as he has never led a diocese as a bishop. However, no high-ranking Church prelate has kept as many secret documents on this issue as Parolin."

Doyle expresses concern about the possibility of Parolin becoming pope, accusing him of defending the interests of the Church while maintaining secrecy and lacking transparency. "We would be disturbed if he became pope, because he continues to cover up information and is not an example of transparency," she notes. "Any request for information about abuse cases went through the secretary of state's office," she charges. She maintains that authorities in Australia, a country severely affected by the abuse scandal, had requested information from the Holy See years ago on cases involving hundreds of abused children but never received a response. "The decision not to cooperate with the Royal Commission is obstruction of justice," Doyle charges, adding that the Holy See refused to publish the 1,200-page report prepared by Maltese Archbishop Charles Scicluna and Spanish prelate Jordi Bertomeu, who were sent by Pope Francis to Chile in 2018 to investigate the abuse scandal that affected the Church in that

---

38. Elisabetta Piqué, "El inédito informe del Vaticano que revela cómo un abusador llegó a ser cardenal en EEUU," *La Nación*, November 10, 2020.

country. "The Holy See doesn't want to release that report, and that is a cover-up and obstruction of justice," Doyle adds.

The director of Bishop Accountability also recalls that Cardinal Parolin exchanged letters with former US Archbishop Theodore McCarrick, the first cardinal dismissed from the priesthood by a pope—Pope Francis—because of allegations of sexual abuse.

The allegations seem strange, first of all because abuse issues are typically handled by the disciplinary section of the Dicastery for the Doctrine of the Faith and not by the Secretariat of State. Furthermore, as Betta points out at the press conference—which is also being streamed—Doyle fails to mention that, at Francis's request, the Vatican conducted a thorough investigation into the McCarrick case and published a public report on it in November 2020.[39] That report made clear that, while there was some kind of cover-up by the Vatican, this occurred during the pontificate of John Paul II (1978–2005).

Bishop Accountability's accusations also target Philippine Cardinal Luis Antonio "Chito" Tagle, whom they accuse of failing to be a firm leader in the fight against sexual abuse. "Tagle has been the most influential bishop in the Philippines in recent years and is a gentleman when he speaks about the issue of abuse and victims. But when we went to the Philippines, what we found shocked us. There, abuse victims are so scared that so far only one has publicly identified herself," notes Doyle. While she does not present evidence that Tagle covered up any specific case, she explains that in this Asian country—one of the most Catholic, along with Mexico and Brazil—the Church remains a very strong and influential institution, with great credibility, which has prevented the scandal from breaking out. According to Doyle, few victims have dared to come forward and report because of the fear that still persists in society. "The Church is so backward that they never published the document with guidelines to prevent abuse. Tagle couldn't even achieve that—the publication of guidelines. What can we expect if he becomes pope?" Doyle asks.

This is when Michal Gatchalian appears via videoconference. Gatchalian, who, at age 17 was a victim of abuse and became the only person in the Philippines who, in 2002, dared to file a complaint with the courts. "I filed my complaint with the police more than twenty-three years ago. I did it on my own, without the support of my family,

---

39. Gerard O'Connell, "Deep Dive: The McCarrick Report and the Popes It Implicates," *America*, November 10, 2020.

my community, or anyone else. Now, twenty-three years later, I'm a lawyer, and very little has changed. Victims face the same pressure and the same difficulties. Those same threats, pressure, and intimidation are still present today," he declares.

Also participating via videoconference is Father Shay Cullen, an Irish missionary priest who has been in the Philippines since 1969, an advocate for children's rights and a well-known whistleblower reporting on abuse in that country. He is the founder of the Preda Foundation, which is focused on rescuing, protecting, healing, and empowering exploited, trafficked, and abused children. Cullen openly criticizes Cardinal Tagle as a leader who performed poorly, although he does not link him to any specific case. Cullen, denounces the "total silence" that has existed for years and explains that, although they managed to bring thirty-four abusers to justice and obtain more than twenty convictions, not a single priest was convicted. "I hope the future pope will be even more firm than Pope Francis, holding bishops accountable and stopping the cover-up. I don't think Tagle is committed to protecting children. We need a true champion for children's rights," he says.

When asked if he has proof or evidence that Tagle had covered up cases, Cullen admits he has no information on the matter. "But he led the Philippine Church, and in every case, we didn't see an effort on his part, as leader of the Archdiocese of Manila, to resolve or stop this. There were no concrete efforts to end the cover-up. Doing nothing is like covering it up."

What's striking is that Cullen, a missionary widely recognized for his defense of human rights, did not hesitate to point out, when asked, that he would consider another Filipino to be a good candidate for the papacy: Cardinal Pablo "Ambo" David, bishop of Kalookan (with whom Betta and I had dinner last night!).

"I am promoting Cardinal Pablo 'Ambo' David, a human rights defender who confronted the murders perpetrated during the administration of former President Rodrigo Duterte. He denounced abuses and maintained that crimes committed by members of the clergy should be tried in civilian courts. He is a person of integrity, and it would be a great thing if Cardinal David were elected pope, representing the Philippines. The time has come for a Filipino pope who defends human rights and protects children," he concludes.

Betta again calls Jesuit Hans Zollner, the Vatican's top expert on abuse, to ask him what he thinks of the Bishop Accountability accusations. "The Parolin thing isn't true. How can they say these things about Parolin?" he asks skeptically, noting that he has spoken several times with Swiss investigators, to whom he tried to explain "what the correct procedure would be for requesting information, through normal diplomatic channels."

SOME CARDINALS ALERT US that they have received a 187-page book titled *The College of Cardinals Report*,[40] which profiles some forty papal candidates and includes a breakdown of their positions on issues such as same-sex blessings, the ordination of deaconesses, and Church doctrine on contraception. The goal of the book is to promote a pope who will lead the Church on a path that is different from that of Pope Francis, whose progressive reforms outraged some conservatives, according to an article written by our friend Chris Lamb for CNN.[41]

The project has been led by two Catholic journalists, Edward Pentin of the United Kingdom and Diane Montagna of the United States. Both work for traditionalist, conservative Catholic news sites. Reuters reports that Montagna has been handing the book to cardinals entering and leaving pre-conclave meetings,.

The report's creators claim they created it to help the cardinals "get to know each other better" and that it was compiled by an "international and independent team of Catholic journalists and researchers."

But there's more. In addition to this publication, several cardinals receive another book, "The St. Gallen Mafia," subtitled "Exposing the Secret Reformist Group within the Church," which also attempts to influence the conclave, as Chinese Cardinal Stephen Chow will later reveal in an interview.[42] Like many others, he is willing to express his displeasure at these operations. "What did the cardinals feel when they received those books? Nothing positive; they felt like they were

---

40. Hard copies of the book were produced for and distributed to cardinals; for public access, the report is available online.

41. Christopher Lamb, "Cardinals Choosing the Next Pope Have Been Offered a Dossier on Candidates—with a Subtext," www.cnn.com, May 6, 2025.

42. Gerard O'Connell, "Cardinal Chow on the Conclave: 'We Voted for a Pastor for the World,'" *America*, May 19, 2025.

being manipulated," Chow comments. Another cardinal, very upset, told us he simply threw those publications in the trash. And a third cardinal suggested we should "follow the money" (investigate who provided the money) to better understand who was behind all this. A very powerful ultraconservative Catholic lobby in the United States?

"They tried to control the conclave, but it backfired," he added.

THE DISTRIBUTION OF THESE TWO BOOKS is but the latest instance of the opposition that Pope Francis constantly encountered during his 12-year pontificate. It appears to be the conclusion to an earlier project started in 2018, called "Better Church Governance," commonly known as "The Red Hat Report" which, as Michael O'Laughlin reported in *America*,[43] would "investigate the cardinals who will vote for the next pope and assess how they handled allegations of sexual abuse and whether they have remained faithful to their own vows." He added, "[They] will use investigators, journalists, and researchers to compile the dossiers on each voting cardinal and will distribute the information online."

Every pope in the last and earlier centuries has encountered opposition, but during Francis's pontificate it gained an unprecedented, global visibility due to social media and online echo chambers, and created a distorted or misleading reading of his ministry and mission.

Some cardinals served, or allowed themselves to be used, as the visible face of this opposition, while at the same time carefully balancing public loyalty to the pope with what seemed to be a responsiveness to their supporters, including some well-heeled backers. These cardinals included Raymond Burke (USA), Robert Sarah (Guinea), Gerhard Müller (Germany), and Walter Brandmüller (Germany). This small but vocal opposition was based mainly in the United States, and involved a former nuncio—the Italian Archbishop Carlo Maria Viganó (who was excommunicated on July 5, 2024)—a few other cardinals, a number of bishops, some Catholic intellectuals and writers, and traditionalist groups.

In general, they strongly disagreed with Francis's refusal to affirm that abortion is the "preeminent" moral issue and to weaponize the Eucharist. They objected to his rejection of the culture wars, his dis-

---

43. Michael O'Laughlin, "Red Hat Report Founders Vow to Investigate and 'Score' Cardinals but Deny Policy Agenda," *America*, October 3, 2018.

taste for "culture warrior" bishops, his detestation of clericalism and a judgmental church. They protested his opening to communion for the divorced and remarried and his openness to the LGBT community. They objected to his denunciation of "the economy that kills," his support of the popular movements, his strong stance on climate change and against the arms trade, his rejection not only of the use but also of the possession of nuclear arms, and his rejection of the death penalty. They protested his overtures to China and Cuba. They denounced his restrictions on the use of the pre–Vatican II Tridentine liturgy (the Latin Mass) and, more recently, his decision to separate the power of governance in the Roman Curia and the Catholic Church from that of orders. Some slammed his style of governing, denouncing him as a dictator or an authoritarian. Others failed to recognize him as the successor of Peter and the center of unity and orthodoxy in the Church, and sought to undermine his papacy.

Nicolas Senéze, a reporter for *La Croix*, the French Catholic daily newspaper, speaks about much of this opposition to Francis in his book, *Comment l'Amérique veut changer de pape* (2019). "They do not want to dialogue because in the integralist mentality truth does not dialogue with error. They are convinced that the pope is in error and is dangerous to the church, but he is dangerous to their vision of the church. They are from very rich groups of the United States that have a very American vision, very liberal on the economy and very anti-liberal on the 'non-negotiable principles': they are pro-life, but in favor of the death penalty." When Mr. Senéze presented the book to the pope on the September 2019 flight from Rome to Mozambique and explained its content, Francis looked at the title and remarked with a smile, "I am honored that the Americans attack me."[44]

Although this opposition never constituted more than a tiny minority of Catholics, numerically speaking, it had powerful megaphones as never before in history, particularly in the United States with the broadcast network EWTN and its affiliates, including CNA, ACI Prensa, the *National Catholic Register*, as well as a very active blogosphere that gives the impression that the opposition is truly a strong force. Francis denounced this abuse of the media in remarks to

---

44. Gerard O'Connell, "Pope Francis to Journalist: 'I am Honored that the Americans Attack Me,'" *America*, September 4, 2019; Elisabetta Piqué, "Las intrigas contra el Papa continúan y tienen al próximo cónclave en la mira," *La Nacion*, September 23, 2019.

Slovak Jesuits during his visit to their country in September 2021, when he referred to "a large Catholic television channel that has no hesitation in continually speaking ill of the pope"—clearly referring to EWTN.[45]

The opposition to Francis also had significant support from the NAPA Institute in California, and other entities. It was well funded, as Christopher Lamb details in his well-researched book *The Outsider: Pope Francis and the Battle to Reform the Church* (2020).

The impression that it was a widespread and significant force in the Church was boosted by some Roman Curia officials and by those US bishops who voted in the USCCB conference for candidates and positions opposed to Francis's vision of Church.

Pope Francis's nomination of cardinals and bishops showed clearly that he was well aware of this.

While the small size of the opposition becomes evident in the general congregations, the moment of truth will come in the conclave.

IN THE DAILY PRESS BRIEFING, Bruni reports that more than 180 cardinals, including more than 120 electors, participated in General Congregation #8 this Friday. Twenty-five cardinals spoke and addressed topics of particular relevance to the future of the Church, including evangelization, which was at the heart of Pope Francis's pontificate, and the need for an evangelizing Church of fraternal communion, capable of speaking especially to the younger generations. Some highlighted the churches of the East, marked by suffering but also by a solid witness of faith; they also highlighted the urgency of communicating the Gospel effectively at all levels of ecclesial life, recalling that the witness of mutual love is the first proclamation. Others spoke of "counter-witnesses" to the Gospel, such as "sexual abuse and financial scandals" in the Church, and of issues that are considered "wounds" that need to be kept "open" in order that awareness of the problems remains alive so that concrete paths to healing can be identified.

Bruni also says that some cardinals emphasized "the centrality of the liturgy, the importance of canon law, and the value of synodality in

---

45. Gerard O'Connell, "Pope Francis Responds to Attacks from EWTN, Other Church Critics: 'They Are the Work of the Devil,'" *America*, September 21, 2021.

relation to mission, collegiality, and overcoming secularism." He adds that "there was also a reflection on the hermeneutics of continuity between the pontificates of John Paul II, Benedict XVI, and Francis."

Bruni confirms that two cardinal electors, from Spain and Kenya, have informed the College of Cardinals that they will not participate in the conclave. Cardinal Antonio Cañizares Llovera, 79, archbishop emeritus of Valencia and known as "Little Ratzinger" for his theological positions, will not attend for health reasons.

Cardinal John Njue, 79, archbishop emeritus of Nairobi, Kenya, on the other hand, will cause a stir worthy of the movie *Conclave* when, in an interview with the Kenyan newspaper *Daily Nation*, he stated that he "was not invited to elect the pope," despite being in good health.[46] The following day, his successor as archbishop of Nairobi, Philip Anyolo, issued a statement stating that the cardinal "was eligible to vote and was officially invited through the Apostolic Nunciature in Kenya," but would not travel to Rome or participate in the conclave "due to his current state of health." Archbishop Anyolo made it clear that it was he, along with the papal nuncio, Archbishop Hubertus Matheus Maria van Megen, who declined the invitation on the cardinal's behalf.

These absences reduce the number of European and African electors by one per continent; Europe will now have 52 electors and Africa 17, which is still more Africans than at any prior conclave.[47]

Four cardinal electors have not yet arrived in Rome, but the Vatican states that they are expected to arrive in time for the conclave.

Bruni also denies reports of Cardinal Parolin's alleged fainting, reported by an American Catholic website,[48] specifying that no such incident occurred. He also denies the involvement of medical or nursing staff. The Italian press dismisses all this as "fake news," considering it "poison" to torpedo the big favorite. Media reports speak of a fainting spell at the end of last Wednesday's general congregation, adding that it was an episode of hypertension that

---

46. Gitonga Marete, "Cardinal Njue: 'I Wasn't Invited to Pick Next Pope,'" *Daily Nation*, May 6, 2025.

47. Africa had 11 electors in the 2013 conclave. See Gerard O'Connell, *The Election of Pope Francis: An Inside Account of the Conclave That Changed History* (Orbis Books, 2019).

48. "Update on Cardinal Parolin Reportedly Suffering Brief Health Scare at Vatican," catholicvote.org, May 1, 2025.

quickly subsided. According to Vatican expert for the daily *Il Sole 24 Ore* Carlo Marroni, various internal sources have confirmed that Parolin did not have any such episode and that his activities in recent days have not been delayed or interrupted.[49] Marroni notes that "the topic of the 'health' of candidates for the papal throne is a recurring one and can be a disturbing element, especially if handled incorrectly. Already in 2013 (and also in 2005), Cardinal Bergoglio had been the subject of rumors about his condition, especially due to the (true) circumstance that in his youth he had had the upper lobe of one lung removed, which did not prevent him from fulfilling his mission as pope. And when he was already pontiff, during the height of the Synod on the Family in October 2015, news circulated that he had been visited by an eminent Japanese oncology specialist. This later turned out to be false," Marroni adds.

The absence of Cañizares and Njue reduces the number of Africans to seventeen, from sixteen countries, more than in any previous conclave, several of whom were created cardinals by Francis.

When I asked a non-elector African cardinal, who requested not to be named, if there were *papabili* among the electors of his continent, where the Catholic Church is growing faster than anywhere else in the world, he responded without hesitation. "Yes, there are two: Cardinals Robert Sarah of Guinea and Fridolin Ambongo Besungu, a Franciscan from the Democratic Republic of the Congo. The problem is that Sarah is too rigid, and Ambongo's main claim to fame is his rejection of the *Fiducia Supplicans* document (on the meaning of blessings)."[50] He commented that "Africa is still too young in the faith to produce a pope."

Cardinal Robert Sarah, who turns 80 next June, is considered a prophet among Church traditionalists. He earned a licentiate in theology from the Pontifical Gregorian University in Rome and a licentiate in biblical studies from the Franciscan Biblical Institute in Jerusalem. As archbishop of Conarky, he demonstrated great courage and pastoral leadership under the Marxist dictator Ahmed Sékou Touré, who included him on a death list. John Paul II called him to Rome in 2001 as secretary of the Congregation for the Evangelization of Peoples. Benedict XVI appointed him president of Cor Unum, the Pontifical

---

49. Carlo Marroni, "Verso il Conclave, sito americano: 'Malore per Parolin.' Ma la notizia è falsa," *Il Sole 24 Ore*, Mat 2, 2025.

50. Dicastery for the Doctrine of the Faith, declarationa *Fiducia Supplicans*, www.vatican.va.

Council for Christian and Human Development, and created him a cardinal in 2010. Pope Francis appointed him prefect of the Congregation for Divine Worship and the Discipline of the Sacraments in 2014, a position he held until 2020 despite his growing opposition to the pope's positions on the family, liturgy, and pastoral care. Those promoting him for the papacy see him as reversing much of what Francis has done.

Cardinal Ambongo, 65, is a Capuchin and member of the Order of Friars Minor, with a degree in moral theology from the Pontifical Alphonsian Academy in Rome. After Ambongo had served as bishop in dioceses in his country, Pope Francis appointed him coadjutor of Kinshasa in 2018, at the request of the legendary Cardinal Laurent Monsengwo Pasinya, whom he succeeded that same year as archbishop of Kinshasa, capital of the Democratic Republic of the Congo. The country has a population of around 112 million, 50 percent of whom are Catholic, making it the country with the fifth-largest Catholic population in the world, after Brazil, Mexico, the Philippines, and the United States.

The Catholic Church enjoys great respect and trust in the Congo; it has played a pivotal role in helping the country navigate numerous crises and political conflicts. Cardinal Ambongo has been a key player as president of the Episcopal Conference's Justice and Peace Commission and its Natural Resources Commission. He worked extensively on issues related to the environment, natural resources, the relationship between these resources and poverty, and the conflicts that are taking place, as he told us in an interview.[51] He has been threatened for his work in this area, even by the government.

Pope Francis created him a cardinal in 2019 and a member of his Council of Cardinal Advisors in 2020. He was elected president of the Symposium of Bishops' Conferences of Africa and Madagascar in 2023, and in that role he voiced the African bishops' staunch opposition to *Fiducia Supplicans*, while insisting that they remained in communion with the pope.[52] His statement of dissent is unlikely to have improved his prospects as a papal candidate.

---

51. Gerard O'Connell, "Cardinal Ambongo: The Congo Faces Similar Problems to the Ones We See in the Amazon," *America*, October 24, 2019.

52. Elisabetta Piqué, "En bloque y con el aval del Papa, los obispos africanos le dicen 'no' a las bendiciones a parejas del mismo sexo," *La Nación*, January 12, 2024.

There is, however, another African cardinal who was considered "papabile" in the 2013 conclave and is still presented as such by the Italian and international media: Peter Turkson, 76, a biblical scholar, much-liked and well-known cardinal from Ghana. John Paul II appointed him archbishop of Cape Coast (1992-2009) and created him a cardinal in 2003. Then, in 2009, Benedict XVI appointed him president of the Pontifical Council for Justice and Peace. In 2017, Francis first named him prefect of the Dicastery for the Promotion of Integral Human Development, a post he held until Francis appointed him chancellor of the Pontifical Academy of Sciences in 2022. He received two votes in the first ballot of the 2013 conclave and one vote in the second ballot.[53] He could also get some votes in this conclave, but his chances of election look slim.

Another African cardinal appointed by Francis in 2016 is Dieudonné Nzapalainga, 58, archbishop of Bangui, capital of the war-torn Central African Republic, where, for the first time in history, a pope inaugurated a Jubilee (of mercy) outside of Rome, as we witnessed in 2016.[54] Although not considered a papal candidate because of his age, the cardinal, whom we have met, is nonetheless an interesting and courageous voice in the conclave. He told Domenico Agasso, Vatican correspondent for the newspaper *La Stampa* and our friend, that he hopes the next pope will be "a man capable of listening deeply." He explains that "in a world marked by tension, violence, and social fractures, those who lead the Church must be sensitive to the signs of the times, capable of discernment, and capable of initiating authentic dialogues—not just simulated meetings, but authentic encounters, capable of opening new paths where there are walls today. A courageous, even audacious, leader is needed, a man of peace, capable of speaking forcefully and holding the helm of the Church steady even in the midst of the storm, to provide stability in a time of great uncertainty. For many today, the Church is a refuge, a point of stability. The pope must be the voice of those without one, the guardian of hope for a wounded and disoriented humanity."[55]

---

53. O'Connell, *The Election of Pope Francis*, 207, 209.

54. Gerard O'Connell, "In Bangui, Pope Francis Seeks to Create the Conditions for Peace in the Central African Republic," *America*, November 29, 2015.

55. Domenico Agasso, "Dieudonné Nzapalainga: 'Il futuro pontefice non ceda e lavori per superare i confini,'" *La Stampa*, April 27, 2025.

DURING THE DAY, the crowd in St. Peter's Square watched with glee and recorded videos as Vatican firefighters installed the chimney on the roof of the Sistine Chapel in preparation for the conclave. People couldn't hide their amazement and fascination at the realization that, in this technologically advanced age, the Vatican still communicates the election or failure to elect the new pope through smoke signals. It captivates millions of people around the world.

While the firefighters install the chimney, inside the Sistine Chapel beneath their feet, another team of workers sets up tables and chairs in preparation for the conclave.

AWAY FROM PUBLIC VIEW, though only a few hundred meters from the Vatican Press Office where now more than four thousand journalists from the international news media have been accredited, a discreet dinner is being co-hosted by the British ambassador to the Holy See, Christopher Trott, and the cardinal archbishop of Westminster, Vincent Nichols, for fourteen cardinals from the Commonwealth, though more had been invited but could not come.

By hosting the dinner, Mr. Trott, a very active ambassador, follows in the footsteps of his predecessor, Mr. Nigel Baker, who held a similar dinner before the 2013 conclave, where Bergoglio's name was mentioned.[56]

For the first time in history, the United Kingdom has four cardinals: Vincent Nichols; Arthur Roche; Timothy Radcliffe, OP; and Michael Fitzgerald MAfr. The first three are electors, but Fitzgerald and the Irish Cardinal Sean Brady, who is also present, are over the age of 80 and cannot vote. Other electors present include: Thomas Collins, Gérald Lacroix, and Frank Leo (all three from Canada); Soane Patita Paini Mafi (Tonga); John Dew (New Zealand); Filipe Neri Ferrão (India); and John Ribat (Papua New Guinea).

Ambassador Trott and Cardinal Nichols welcome the guests on arrival, and offer aperitifs. Earlier, Nichols had told the BBC, "I feel quite intimidated knowing that the outcome of this election is awaited by people all over the world and of many faiths."[57] And he

---

56. O'Connell, *The Election of Pope Francis*, 145.

57. Paul Burnell, "Choosing the Pope: 'The Conclave Is Intimidating,'" www.bbc.com, April 24, 2025.

told CNN, "His [the pope's] first duty is to preserve and deepen the unity of the Church."[58]

At the end of dinner, the ambassador offers digestifs and then graciously retires from the table to allow the cardinals to converse in private about the forthcoming conclave. They naturally talk about the *papabili*, and I learn later from a source that "there was no strong plugging for an Italian, but no strong opposition." More interestingly, however, "those who had experience of the Dicastery for Bishops were ready to speak about Robert Prevost for pope."

This is but one of the many meetings taking place across Rome in these days; some have taken place in the apartments of cardinals, others in colleges or religious houses, and even a few at restaurants. It is what normally happens before a conclave.

*Le Monde* publishes an article today about some prior meetings that attracted a lot of attention, under the headline: "In Rome, rumors swirl of a Macron plot to influence the election of the next pope."[59] The subheading reads: "Some Italian media suspect that French President Macron is maneuvering with the Catholic Sant'Egidio movement, close to the late pope, to push his candidate for the chair of St. Peter."

It adds that right-wing Italian newspapers allege that Macron is interfering in the conclave: "Macron even wants to elect the pope," proclaimed a headline published by *La Verità* on Tuesday, April 29, while another right-wing newspaper, *Libero*, wrote: "Macron even breaks into the conclave." Meanwhile, *Il Tempo*, a conservative Roman daily, criticized the French leader's "interventionism" as worthy of a modern-day Sun King. The alleged interference is based on two meals, around the time of Pope Francis's funeral, both attended by the French president.

The first took place on April 25, the eve of the funeral. President Macron and Professor Andrea Riccardi, founder of the Sant'Egidio community, a Catholic lay community, dined together at the famous Dal Bolognese restaurant in Piazza del Popolo. The two are known to be close friends and have dined together on previous occasions in

---

58. Christopher Lamb, "Cardinals at a Crossroads: While Some Want to Continue Francis's Reforms, Others Want a Different Kind of Pope," www.cnn.com, May 2, 2025.

59. Allan Kaval, "In Rome, Rumors Swirl of Plot by Macron to Influence Choice of Next Pope," *Le Monde*, May 2, 2025.

both Rome and Paris, most recently following the reopening of Notre Dame Cathedral in Paris. What was striking here is that Cardinal Matteo Zuppi, archbishop of Bologna, a close friend of Riccardi and the first member of the Sant'Egidio community to be ordained a priest, is being considered *papabile*.

The second meal was the following day, April 26: a luncheon hosted by the French ambassador to the Holy See, Florence Mangin, at her residence, which, according to *Le Monde*, "brought together President Macron and four of the five French cardinal electors: Jean-Marc Aveline, archbishop of Marseille, considered a *papabile*; François Bustillo, bishop of Ajaccio; Christophe Pierre, apostolic nuncio to the United States; and Philippe Barbarin, archbishop emeritus of Lyon." *Le Figaro*, the right-wing French daily, was the first to report on this luncheon.

Coincidence? Perhaps. A source at Sant'Egidio denounced the rumors as unfounded, since "Macron seeks to understand the process, not influence it," wrote *Le Monde*.

But it is no secret that Cardinal Aveline maintains a close relationship with the Sant'Egidio community. In fact, he presented his new book, *Il dialogo della salvezza. Piccola teologia della missione* (The Dialogue of Salvation. A Brief Theology of Mission), at the Sant'Egidio headquarters in Rome on May 2, 2024, an event attended by prominent members of the community.

According to what we learned, Cardinals Aveline and Zuppi had lunch together before the conclave, which further underscored the close ties between them.

CONTINUING WITH THE TOPIC OF FOOD, I have lunch with Japanese Cardinal Tarcisio Kikuchi at the I Tre Pupazzi restaurant in Borgo Pio. Because Betta had just made a live appearance on television, she arrives a little late, but in time to order some delicious *spigole* and baked *orate* with potatoes. We chat, of course, about the impending conclave and the mad climate surrounding it, in which the poor cardinals, upon leaving and entering the general congregations, are harassed by journalists who ask them tactlessly and point-blank, "Who are you going to vote for?" without understanding that the conclave is something very different from a political election....

So much so that at lunch Betta advised Kikuchi, who is very reserved and shy, that instead of running away—something that wouldn't suit him because, after all, these reporters are obeying orders from their directors who are looking for images—he should still respond to the questions on camera with a smile, using pleasantries. Famous last words. As we leave the restaurant, Kikuchi is intercepted by a reporter from Tg1, RAI's main news program, who chases him for several meters, bombarding him with questions, as will be seen in the evening edition of the news.

THE DAY CONCLUDES with Betta as the star guest on the RAI 3 television program run by prestigious Italian journalist Marco Damilano, entitled "Il Cavallo e la Torre" (The Horse and the Tower), which covers the day's news. The program lasts barely ten minutes and has a different guest every night. Damilano, who follows Elisabetta closely, has invited her because he wants to dedicate this Friday's episode to the chimney installed in the ceiling of the Sistine Chapel and wants to present an informed but alternate voice. From her widely read article on Parolin's weaknesses, as well as our article on his campaign strategist, Cardinal Stella, he sees that our coverage of the conclave is very different from that of the Italian media. In the midst of an impressive campaign boosting an Italian pope, these people seem to be muzzled and don't dare—or aren't allowed—to report on the reality that very few hint at, but that she has made very clear: that Cardinal Parolin, although he was the second-in-command, is not a continuation of Francis's pontificate, nor Francis's hand-picked successor.

MAY 3, SATURDAY [BETTA]
*Counterattack*

THE ATMOSPHERE IS FEVERISH. There are only three days left to continue collecting votes, and the negotiations and meetings to organize the *cordate* continue at a frantic pace. And with much uncertainty about what will happen next Wednesday afternoon in the Sistine Chapel, when 133 cardinal electors from seventy countries—never before a number so high and so global—will hold the first vote to elect the new head of the Catholic Church.

While the conservative wing seems ready to vote for the strongest, most well-known candidate, Cardinal Pietro Parolin, former secretary of state to Pope Francis, a 70-year-old diplomat who presents himself as someone who would bring order to the "Bergoglian revolution," the other side continues searching for the best way to ensure there is no turning back and consolidate the reformist path of the pope from the end of the world

Gerry learns that at this morning's General Congregation #9 there has been a virtual counterattack by the progressives, who are fighting for the election of a pope who will ensure the continuation of Francis's legacy of openness. For the first time, they state what quality they seek in his successor: "a prophetic profile, one that inspires hope."[60]

"Cardinals very much in line with Francis spoke. Since they came from distant lands, no one among the conservatives seemed particularly interested in what they had to say," an elector confided. And of the twenty-six interventions made in the Synod Hall, one speech was considered "a bombshell" by the progressives.

Hendro Munsterman, the Vatican correspondent for the Dutch daily Nederlands Dagblad, reported[61] that this speech was given by the Filipino Cardinal "Ambo" David, who asked why Italian has to be the main language in the Vatican, and why there are no women in the College of Cardinals. Munsterman quoted David as saying: "We are a Catholic, universal Church. So I asked ChatGPT what the most spoken languages in the world are. And Italian, with 66 million people, only comes in 22nd." Cardinal David also recalled how the apostles locked themselves in the upper room after Jesus's crucifixion and, "while they were hiding there, the risen Jesus had already shown himself to the women. But of course, they didn't believe the women! And two thousand years later, we're still a men's club; there's not a single woman here. Perhaps, deep down, we still struggle to trust the voices of women in the Church."

---

60. Elisabetta Piqué, "El contraataque del ala progresista: defendió el legado de Francisco y pidió que el perfil del próximo papa 'sea profético,'" *La Nacion*, May 4, 2015.

61. Hendro Munsterman, "Vier stemrondes en een opvallende toespraak: dit weten we van het geheime conclaaf waarin Leo XIV paus werd," *Nederlands Dagblad*, July18, 2025.

In his regular press conference, Bruni seemed to confirm this pushback from the progressives, listing the issues raised during the deliberations. "Among the topics discussed," he said, "were the Church's dual mission: internal communion and universal brotherhood. Gratitude was also expressed to Pope Francis, with frequent references to the apostolic exhortation *Evangelii Gaudium*, the programmatic document of his pontificate, and the call to continue the processes he has initiated was also reiterated.

"Furthermore, the importance of collaboration and solidarity among the churches was highlighted, and the role of the Curia in its relationship with the pontiff in the service of the Church, and of the pope in particular, in favor of peace was addressed. Reference was also made to education as a fundamental value in pastoral action. Likewise, it was hoped that the next pope would have a prophetic profile and encourage the Church to 'come out of the cenacle' to bring hope to the world, in harmony with the Ordinary Jubilee of 2025," he added. This appeared to be the first time such topics had been raised in the pre-conclave meetings.

"Other points of discussion included synodality and collegiality as key pillars of the ecclesial journey and the role of the Jubilee as a sign of hope," Bruni said, adding that "there was no shortage of reflections on the attention with which the world views the Church, as well as on the need not to isolate oneself from reality. Finally, the cardinals analyzed the urgency of ecumenical dialogue and the evangelizing mission."

It seems clear that those who spoke were the "Bergoglian" cardinals who, after days of hearing "complaints" against Francis's "confusing" papacy and the need for order, came out to defend his legacy and propose a profile in keeping with their outward-looking Church.

Within the group of cardinals from this faction, who see the conclave as a virtual referendum on synodality—the journey of hierarchy and baptized together—the names that most resonate are those of many high prelates who lent their support and enthusiastically endorsed the recent Synod on Synodality, the three-year process of global consultation and listening, the great challenge of the final phase of Francis's pontificate. Sixty-one of the cardinal electors participated in this synod. Now, in addition to Luxembourg Cardinal Jean-Claude Hollerich, a Jesuit like Francis and among the most outspoken, and Maltese Cardinal Mario Grech, who served as his right-hand man as secretary general of the Synod, as well as Frenchman

Jean-Marc Aveline, archbishop of Marseille and president of the French Episcopal Conference, and Filipino Cardinal Luis Antonio Tagle, other names are beginning to be mentioned.

Among them is that of the Augustinian Cardinal Robert Prevost, former prefect of the Dicastery for Bishops and president of the Pontifical Commission for Latin America. Completely aligned with Francis, he is a 69-year-old Chicago-born missionary prelate who was prior general of the Augustinians and who worked in Peru for almost twenty years, during more than eight of which he spent serving as bishop of Chiclayo, in the northwest part of the country, a position to which he had been appointed in 2014. Pope Francis brought him to the Roman Curia in 2023 to replace Cardinal Marc Ouellet as head of one of the most important ministries

Another "dark horse" who could emerge in the second round of the vote count if Tagle's candidacy is blocked (he has been criticized for his management of Caritas Internationalis and the Dicastery for the Evangelization of Peoples) is another Filipino already mentioned, Cardinal Pablo Virgilio David, 66, bishop of Kalookan. He is also a synod enthusiast—he participated in the two sessions—is multilingual and very popular in his country because he came out to help the victims of former President Duterte's repression in his brutal war against drug trafficking. A true reflection of his courage: on his Facebook page, alongside the photo of Donald Trump dressed as the pope[62]—generated by AI and reposted a few days ago by the president, causing widespread controversy—he wrote in all languages: "Not funny, sir."

WE LEARNED THAT among those who traveled to Rome for the funeral was Greg Burke, the American layman whom Francis appointed as director of the Holy See press office in July 2016, together with Paloma Garcia Ovejero, the first woman ever to serve as deputy director.[63] They both resigned in December 2018.[64]

---

62. Max Matza, "No hay nada inteligente ni gracioso en esta imagen, señor presidente," BBC News Mundo, May 4, 2025.

63. Gerard O'Connell, "Pope Francis Appoints American Layman Greg Burke as Vatican Spokesman," *America,* July 11, 2016.

64. Gerard, O'Connell, "Director and Deputy Director of Vatican Press Office Resign on Last Day of 2018," *America*, December 31, 2018.

Ever well-informed and tuned in to the Vatican, after speaking with sources, Burke on April 24 wrote a prediction for the conclave that he summarised as the "3 Ps": 1. Prevost, 2. Parolin, 3. Pizzaballa. He took a photo of his prediction and sent it to Paloma.

To provide an idea of what the allure of an ardently desired Italian papacy is triggering in Italy and the Italian press, Professione Reporter,[65] a website that defends the journalistic profession, reveals today that the progressive weekly *L'Espresso* decided at the last minute to cancel an unflattering article titled "Parolin, the Diplomacy of the Invisible," which examined the cardinal's relations with the palaces of Roman power. Although they managed to remove the article at the last minute and replace it with a two-page advertisement, the title remained in the magazine's summary. This sparked a protest from the publication's journalists, who denounced a "unilateral act," not to say censorship, at the last minute on the part of management.

IN THIS TENSE ATMOSPHERE, the Vatican announces that all the cardinals, including those who will celebrate Mass tomorrow in the Roman churches of which they are the titular heads, will have a full day of work on Monday, their last: there will be a general congregation in the morning and in the afternoon, so that all can express themselves.

On Tuesday evening, May 6, those who wish to will be able to enter Santa Marta and the adjacent Old Santa Marta residences (which have been renovated for the "big event") to take possession of their rooms. As always, and as the rules indicate, there will be a lottery for the rooms. The cardinal electors will be under a communications blackout so they will not be able to have any contact with the outside world (goodbye cell phones, tablets, computers, radios, smart watches, and the like). The staff who will assist them in their confinement must swear to secrecy about everything they see and hear.

The rest of the cardinals will enter their cloistered accommodations in the new and old Santa Marta residences early Wednesday morning, allowing them time to prepare for the *Pro eligendo Pontifice* Mass, which will be presided over at 10 AM by the dean of the College of Cardinals, Giovanni Battista Re.

---

65. "L'Espresso, pezzo sul cardinale Parolin cancellato quasi in edicola," May 3, 2025, www.professionereporter.eu.

AFTER BRUNI'S DAILY BRIEFING—he's starting to go crazy because unversed outsider TV journalists are asking him about the times the *fumata* (smoke signals) will be released and details of that nature—we walk back home. We meet Irene at the door of the Jesuit Curia, where she will interview Argentine Cardinal Ángel Sixto Rossi, whom I've known well for some time and with whom I put her in touch.

The 66-year-old is one of the four Argentine cardinals who will enter the Sistine Chapel next Wednesday afternoon to elect Francis's successor. He will be accompanied by his three other compatriots: Cardinals Víctor Manuel "Tucho" Fernández, former prefect of the Dicastery for the Doctrine of the Faith; Mario Poli, archbishop emeritus of Buenos Aires; and Vicente Bokalic, archbishop of Santiago del Estero and primate of Argentina.

A Jesuit like Pope Francis, whom he met at a very young age, the archbishop of Córdoba Rossi makes no secret of his nervousness. "It's so hot! I don't understand how all these fabrics hold up. During ceremonies, my miter falls off, one thing falls off, another falls off," he told me, laughing, when I interviewed him yesterday.[66] He has gone viral for his Spanish pun, "Papa, me? Sure, French fry!" Opening his cell phone (which he rarely uses), he showed me a cartoon that appeared on social media with that expression. (In Spanish, *papa* means both pope and potato.)

Founder of the Manos Abiertas Foundation in 1992, which provides aid to the poorest and most vulnerable people in various social assistance centers in ten Argentine cities, Rossi shared eight years under the same roof with Jorge Bergoglio, first at the Colegio Máximo of San Miguel and then at the Iglesia del Salvador. Now about to elect his successor, he admits that it will be a complex election since "there are different views" among the cardinals. The possibility of a reversal exists, although he remains optimistic and predicts that "common sense and prudence will be stronger" among the cardinal electors.

When I ask him the classic question about what qualities the successor should have—not Francis's as everyone says, but rather Saint Peter's—Rossi displays character. "No, I say, instead, the successor of Francis, the successor of Peter. We will vote for the successor of Francis, who was Peter," he replies. "What qualities? I would say a sense

---

66. Elisabetta Piqué, "Rossi, uno de los argentinos que elegirá al papa, teme que se revierta el legado de Francisco: 'Espero que sea más fuerte la sensatez,'" *La Nacion*, May 2, 2025.

of mercy. It seems essential to me. If I had to choose a single noun from Francis's pontificate, I think mercy is the one that tops them all. And then, exquisite charity, in that Ignatian motto that Pope Francis himself is said to have used a lot: don't be afraid to dream big. I don't dream according to the world, but according to the Kingdom, according to the Gospel. Don't be afraid to dream big, and at the same time, take care of the small details. This is a sign of God: a big vision expands the big dream, and at the same time, also the small details. Well, I think it would be nice if whoever comes would also be encouraged to do that and be encouraged to live the Gospel. Furthermore, I believe that the revolutionary part of Francis is simply returning to the Gospel, which brings relief to the good, the simple enjoy it, and the mediocre suffer it. And those who don't like it, fight it."

What about the possibility of a reversion? "There may be a possibility, I suppose, and I hope and wish that it doesn't happen, that common sense and prudence will prevail. And above all, realizing that there's a whole open path, several open paths that Francis has opened up, and well, it's almost common sense to keep up with him.... A turning back would be very sad, and I think it won't happen. ... We have to take the baton without losing individuality, because whoever comes doesn't have to be a Francis, right? But we do have to take charge. Let's say, take advantage of the path he opened to continue growing in dialogue, in listening, in a Church that isn't courtly but rather a servant. In short, a path of synodality, where we are not the landowners, but rather we walk with our people so that together we can discern what is most appropriate without losing authority. In other words," the pope said, "sometimes we have to go ahead of the flock, at other times walk among them to listen to them, and at still other times be at the back of the flock to see where God is guiding his people."

When I ask him about the media pressure—and pressure within the conclave—from the Italians to have a fellow countryman again after forty-seven years, Rossi, like many, says it's not a question of nationality. "Let someone come from China, Italy, Finland: the point isn't about geography or maps, but rather a matter of the heart. So, I don't care where they come from, but rather what their heart is like," he asserts. And, as an Argentine and a Jesuit, and with that sense of humor he learned from his beloved Father Jorge, he appears "totally calm." He makes a joke, saying it will be another three thousand years before there is another Argentine Jesuit pope. "I won't last [that long]...and I don't think I'll be considered...which gives me a lot of freedom."

GERRY, WHO HAS BEEN CALCULATING for days, reviews the situation:

The composition of the 2025 conclave differs significantly from that of the 2013 conclave, in which 115 electors from forty-eight countries voted to elect the first Latin American Jesuit pope. In the 2013 conclave, 60 electors came from Europe (including 28 Italians), 19 from Latin America, 14 from North America (11 from the United States, 3 from Canada), 11 from Africa, 10 from Asia, and 1 from Oceania (Australia). [67]

From the beginning of his twelve-year pontificate, Francis set about changing the composition of the College of Cardinals, internationalizing it even more than his predecessors had, so that it would more fully reflect the universality of the Catholic Church. He did this by reducing the number of European and Italian electors while increasing the number of Asian, African, and Latin American electors. He selected many electors from the world's peripheries that had never before had a cardinal. In this way, he gave greater voting power and influence to the electors of the Global South, where the majority—about 72 percent—of the world's Catholic population currently resides.

As a result of his changes, 133 electors from seventy countries will enter the Sistine Chapel to elect the next pope: 52 from Europe, 23 from Asia, 23 from Latin America, 17 from Africa, 14 from North America (10 from the United States and 4 from Canada), and 4 from Oceania.

On the day when the conclave begins, 80 percent of the electors will have been appointed cardinal by Pope Francis—108 of the 133 electors, while 20 were appointed by Benedict XVI and 5 by John Paul II.

This fact, coupled with the strong emotional impact of Pope Francis's funeral on the cardinals, seems to increase the likelihood that the chosen cardinal will share Francis's vision of a missionary and synodal Church.

BEYOND THE NUMBERS, Gerry finds a shockingly frank *Paris Match* interview published a few days ago with 74-year-old French Cardinal

---

67. O'Connell, *The Election of Pope Francis*, 197.

Philippe Barbarin. Former archbishop of Lyon, Barbarin participated in the 2005 and 2013 conclaves and is one of the French cardinal electors. Barbarin doesn't mince words when he dismisses Cardinals Parolin and his compatriot Jean-Marc Aveline as being unfit to be pope.[68]

It's rare to hear a cardinal speak so frankly. Asked by *Paris Match*'s Vatican correspondent Arthur Herlin his opinion of the favorite, Parolin, Barbarin blasts with heavy ammunition. "I don't see Cardinal Parolin as the next pope for structural rather than personal reasons. As secretary of state, his role is fundamental to the day-to-day governance of the Vatican. He is responsible for ensuring the efficient functioning of the administration, but his performance has not met expectations. Furthermore, the pope's mission is of a different nature: he must look toward the universal Church and the entire world. Being pope requires a comprehensive pastoral vision, while the secretary of state must focus on the internal organization of the Roman Curia. Each dicastery requires specific profiles. Both the Doctrine of the Faith and the Secretariat of State require people of exceptional intellectual stature and leadership ability. Frankly, I believe that Cardinal Parolin, although competent, does not have the stature one would ideally expect from a secretary of state, let alone a pope."

He considers Archbishop Aveline of Marseille similarly unsuited. "Cardinal Aveline is undoubtedly a highly prestigious figure. However, I must say that in the conversations I have had, his name has not come up particularly. I have not heard any cardinal explicitly campaigning for him," he said. "It must be acknowledged that his French nationality could constitute an obstacle. Historically, France has often been perceived as a hegemonic power, which is not always well received in international ecclesiastical circles. Even when we had such an exceptional figure as Cardinal Lustiger (Jean-Marie), who enjoyed considerable influence, this did not translate into significant support in previous conclaves. Jean-Marc Aveline undoubtedly has great qualities, but he does not have the same international stature," he concludes. The remarks cause quite a stir.

---

68. Philippe Barbarin, "Le prochain pape devra être un pasteur et un solide théologien," *Paris Match*, April 30, 2025 (English translation from: "Cardinal Barbarin Unleashes on Cardinals Aveline and Parolin," Cathcon. blogspit.com, May 1, 2025.

AFTER ANOTHER EXHAUSTING DAY, I am not up to cooking. We go out to eat with Irene and Cristina Taquini at our reliable "Da Luigi," close to home in Piazza Sforza Cesarini. Gerry stays behind, preferring to rest. He's not at 100 percent because he caught a cold the morning of Francis's funeral when he had to make live television appearances from the Augustinian terrace. That was a week ago, but it seems like ages.

Another gentleman will be joining us: Juan Pablo! As always, I order the exquisite octopus carpaccio as a starter, which Juampy and Irene also enjoy. Afterward, I go for delicious grilled calamari. Cristina orders ham with melon—the first of the season—and Juampy and Irene order a Roman classic: spaghetti *alla carbonara*. We toast with house red wine.

MAY 4, SUNDAY [GERRY]
*Abnormal Sunday*

TODAY IS THE LAST SUNDAY WITHOUT A POPE in Rome. It is assumed that by next Sunday, Francis's successor will have been elected, and he will likely make his debut with his first Marian Regina Caeli prayer from the window of the Apostolic Palace. Who will it be? Where will he come from?

It's not a normal Sunday, but one marked by these questions and a climate of growing anxiety. The 133 cardinals who will enter the Sistine Chapel, although they haven't held general congregations today, are not resting. While many continue talking at meetings, lunches in Roman trattorias, private homes, and religious houses, seeking to discuss strategies for promoting the candidates of the various factions, others are celebrating Mass in their respective titular Roman churches.[69] This is an ancient tradition, in which cardinal electors celebrate a public Mass in their titular church in Rome, that is, the

---

69. Elisabetta Piqué, "Máxima expectativa por el cónclave: gestos, campaña y cálculos de los cardenales en el último domingo sin papa," *La Nacion*, May 5, 2025.

church the pope assigned to them in the Consistory when he also gave them the red biretta, making them pastors of the diocese of Rome and affirming their special relationship with the pontiff.

Many, especially those on the papal candidate lists, are so harassed by legions of journalists, cameramen, and photographers. For this reason, the two cardinals considered favorites, the Italian Parolin and the Filipino Tagle, choose not to go to their churches to avoid national and international media attention. The other two Italian papal candidates, Cardinals Zuppi and Pizzaballa, do the same. Still others, such as the French Cardinal Aveline and the Hungarian Cardinal Erdő, have no such qualms. Meanwhile, Cardinals Dolan of New York and Ambongo Besungu of Kinshasa seem to enjoy this moment of glory.

Aveline, the 66-year-old archbishop of Marseille, who was born in Algeria, demonstrated that he speaks Italian much better than previously thought (something considered a weak spot in his candidacy) during a Mass he celebrated at "his" Church of Santa Maria dei Monti near the Colosseum. Although he read the text of his homily—which lasted fewer than seven minutes, as Pope Francis recommended so as not to bore the faithful—he celebrated the rest of the Mass in Italian without any difficulty and with a French accent, as we were able to verify through an audio recording kindly sent to us by a French colleague.

In his sermon, Aveline emphasizes inclusion: "Only love is worthy of faith. Do not be afraid of the truth or of diversity. Every man and every woman is our brother and sister," he says.

Curiously, when Aveline was at the church of Santa Maria dei Monti last Sunday (April 27) to administer the sacrament of confirmation to some young people, his briefcase had been stolen. It contained his personal belongings and car keys. But the briefcase was "found" three days later and returned to him when he went back there to celebrate Mass this Sunday. "It was a miracle of Our Lady, with a little help from us," joked the parish priest, Father Francesco Pesce, as he handed the briefcase to him. The cardinal laughed.[70]

Because he physically resembles and has the same good-natured and affable demeanor as John XXIII (1958–1963), some French journalists comment that they already imagine Aveline, president of the

---

70. Rubano la borsa al cardinale Aveline: ritrovata pochi giorni dopo vicino alla "sua" chiesa a Monti, *La Repubblica*, May 4, 2025.

French bishops and a rising star, in line with the emerging Church of Francis, as a possible "John XXIV."

His compatriot, the Cardinal of Ajaccio, Corsica, François-Xavier Bustillo, who is celebrating in "his" parish of Saint Mary Immaculate of Lourdes in the Roman neighborhood of Boccea, recalls in his sermon that Jesus "doesn't ask if you are strong, if you have a marketing strategy, or if you know how to speak languages," but rather asks us to "love him to the end," and adds that we must "be docile and responsible. God doesn't ask us for strategies, he asks us to listen to him." Afterward, people crowd around him, as parish priest Father Carmine Cipolla downplays the situation by calling on the children to immortalize the moment: "Take a selfie with our cardinal. You never know, he could become pope!"[71]

Cardinal Timothy Dolan of New York, celebrating Mass at the Church of Guadalupe at Monte Mario, is very relaxed and animated, joking, smiling, also taking selfies with many people, asking a woman what she's cooking for lunch, and then requesting that those present pray for the conclave. "The experience of 2013 helped me, so I'm calm this time, but I was tense then!" he reveals, with a big smile. His homily is brief because "Pope Francis told us to be brief!" he explains. When the press asks him if he found the AI-generated photo of President Trump dressed as the pope "offensive," Dolan replies: "It wasn't good at all." Asked what he thinks of Trump's endorsement of his papal candidacy, the cardinal dismisses the idea with a frown and a hand gesture. On April 30, Trump appeared to have endorsed Dolan for the papacy when he told reporters at the White House: "I must say, we have a cardinal who happens to be from a place called New York, and he's very good, so we'll see what happens."[72]

Dolan, a conservative who's seen as pro-Trump and who, by invitation, attended his inauguration on January 20 in Washington, has long been critical of Francis. When asked if a "Francis II" is possible, he responds diplomatically: "Hopefully. I think we're fortunate because we could even do a mix of the recent popes, the heart of Francis, but I also think of the intellectual intensity of Benedict XVI and John Paul II, with their courage and their call to follow Jesus. . . .

---

71. Card. Bustillo, Dio non ci chiede strategie ma di ascoltarlo, Ansa.it., May 4, 2025.

72. Kathryn Palmer, "Who Is Timothy Dolan? The New York Archbishop Is Trump's Pick to Be the Next Pope," *USA Today*, April 30, 2025.

I think if we can combine these great characteristics, it would be a blessing."

Another cardinal who always attracts attention in the media is the German Gerhard Müller, who celebrates Mass in the seventeenth-century Baroque church of Sant'Agnese in Agone in the spectacular Piazza Navona, where many come to greet him.

His role in this conclave is no small feat: we learned that long before Pope Francis's death, Müller was organizing dinners in his Vatican apartment in Piazza Leonina, to which he invited several cardinals, reportedly including Raymond Burke, Beniamino Stella, and Robert Sarah, with the succession as a major topic of conversation. Once the general congregations began, he invited many other cardinals to his apartment, but it is unclear whether he invited his neighbor and fellow German, Walter Kasper, a theologian in his nineties who is age-barred from entering the conclave and who has a different vision of the Church and lives in the same building.

American Cardinal Joseph Tobin from Newark arrives by subway, wearing a clergyman's suit, to his titular church Santa Maria delle Grazie (St. Mary of Grace) in Rome's Trionfale neighborhood. As our friend Cindy Wooden reports,[73] it was First Communion day and the cardinal prayed that his "little brothers' and sisters'" first encounter with the risen Lord in the Eucharist would lead them, like St. Peter in the day's Gospel, to respond, "Lord, you know everything; you know that I love you."

He told the journalists present, "There is a growing consensus about the qualities needed for the next Holy Father, but not names. A lot depends on the Holy Spirit." He predicted a fairly short conclave "because the majority of cardinals, including me, are diocesan bishops and we need to get back." He said there is a desire "to have continuity" with the papacy of Pope Francis, but not an "exact" replica. "There is no going back," he added.

The intellectual Hungarian Cardinal Péter Erdő, on the other hand, arrives in a car with tinted windows to the Church of Santa Francesca Romana in the Forum, packed with Hungarians, many of them residents of Rome, while others are passing through on Jubilee pilgrimages. In his homily, he emphasizes that evangelization is the

---

73. Cindy Wooden, "Cardinal Tobin, at Rome Parish, Focuses on Eucharist, Not Conclave," www.usccb.com, May 4, 2025.

number-one priority for the Church today and that the new pope "has a mission that goes beyond human strength." He avoids making statements to journalists, but offers discreet smiles to the crowd, blesses a child, and leaves quickly after Mass.

The Hungarian cardinal arouses great interest in the media because he is considered the leading candidate among the most conservative and traditionalist group of electors in the conclave. There is speculation that if the cardinals supporting him and those backing Parolin were to unite and vote for either of them, one of them could become a very strong, perhaps unstoppable, force in the conclave.

This speculation appears to have arisen after Cardinal Stella, Parolin's main proponent, attacked Francis at the April 30 general congregation, perhaps a not-so-veiled appeal to the conclave's most conservative and traditionalist bloc to vote for Parolin.

All this reached the ears of the Hungarian ambassador to the Holy See, Eduard Habsburg, a friend of Erdő, who considered it so serious that he took the unusual step of publishing a post on X that reads: "Any speculation about a pre-conclave agreement between Hungarian Cardinal Péter Erdő and former Vatican Secretary of State Pietro Parolin is completely false. Cardinal Erdő has not held any such conversations." Later, we learned that some cardinals were wondering whether Habsburg—a member of the House of Habsburg-Lorraine, the former ruling family of Austria-Hungary, and very active on X—had posted the tweet at Erdő's request.

Meanwhile, Democratic Republic of the Congo Cardinal Fridolin Ambongo Besungu drew warm applause and laughter as he posed for selfies like a star in the church of San Gabriele Arcangelo, built in 1956 north of Rome. "I'm not here for Africa, but for the universal Church," he said. He emphasized that this was his first conclave, "and I don't know what will happen; we don't have any names yet." He urged people to "pray at this very important moment for the Holy Spirit to guide the election" of the new pope. "It will take time; it took years before, but," he said with a smile, "let's hope it won't be like that this time."

Cardinal Mario Poli, archbishop emeritus of Buenos Aires and one of the four Argentine electors, celebrates Mass at the Argentine National Church of Santa Maria Addolorata on Viale Regina Margherita before dozens of compatriots who know that the odds for another pope "from the end of the world" this soon are very remote.

IN THIS CLIMATE OF ENORMOUS EXPECTATION, Italy's major newspapers continue a clear media campaign in favor of the "strongest" papal candidate, Cardinal Parolin. A 70-year-old diplomat, moderate, but inexperienced in pastoral matters, he is promoted as a peacemaker in a seemingly divided College of Cardinals and as someone who would bring some "calm" and order after an informal and disruptive papacy. But he lacks charisma.

"The risk is that the candidates with the most votes will be stalled after the first ballots," writes Franca Giansoldati, Vatican expert for the daily *Il Messaggero*, who, like everyone else, identifies the 67-year-old Filipino Cardinal Tagle as the other big favorite.[74] She, like other experts, estimates that Parolin could count on a good number of votes at the start (between 40 and 50), and that the problem is that he could remain stagnant with those numbers and not grow. In fact, she sees no cardinal coming close to the magic number of 89, the two-thirds needed to be elected.

"Time is needed" for agreement among all, some cardinals admit. Tomorrow, since the *novemdiales* end tonight, they will hold pre-conclave meetings for the first time in the morning and in the afternoon.

Because there have never been so many cardinals in a conclave, many have yet to speak, a crucial detail. Everyone remembers that the brief speech given by the archbishop of Buenos Aires on March 9, 2013—when he called for a Church that is not self-referential and that seeks to reach out to the existential and geographical peripheries of the world, shining a light on others—was pivotal.

But this time it is different. The electors complain that the aged non-electors have consumed floor time, delivering extremely long speeches that far exceed the five minutes each one is theoretically allowed. This has had a negative impact, with nonagenarian meeting leader Cardinal Re unable to stop them. "Many of us are asking ourselves, 'What is this?'" one cardinal told us, criticizing the dynamic that has been established in the general congregations.

The main headline on the front page of *La Stampa*, based on a poll, states that "six out of ten Italians want a progressive pontiff,"[75] which

---

74. Franca Giansoldati, "Conclave, mediazione tra i cardinali: sei cordate per sei nomi. Ecco i favoriti (mentre continuano i veleni su Parolin)," *Il Messaggero*, May 5, 2025.

75. Alessandra Ghisleri, "Papa, il 57% di italiani vuole un progressista: sorpresa dei giovani, i più conservatori," *La Stampa*, May 4, 2025.

would indicate that they prefer a non-Italian successor to Francis. The same newspaper, however, also estimates that Parolin would enter the conclave with 45 votes, a number that no one else has, according to its Vatican expert, Domenico Agasso.

Bologna Archbishop Cardinal Matteo Zuppi of the community of Sant'Egidio, although he presents himself as someone aligned with Francis's pastoral approach of concern for the poor and marginalized, as president of the Italian Episcopal Conference (CEI), "distanced himself" from Francis, an Italian bishop who requested anonymity told us. "He built the CEI in his own image, not in the image of Francis. In recent years he has distanced himself from Francis because he even allowed Mass to be celebrated in Latin in Bologna," he added.

The same source revealed that Zuppi, famous for having mediated various conflicts in Africa and who reportedly has the support of several conservative cardinals on that continent, is telling several fellow electors to vote for Parolin, as a tactic "as if to test the waters." But we could not verify this.

The other Italian papal candidate, the Latin patriarch of Jerusalem, Pierbattista Pizzaballa, 60, is being promoted by conservative groups.

On an unusual Sunday afternoon, when all the talk is about the conclave and many are still studying the lists and doing the math, two-hundred-plus cardinals concelebrate the final *novemdialis* Mass for the deceased pope in St. Peter's Basilica.

"We all admired how Pope Francis, animated by the love of the Lord and led by His grace, was faithful to his mission to the very end of his strength," says presiding Corsican-French Cardinal Dominque Mamberti in his sermon.

"He warned those in power that they must obey God before men and proclaimed to humanity the full joy of the Gospel, the Merciful Father, Christ the Savior. He did this in his teaching, in his travels, in his actions, in his lifestyle. I was close to him on Easter Day, in the blessing loggia of this basilica, a witness to his suffering, but above all to his courage and his determination to serve the People of God until the end," recalled Mamberti, who will, in a few days from that same Loggia of Blessings, announce to the world in his role as cardinal protodeacon the name of the new pope. Dressed in a striking white miter with gold embroidery—reminiscent of those of Pius XII, completely different from the simple and austere ones of Francis—Mamberti calls for rediscovering the flavor of adoration. "This capacity for adoration wasn't difficult to recognize in Pope Francis," he notes, recalling that "his intense pastoral life, his countless meetings, were based on long moments of prayer that the Ignatian discipline had instilled in him."

Mamberti, a 73-year-old diplomat who is presumed to support Parolin's candidacy (like most cardinal diplomats), mentions in his homily Benedict XVI and John Paul II, two conservative popes with a much more rigid and formal style than the Argentine, an appeal to traditionalist sensibilities.

MAY 5, MONDAY [BETTA]

*Under the Radar*

The countdown has begun; less than forty-eight hours until the start of the conclave. Gerry continues to calculate, and although the Italian newspapers insist that the overwhelming favorite, the best-known papal candidate, is Pietro Parolin—considered the peacemaker, the candidate for order and unity after the Argentine pope's revolution—he thinks the secretary of state does not have the forty-plus votes the media is claiming.

While the Italian lobby wants to reclaim the papacy after forty-seven years in foreign hands (John Paul II, Benedict XVI, Francis) and moves at full speed, this media offensive could backfire.

"Although it's normal and we saw it in 2013, these kinds of media campaigns ultimately destroy the favorites because the others are alerted and organize," a Vatican monsignor friend in contact with several cardinals tells me by phone. "If they think these campaigns are doing Parolin a favor, they'll inflate the situation even more, creating more organized opposition," adds the prelate, who emphasizes that, beyond the speculation, the atmosphere prevailing in the pre-conclave meetings "is very spiritual and engaged in a search for the right person for this moment."

Italian newspapers are filled with interviews with cardinals that reflect that the game is on.

"Look carefully around St. Peter's Square and Saint Mary Major and ask the crowd: they will all answer that they are waiting for a new Francis," says German Cardinal Walter Kasper, a 92-year-old progressive theologian and president emeritus of the Pontifical Council for Promoting Christian Unity. "Without looking for a carbon copy, I am convinced that we will continue along Bergoglio's lines. I spoke about it with several cardinals," adds the cardinal, whom we know well. He participated in the last conclave, but will not be able to attend this one because of his age. "It seems to me that in the general congregations the opposing factions are a small group. The Church cannot afford to back down now," he asserts.[76]

African Cardinal Ignace Bessi Dogbo, 73, archbishop of Abidjan, Ivory Coast, agrees: "The next pope must follow in Francis's footsteps, that is, with a missionary, synodal Church, reaching all people and excluding no one," he tells Gerry.

Stockholm Archbishop Cardinal Anders Arborelius, 75, the first cardinal in Scandinavia's history, a moderate-conservative whose name appears on some lists of papal candidates, begs to differ. When our friend Iacopo Scaramuzzi, Vatican expert for *La Repubblica*, asks him if it's time to continue on Francis's path or slow down, Arborelius says he thinks "both are possible... because Francis's personality and heart have been well received all over the world, but at the same time, we must unite the Church and find time to reflect and try to address both internal and external problems."

Arborelius emphasizes that while no one knows where the next pope will come from geographically, "many hope he will come from outside Europe because our continent is old and tired, while the Church in other parts of the world is more dynamic and lively. It would therefore be more natural for the next pope to come from Africa or Asia, but I don't know if we will ultimately manage to find a suitable candidate in that part of the world."[77]

---

76. Domenico Agasso, "Il cardinale Kasper: 'Vogliono tutti un nuovo Francesco. Una guida nei drammi del mondo,'" *La Stampa*, May 5, 2025.

77. Iacopo Scaramuzzi, "Il cardinale svedese Arborelius: 'Europa stanca, è ora di guardare all'Africa o all'Asia,'" *La Repubblica*, May 4, 2025.

UNDER THE RADAR AMIDST ALL THIS WHIRL, Cardinal Robert Prevost is beginning to be mentioned more as a papal candidate—though not among the big favorites. While some say it would be impossible because he is American (born in Chicago), he could attract those who want to continue the openness and support of Francis's recent policies.

"Prevost is not a pope from the United States, he's a Latin pope," a Vatican source in contact with cardinals tells me by phone. He says that this prelate, who was head of the Augustinians, lived in Peru for more than twenty years, where he first served as a missionary and later as bishop of Chiclayo.[78]

Experts emphasize that Prevost, a low-profile man, has an advantage in that—like Parolin—he knows the Roman Curia and "all its virtues and defects," given that he has been in Rome as prefect for the Dicastery for Bishops since April 2023.

Although he would break the taboo against an American pope, some emphasize that he would be an "anti-Trump" pope, capable of standing up to an American president who, days ago, posted an image on his social media that was seen in the Vatican as almost a Mafioso "message."

"Trump dressed as a pope wasn't a joke, but a clear and resounding message: 'Be careful who you elect, I don't want opposition to my policies.' It was a way of saying, 'I'm watching you and I want a domesticated Catholic Church,'" explains the same source.

"And not just anyone can stand up to that. In this sense, Francis has restored the freedom of the Church, which during the times of John Paul II and Benedict XVI was aligned with the United States, but which, under him, sided with the weak, the 'bad guys'—like the Lulas, the Maduros, the Petros, Gaza—and one of the challenges for the next pope is to maintain this line and put a stop to Trump, something Prevost could do," he insists.

"Furthermore, with Prevost, an American pope, that $500 million financial pension shortfall would be immediately closed, because donations from American Catholic billionaires would begin to pour in," he adds enthusiastically.

---

78. Elisabetta Piqué, "Las matemáticas del cónclave: el techo que limita a los dos favoritos, el cardenal norteamericano que se afianza y los indecisos," *La Nación*, May 6, 2025.

*The Quest for a New Pope* 133

IN A VERY FLUID ATMOSPHERE, today the cardinals for the first time hold two pre-conclave meetings—one in the morning and one in the afternoon—at which a total of forty-six cardinals speak, reports Bruni in two separate press conferences.

At the morning General Congregation #10 several cardinals emphasize "the missionary nature of the Church," meaning that "the Church must not withdraw into itself, but must accompany every man and woman toward the living experience of the mystery of God." Some highlight the challenges facing the Church today, such as "the transmission of the faith, the care of creation, war, and the fragmentation of the world." Others express "deep concern about the divisions within the Church" and "the shortage of vocations," as well as "about the family and the educational responsibility toward children."

In General Congregation #11, which begins at 5 PM—forcing Bruni to hold a second briefing at 8 PM—the topics discussed are ethnicity within the Church and society, immigration as a gift, war on some continents, the synod, the ecclesiology of communion, and the cardinals' commitment to supporting the pope. The need for a "pastor pope" with a "perspective that goes beyond the Catholic Church" and with a capacity for dialogue with diverse cultural and religious worlds and the challenge of sects in some parts of the world are again discussed.

Bruni confirms that the final General Congregation #12 will take place tomorrow morning. Before it begins, the 133 cardinal electors can leave their belongings at the Santa Marta and Old Santa Marta residences, which have been prepared for them. Cardinal Camerlengo Kevin Farrell conducted the drawing of lots for the rooms last Saturday. The premises will be isolated from all outside influences. The cardinals will participate Wednesday in the *Pro eligendo Pontifice* Mass, which will take place at 10 AM in St. Peter's Basilica.

In addition to the 133 cardinal electors housed in the new and old Santa Marta, there will be all the people who provide essential assistance to them, including security personnel, two doctors, nurses, chauffeurs, cooks, cleaning staff, dining room staff, assistants, masters of ceremonies, and drivers. They are so numerous that some will live in the Ethiopian College, another building within the Vatican walls. These are at least one hundred people, including gendarmes, priests, lay people, consecrated women, and others, Bruni explains.

In a solemn ceremony in the Pauline Chapel, they all swore before the cardinal *camerlengo* "to observe absolute secrecy with anyone who is not part of the College of Cardinal Electors, and this in perpetuity."

Furthermore, they promised and swore, as indicated in the apostolic constitution *Universi Dominici Gregis,* to refrain from using any means of recording, hearing, or seeing what will happen during the election period. And with their hands on the Gospel, they declared they were taking the oath, aware that "a violation of the same would entail the penalty of excommunication *latae sententiae* reserved to the Apostolic See."

TOKYO ARCHBISHOP CARDINAL TARCISIUS ISAO KIKUCHI, 66, speaks at the general congregation about the work of Caritas Internationalis, of which he is president, whose task is "not only to provide relief, but also to defend the poor, bearing witness to the justice of the Gospel."

Interviewed by *La Repubblica*,[79] Kikuchi states that while "Europeans have the majority percentage-wise, and if they were to unite they would form the strongest bloc, they do not seem to be [united]. We Asians, on the other hand, will most likely show ourselves more united in supporting one or two candidates." He adds that he is "certain" that one of the names that emerges among the top candidates in the first ballot "will be from Asia."

Describing the nature of their close-knit fellowship, an Asian cardinal tells us they have formed a WhatsApp group to stay in touch while it is permitted to do so.

The Governorate of Vatican City State announces this afternoon that, starting at 3 PM the day after tomorrow, May 7, all mobile radio telecommunications signal transmission systems within Vatican City State will be deactivated, except for the Castel Gandolfo area. This guarantees the isolation of the cardinals during the conclave. The signal will be restored after the announcement of the election of the next Pope, delivered from the central loggia of St. Peter's Basilica.

JAPAN'S CARDINAL KIKUCHI is a member of the Divine Word Missionaries, and just one of the thirty-three members of religious orders

---

79. Iacopo Scaramuzzi, "Cardinale Kikuchi: 'Scommetto che nelle prime fasi emergerà un asiatico,'" *La Repubblica,* May 5, 2025.

who will vote in the conclave. Never in history have so many members of religious orders participated in the election of a pope; they represent 25 percent of the electors.[80] Although these thirty-three electors differ from each other, and not only geographically, if they were to unite, they could significantly influence the course of the conclave.

The historical record shows that thirty-four of the 266 popes have belonged to religious orders; the majority came from the diocesan clergy. Among those belonging to religious orders, seventeen were Benedictines, four were from the Franciscan and Dominican orders, two were Cistercians, one was Theatine, and one was a Jesuit, Francis. Before Jorge Bergoglio, the last pope from a religious order was Gregory XVI (1831–1846), a Camaldolese monk.

The thirty-three electors from religious orders present at this conclave come from eighteen different religious communities. Five are Salesians; four are Friars Minor; four are Jesuits; and two each are Dominicans, Redemptorists, and Missionaries of the Divine Word. Several other orders, such as the Augustinians, the Capuchins, and the Scalabrinians, have just one elector.

It is also worth noting that five of these cardinal electors were major superiors, that is, heads, of their orders: Robert Prevost, former prior general of the Augustinians; Joseph Tobin, former superior general of the Redemptorists; Gérald Lacroix, former superior general of the Pius X Secular Institute; Timothy Radcliffe, former master of the Dominicans; and Ángel Fernández Artime, former rector major of the Salesians.

Father Ricardo da Silva, SJ, associate editor of *America*, remarks that "their presence in the College of Cardinals signals a recovery of religious charisms rooted in community, mission, and prophetic witness, at the very heart of ecclesial governance."

Could the fact that one in four electors in the conclave belong to religious orders, and almost all were appointed by Francis, increase the chances of a member of a religious order, such as Prevost, becoming pope?

---

80. Ricardo da Silva, SJ, "The rise of religious orders among the conclave's cardinal electors," *America*, May 6, 2025. The 2013 conclave had 18 religious (O'Connell, *The Election of Pope Francis*, 197).

CARDINAL PREVOST MET BERGOGLIO, then archbishop of Buenos Aires, when he was prior general of the Augustinian Order (2001–2013). He visited the Augustinian community in the Argentine capital on several occasions, and among other things inaugurated a library, the Biblioteca Agustiniana, in the Buenos Aires neighborhood of Villa Pueyrredón.

He and the archbishop had had some disagreements, Prevost revealed in 2023, when he said goodbye to his beloved Peru to serve in the Curia in Rome. He recalls that, when Francis was elected pope, he told his friends, "Well, thank God I'll never be a bishop"—as can be seen in a very interesting video from the Peruvian Episcopal Conference.[81]

"Well, I said that specifically in relation to Bergoglio, who had then been elected pope, and it was because of a couple of incidents when he was archbishop of Buenos Aires and I was prior general of the Augustinians. He had asked me for something. It had to do with personnel issues, and I made decisions that were contrary to what he had requested. So, when he became pope, I thought, 'Well, he knows who I am, he's not going to call me to be a bishop, because he knows I'll say no, depending on the matter.' Obviously, the opposite happened for reasons that... you would have to make a book about Pope Francis, about some of his ways of thinking and doing things," Pope Leo said in the interview for the biography of Elise Ann Allen, *León XIV, Ciudadano del Mundo misionero del siglo XXI*.[82]

There he revealed an important fact: "At one point,...there was another matter in which I actually sided with him and against an official of the Holy See. I won't go into detail there.... I confronted someone in the Holy See and he [Pope Francis] said to me, as I was finishing my term as prior general: 'I will never forget what you did on that occasion.' And, apparently, he did not forget it. Everyone knows that he had a very keen memory, but, because he knew that I was frank and said things as I saw them, and then was very willing to talk about them, he respected that. And I think that had something to do with him considering me for the possibility of an episcopal appointment."

---

81. Conferencia Episcopal Peruana, "Papa León XIV (Robert Prevost) recibe la Medalla 'Santo Toribio de Mogrovejo' del Episcopado Peruano," youtube.com, May 10, 2025.

82. Elise Ann Allen, *León XIV, Ciudadano del Mundo misionero del siglo XXI* (Penguin Peru, 2025), 137.

In the video of the Peruvian Episcopal Conference, he also recounted that Francis surprised him when, on August 28, 2013, he went to preside at a Mass at the Church of San Agostino for the opening of the General Chapter of the Augustinians. In that church in the historic center of Rome is the tomb of Augustine's mother, Saint Monica. Prevost had requested an audience with Francis for the members of the General Chapter—a normal but difficult request, as everyone told him "the Pope won't accept"—but to his great surprise, Francis agreed to go and preside over Mass with them.[83] After Mass, Francis told Prevost: "Now, get some rest."

The Augustinian priest could never have imagined then that this phrase would mean that, just over a year later, on November 3, 2014, the pope would appoint him apostolic administrator of the Peruvian Diocese of Chiclayo. Nor that, less than a year after that, on September 26, 2015, he would appoint him bishop of that diocese.[84] Prevost then chose as his episcopal motto "*In Illo uno unum*," words spoken by Saint Augustine in a sermon on Psalm 127 to explain that "although we Christians are many, in one Christ we are one." In March 2018, he was elected second vice president of the Peruvian Episcopal Conference.

Clearly Pope Francis had his sights set on him: in July 2019, he appointed him a member of the Vatican's Congregation for the Clergy.[85] In April 2020, during the COVID-19 pandemic, he sent Prevost as apostolic administrator to the diocese of Callao after having obtained the resignation of Bishop José Luis del Palacio y Pérez-Medel who had tried to impose the neo-catechumenal model on the whole diocese and caused enormous problems there. Prevost drove 800 km to Callao every two weeks and succeeded in bringing healing and stability to the diocese by May 2021, when a new bishop was installed. It seems that Pope Francis, who had already been informed about how well Prevost was doing in Chiclayo, was now highly impressed by how he dealt with this extraordinarily difficult situation in Callao, as Elise Ann Allen tells us in her biography of Pope Leo.[86] In the following year, 2022, he asked Prevost to be prefect of the Dicastery for Bishops.

---

83. Cindy Wooden, "Pope Says Christians Should Have Restless Hearts," www.ncronline.com, August 28, 2013.

84. "Biography of Pope Leo XIV, Born Robert Francis Prevost," www.vaticannews.va, May 8, 2025.

85. Congegations were renaned dicasteries in 2022.

86. Elise Ann Allen, *León XIV*, 102.

This reshaped the landscape for several reasons. First, this dicastery's prefect has tremendous influence over the long-term direction of the Church, producing the refined shortlist of bishop candidates to the pope for Europe and the Americas.[87] Second, the new prefect replaced longtime conservative stalwart Cardinal Marc Ouellet, the third runner-up in the 2013 conclave[88] who was approaching his seventy-ninth birthday. Many Vatican watchers, especially on the progressive side, were anxiously watching whom Francis would place in that role. Third, this prefect is automatically the president of the Pontifical Commission for Latin America. Although this role might take only 10 percent of his time, it gives him exposure to the people and issues of the Church's largest region, with 450 million baptized Catholics.

Prevost assumed the office of prefect on April 12, 2023. The pope and the prefect of the dicastery for bishops have a standing meeting on Saturday mornings when both men are in town to discuss upcoming bishop appointments. An anecdote circulated that each man competed to arrive first to the meeting, and their 8 AM gathering would start as early as 7:15. The Press Office's daily bulletins list fifty-four Saturday meetings between the two over the twenty-four-month period before Francis's death. Francis was known to be unrushed and expansive in his one-on-one meetings, and surely the two men discussed Church leadership issues beyond the immediate topic at hand. Very few other people would have such significant face time with the Holy Father.

In September 2023, Francis created Prevost a cardinal, naming him first on the list, which gave him the privilege of delivering the induction remarks on behalf of the incoming cohort at the ornate Consistory ceremony.

Keen-eyed Vatican observers arched an eyebrow when Pope Francis invited Prevost to accompany him on his last two trips abroad: to Luxembourg and Belgium (September 26–28, 2024), and to Corsica (December 15 of the same year).

Then, in a niche maneuver that only attentive insiders noticed at the time but was quietly consequential, on February 6, 2025, just two months before his death, Pope Francis promoted Cardinal Pre-

---

87. African and Asian bishop recommendations are processed through the Dicastery for Evangelization.

88. O'Connell, *The Election of Pope Francis*, 226.

vost to the order of cardinal-bishops, the highest rank in the College of Cardinals, placing him in a position of greater prominence and responsibility in the Catholic Church.[89] There are three orders of cardinals, with Curial cardinals being placed in the Cardinal Deacon class, which is the lowest in the order of precedence. When Francis made this subtly impactful promotion, Prevost leapt from number 241 in order of precedence to number 11. This would be noted during processions. Prevost was the only cardinal to receive this honor recently.

THE FIRST TIME WE HEARD PREVOST'S NAME mentioned as a papal candidate was in March 2024, more than a year before the conclave, when a cardinal elector told us over dinner, "He's *papabile* because, although he was born in Chicago, he is not considered an American."

At first, we were skeptical, since for many years cardinals kept telling us, "There can't be an American pope."

Later, we learn that some of Prevost's early supporters for the papacy came from the group of twenty-three cardinal electors who are part of the thirty-plus-member Dicastery for Bishops,[90] which meets at the Vatican every two weeks between September and the end of June.

Prevost presided over all of those meetings after having taking office as prefect of the Dicastery, and he earned respect and high marks for his listening skills and management of the meetings, in which members typically discuss the backgrounds of the proposed bishop candidates and then vote on them. Prevost then would present the names at the Saturday morning meeting to the pope, who made the decision regarding whom to appoint.

---

89. Elisabetta Piqué, "Una decisión del papa Francisco con impacto en el cónclave abre especulaciones sobre su sucesión," *La Nación*," February 7, 2025.

90. The 23 cardinals members of the Dicastery for Bishops, according to the *Annuario Pontificio 2025*, are: Parolin (Italy), Sandri (Argentina), Koch (Switzerland), Braz de Aviz (Brazil), Nichols (UK), Rocha (Brazil), Cupich (USA), Tobin (USA), Omella (Spain), Arborelius (Sweden), Advincula (Philippines), Lojudice (Italy), Aveline (France), Cantoni (Italy), Ryś (Poland), Cobo Cano (Spain), Mendonca (Portugal), Grech (Malta), Roche (UK), You Lazzaro (South Korea), Gugerotti (Italy), Fernández (Argentina), and Tscherrig (Switzerland).

ONE OF THE FIRST TO SUPPORT PREVOST is Chicago Archbishop Cardinal Blase Cupich, who has known him since he became a member of the Dicastery for Bishops in 2020. Cupich, an American of Croatian origin, is known for his sense of humor, affability, and network of contacts.

Another early backer of Prevost, this time a European and also a member of the Dicastery for Bishops, is German Cardinal Reinhard Marx, according to Ludwig Ring-Eifel, Rome bureau chief of the German Catholic News Agency (KNA).

He told Gerry that Marx greatly respects Prevost because he credits him with "saving the German Synodal Path" from a canon law closure through a compromise formula. Prevost's predecessor, Cardinal Marc Ouellet, had adopted "a tough, confrontational stance," demanding a moratorium on the proposed Council of German Catholics, a demand that Marx had considered "a declaration of war." Cardinal Parolin had also taken a firm stance by issuing a statement "in the name of the Holy See," warning that the German Synodal Path would threaten the unity of the Church and risk a schism. Prevost then proposed not using the word "council" because the Evangelical Church in Germany uses that title for those who govern the Luther an Church.

Marx backs Prevost for an additional reason, says Ring-Eifel. As coordinator of the Vatican's Council for the Economy, he is deeply concerned about the Holy See's precarious financial situation; he believes it cannot recover without substantial aid from Catholic donors in the United States. Furthermore, he believes an American pope would be more likely to address this problem adequately.

Marx organizes private meetings to discuss qualities of the next pope and Prevost's candidacy. These meetings take place at his Roman residence, a twenty-room building that the Archdiocese of Munich purchased and renovated in 2015 on the Monte Mario hill, four kilometers from the Vatican, according to Ring-Eifel. The residence is called "Casa Maria," but is also known as "Casa Marx," and guarantees a certain amount of privacy to visitors. Marx invites cardinals there on several occasions during the general congregations prior to the conclave. We learn that up to fifteen cardinals were present at one meeting shortly before the conclave.

In addition to the cardinal electors who are members of the Dicastery for Bishops, there are also some non-bishops—men and women—working in the Roman Curia who are actively seeking to convince the Latin American electors that Prevost is the best choice. They present him as someone who has spent about twenty years of his life as a missionary in Peru and who fully shares Pope Francis's vision of a missionary and synodal Church. One of the Latin American cardinals who began to support Prevost—after realizing that Parolin was not at all Francis's candidate—is the archbishop of Lima, Carlos Castillo. He tells several of his Latin American colleagues that Prevost, "although a '*gringo*,' is one of us." The Venezuelan cardinal, Baltazar Porras Cardozo, who is over 80 and so cannot enter the conclave, is of the same view and says, "Almost all of us know him. He is one of us."

AS THE COUNTDOWN TO THE CONCLAVE CONTINUES, a network of Prevost supporters is building, quietly, slowly, and surely, without attracting media attention. According to information obtained by Gerry, this will allow the American missionary cardinal to enter the conclave with more than twenty votes secured in the first round.

Of course, there is no shortage of those who will attempt to torpedo Prevost's candidacy. Media outlets linked to Sodalitium Christianae Vitae, a powerful and controversial right-wing Catholic lay movement founded in Peru in 1971 and active in the United States, will begin to attack him, through "corrupt" information, for his role, alongside Francis, in what will be its dissolution on April 14, 2025.

He will also be criticized by SNAP (Survivors Networks of Those Abused by Priests) for an alleged problem in Chicago. Just today, *The Pillar*, a North American investigative journalism website focusing on the Catholic Church, published an article by its editor-in-chief JD Flynn repeating the same accusations of mishandling abuse cases as part of a backlash from survivor groups. The article mentions that Prevost's candidacy is gaining traction with the support of "high-profile advocates among the cardinals," including Christophe Pierre, apostolic nuncio to the United States, and Oscar Maradiaga, the 82-year-old Honduran cardinal credited with helping elect Francis in 2013.[91]

While these accusations garner media coverage, without hard evidence they have little or no impact on the cardinal electors.

IT'S WORTH NOTING HERE that although the 133 electors come from seventy countries, only fourteen of these countries have more than one

---

91. JD Flynn, "Why Prevost's Papal Prospects Prompt Pushback, *The Pillar*, May 5, 2025.

elector. Italy, as always, heads the list with 19 electors, followed by the United States with 10; Brazil 7; France and Spain 5 each; Argentina, Canada, Portugal 4 each; Germany, the Philippines, Poland, and the United Kingdom 3 each; and Ivory Coast and Switzerland 2 each. As is well known, both from the 2013 conclave and from an early analysis of the present one, the electors in many of these countries have different views. Nevertheless, from our conversations with many cardinals—not all of whom are named in this book—it seems the vast majority of the electors are committed to a missionary, synodal church, and Francis's vision of a church that reaches out to people and is inclusive.

UNLIKE THE 2013 CONCLAVE, when accredited journalists were able to visit the Sistine Chapel already prepared for voting, this time it will be impossible. The Vatican Gendarmerie has already sealed the chapel off. However, images showing the prepared interior will be released, and Barbara Jatta, director of the Vatican Museums, will explain its history in a briefing.

What a shame! Gerry and I still have photos from 2013. It was a unique experience.

After a full day at the Press Room, between Bruni's two briefings and various live broadcasts for LN+ and CNN, I walk home as usual to refresh my brain and do a little exercise.

Juampy prepares some delicious *mezze maniche all'amatriciana*—with *guanciale* and pecorino Romano. We eat late, as always. While we talk and speculate about who will succeed our beloved Francis, Irene tells us over and over again that we'll have to write a book about the conclave, which is just around the corner and becoming more intriguing than ever.

MAY 6, TUESDAY [BETTA]
*Great Anxiety*

ANXIETY HEIGHTENS WITH EVERY PASSING MOMENT. It is evident in the morning as the cardinals make their way into the synod hall for General Congregations #12, besieged by a crowd of excited journalists on the hunt for a statement. This is the last meeting before tomorrow's conclave. The atmosphere is electric. Such is the interest and anticipation that the news channels broadcast the moment of the cardinals' entry live. Police call in reinforcements in Piazza del Sant'Uffizzio to prevent a media siege.

We read the newspapers. Gerry meets with his team from *America*, which includes the seven people who have traveled to cover the conclave. One of them asks ChatGPT: According to newspaper reports, who will be the next pope? Answer: Italian Cardinal Matteo Zuppi.

I head to Bruni's last briefing at the Vatican Press Office. A bus takes me to the Santo Spirito Hospital. Walking toward the Press Room I run into our friend Darío Menor, a Spanish journalist and correspondent for *Telecinco*, who is speaking in front of the Curia of the Society of Jesus with a cardinal who has just left the final general congregation. It is Venezuelan Baltazar Enrique Porras Cardozo, who graciously agrees to answer a few questions.

"The tone is that there is no desire or possibility of backing down, quite the opposite," says the cardinal, when I ask him if the conclave will respect Francis's legacy. Porras Cardozo, archbishop emeritus of Caracas and Mérida, who will not participate in the conclave because he is over 80, is more than convinced that there is consensus that we must "continue the fundamental projects of Francis." His successor must be "a shepherd with the smell of sheep," he asserts.

Asked if he could be an Italian, he offers a clue: "Where are the world's Catholics today? More than 80 percent of the world's Catholics are not in Europe." He predicts that there will be white smoke "between Friday and Saturday."

IN THE PRESS ROOM, expectations are sky-high. The crowd is thick, the water vending machine is empty, and there are lines to use the bathroom.

The good news from the final briefing is that all 133 cardinal electors are in Rome. Bruni reports that 173 cardinals participated in this morning's meeting, but three electors did not attend, he says, without giving an explanation.

Among the last twenty-six cardinals who were able to speak, some strongly emphasized "the need to continue many of the reforms promoted by Pope Francis," especially those related to "the fight against abuse, the need for economic transparency, the reorganization of the Roman Curia, and synodality." Others spoke of the importance of continuing "the commitment to peace and care for creation," and addressing climate change "as a global and ecclesial challenge," as well as to better link the World Day of the Poor to the feast of Christ the King. Some again raised the question of the role of cardinals in relation to the papacy, and the need to make the meetings of the College of Cardinals more meaningful when consistories are held.

Others affirmed the need, through ecumenical dialogue, to arrive at a common date for Easter with the Orthodox churches and to celebrate the seventeen-hundred-year anniversary Council of Nicaea. They spoke of the martyrs of the faith and the need to care for Christians in countries where they suffer persecution or are deprived of religious freedom.

Most important, however, the cardinals finally completed their "identikit" of the new pope. Bruni summarizes it as "the profile of a pastoral pope, a teacher of humanity, capable of embodying the face of a [Good] Samaritan Church, close to the needy and the wounds of humanity."

"In times marked by war, violence, and strong polarization, the need for a spiritual guide that offers mercy, synodality, and hope is strongly felt," Bruni adds, capping his final meeting before the election with many of the four-thousand-plus journalists who have come from around the world to cover the conclave.

The influx of journalists is not due to a heightened interest thanks to the film *Conclave*, Bruni says in response to a question on the matter. He explains that it is "normal" that the election of a pontiff, leader of more than 1.4 billion Catholic faithful worldwide, is viewed with enormous interest.

AT THE FINAL PRE-CONCLAVE MEETING, in the presence of members of the College of Cardinals and in accord with the new rules envisioned by the pope, Francis's Fisherman's Ring and lead seal are formally destroyed. Curiously, it is done by a woman.[92]

---

92. La "biffatura" dell'Anello del Pescatore e del Sigillo di piombo del Papa, www.vaticannews.va, May 7, 2025.

The new Fisherman's Ring for the next pope will bear the identical image of Peter casting his net, but with the new pontiff's name inscribed above it.

Indicating that they, like Pope Francis, are concerned about a world in flames, the cardinals—many of whom come from theaters of war—issue a statement[93] lamenting that there has been no progress toward peace in Ukraine, the Middle East, and other parts of the world, but that "attacks against civilians have intensified," and they call for a permanent ceasefire and prayers for a just and lasting peace. By the end of today's session, a total of 218 cardinals had spoken at the general congregations, some of them more than once.

As many emphasized the need to "continue the process initiated by Pope Francis to build a synodal Church," Gerry believes this issue could become a litmus test in the election of the next pope.

From near the reporters' pen in St. Peter's Square, I broadcast live on various LN+ programs. In one, we appear simultaneously with beloved Father Guillermo Marcó, who was spokesperson for then-Archbishop Jorge Bergoglio and whom we have known for more than twenty years.

We go to a bar on Via della Conciliazione and have a *tramezzino* and a Coke with our young Argentine journalist friend Clara Fontan. She was the head of the research team I had put together to write my biography of Francis.[94] She is covering her first conclave and, like everyone else, is disoriented.

Gerry explains to her that, as several cardinals have also told us, on the eve of the conclave, there is no obvious *papabile* who stands out above the others.

In fact, Indonesian Cardinal Ignatius Suharyo Hardjoatmodjo, 74, archbishop of Jakarta, who was the last elector to arrive yesterday, said that "there have been many interventions, but no progress on the name, except that [he] has to follow the line of Francis," who visited his country last September (a spectacular trip that Gerry and I covered).[95]

---

93. "Bollettino," Comunicato della Santa Sede, Sala Stampa della Santa Sede, May 6, 2025.

94. Elisabetta Piqué, *Francisco, vida y revolución* (Loyola Press, 2013); *Francis, Life and Revolution* (Loyola Press, 2014).

95. *Corriere della Sera*, May 6, 5.

The jovial 63-year-old French-born Cardinal Jean-Paul Vesco, OP, archbishop of Algiers, the capital of Algeria, seemed to agree when, passing St. Peter's Square and hounded by journalists, he told us that "the most important characteristic" of the next pope is "the pastoral dimension." He went on to say, "We need a pastor, a witness [of the faith], a father. This is what the people asked of us at Francis's funeral: 'Give us a pastor!'"[96] For Cardinal Vesco, "at least five or six cardinals fit that profile."

Gerry explains to Clara that, given that Church history shows that more than 80 percent of popes—that is, 217 out of 266—have been Italian, it's not surprising that the Italian press insists on the need to return the papacy to the peninsula. But many cardinals do not share this way of thinking.

When asked about this by a group of journalists, including us, a few days ago at the Chiesa Nuova, Luxembourg Cardinal Jean-Claude Hollerich replied: "We mustn't put geographical limits on the Holy Spirit."[97]

German Cardinal Gerhard Müller, with whom we met a few days ago, agreed: "I think talking about nationalism, about national selfishness, is out of place. Anyone who thinks with a Catholic mentality is always open to where the Holy Spirit points."[98]

Italian Cardinal Baldassare Reina shared this sentiment, saying, "I don't think nationality should be the primary concern. The College of Cardinals' real concern should be finding the right man for this moment. Whether he's Italian or from another country doesn't matter. What matters is that the work begun by Francis continue."[99]

THE TRUTH IS THAT, although no cardinal stands out above the others as a papal candidate, two are known throughout the world and by all electors: the Italian Pietro Parolin and the Filipino Luis Antonio "Chito" Tagle.

---

96. *Corriere della Sera*, May 6, 8.

97. Gerard O'Connell, "Conclave Watch: Which Cardinals Are Likely Contenders?" *America*, May 7, 2025.

98. Gerard O'Connell, "Interview: Cardinal Müller on if Pope Francis Was a Heretic and What He Wants in the Next Pope," *America*, May 3, 2025.

99. Gerard O'Connell, "Cardinal Reina: The Next Pope Must Continue the Reform Francis Began," *America*, May 3, 2025.

Cardinal Parolin, 70, a highly experienced Vatican diplomat, is seen as the favorite. He is a moderate figure, strong in the institutional aspect of the Church, and the most viable Italian candidate. He joined the diplomatic corps of the Holy See in 1986, and after serving on diplomatic missions in Nigeria and Mexico, he was called to work in the Vatican Secretariat of State in 1992, where he handled reports on China, Israel, North Korea, and Vietnam. Benedict XVI sent him as nuncio to Venezuela in 2009. Pope Francis called him to Rome to become secretary of state in August 2013, and made him a cardinal in 2014. Since then, he has traveled to numerous countries on all continents and is fluent in several languages. He suffered serious health problems in 2014, but seems to have recovered. His biggest handicap is, as mentioned earlier, that he lacks pastoral experience (he has never led a diocese—in contrast to 92 of the 133 electors who have done so). Also, he has not been a strong secretary of state. "A weak secretary of state will not make a strong pope," a senior Vatican prelate told us on the eve of the conclave.

Although the Italian and other media have presented him as Pope Francis's "strongman," he has not been.

Even though he is promoted daily in most Italian media, he has been harshly attacked in the United States, the United Kingdom,[100] parts of Italy,[101] Eastern Europe, and parts of Asia[102] for being the architect of the Vatican's provisional agreement with China on the appointment of bishops. And in what seemed like an effort to derail his candidacy, false rumors about his current health circulated on May 1,[103] which Vatican media outlets, supporting him, quickly denied.

Although many consider him to be in the leading position on the eve of the conclave, and some cardinals claim he already has 40–50 votes,[104] Gerry thinks this is not the case. Based on his private conversations with many cardinals and his reckoning, he estimates that at least

---

100. Damian Thompson, "Does China have Vatican City in its sights?" *The Spectator,* March 22, 2025.

101. Sandro Magister, "Parolin Is the Candidate Being Noised About, But He's a Lame Duck," *Diakonos,* April 10, 2025.

102. Daniel Williams, "Bad Vatican Deal with China May Sink a Papal Conclave Favorite," *Asia Times,* May 8, 2025.

103. Nico Spuntoni, "Becciu, il caso scuote il Conclave. Paura per Parolin, arrivano i medici," *Il Tempo,* May 1, 2025.

104. Franca Giansoldati, "The Conclave's Intrigue Unfolds," *Il Messaggero,* May 4, 2025.

55 of the 133 electors will not vote for Parolin, making it highly unlikely that he will get the necessary 89. Of course, the electors can change their minds during the conclave—as has happened several times in history—but his chances of election will depend on how many votes he receives on the first two ballots.

The second most well-known *papabile* is Cardinal Luis Antonio "Chito" Gokim Tagle, 67, former archbishop of Manila, the largest diocese in Asia, and previously bishop of a smaller diocese in the country. A charismatic figure of Chinese descent who hosted his own television show before coming to Rome, he is capable of inspiring young people. Due to his simple lifestyle and outreach to the people, he is known as "The Francis of Asia." The Argentine pope called him to Rome in 2019 to lead the Dicastery for the Evangelization of Peoples, which oversees the churches in missionary lands and the appointment of bishops to them. Fluent in several languages, Tagle was elected president of Caritas Internationalis, the Catholic Church's international charity federation in 2015, and in that role traveled extensively. However, Pope Francis dismissed the entire leadership of that organization, including Tagle, in 2022 because of serious internal administrative problems. On the eve of the conclave, his candidacy is harshly attacked on social media because he is seen as the main challenger to Parolin. He is attacked especially in North America and Italy because of a "karaoke" video in which he is seen singing and dancing to John Lennon's song "Imagine." That video, coupled with the fallout from the Caritas crisis, which had a major impact in the United States and Germany, could have a negative impact on voters. This could also contribute to the perception in Rome that he is considered an emotional man, overly cautious in his decision-making, and not a great administrator at the Dicastery for Evangelization. As in the case of Parolin, it seems unlikely that he will obtain the necessary votes to be elected.

ASIDE FROM THESE TWO well-known main contenders, we gather from conversations with cardinals that there are other papal candidates who, although less well-known, could garner solid support and seem to have no limits on the number of votes they could obtain.

The first is Cardinal Robert Francis Prevost, 69, who was born in Chicago but has been described as "the least American of Americans" for having lived more than half of his life outside the United States.

He spent about twenty years of his life as a missionary in Peru (1985–1987, 1989–1999), including more than eight years as a bishop (2013–2023), and became a citizen of that South American country. He lived fifteen years in Rome, first as a graduate student in canon law (1984–1987) and from 2001 to 2013 as prior general of the Augustinian order. As head of that order, he traveled around the world, visiting members of the order in some fifty countries, including China and India. Shortly after Prevost completed his term as prior general, Pope Francis appointed him first as apostolic administrator and then bishop of Chiclayo, Peru, and later brought him to the Roman Curia. Known as a careful listener with excellent administrative skills, he is fluent in several languages.

On the eve of the conclave, several cardinals tell us they are unsure whether the electors would vote for an American pope. However, unlike Parolin and Tagle, who have been constantly in the media spotlight, Prevost has had the advantage of flying under the radar. And although his name has been mentioned in the Italian and international media, he has never been considered a front runner and has therefore largely avoided media scrutiny, much like Bergoglio did in the 2013 conclave.

Prevost could receive more than 20 votes on the first ballot, Gerry estimates, but it remains to be seen whether—like Bergoglio—he will garner more votes in the second and third ballots to have a realistic chance of succeeding Francis.

ANOTHER CARDINAL WHO appears to have some support is the 66-year-old French cardinal of Algerian origin, Jean-Marc Aveline. Francis appointed him bishop in 2013 and archbishop of Marseille in 2019. Hailed as one of France's finest theologians, he is a charismatic pastor and can inspire crowds, as we saw when Francis visited Marseille in September 2023. He apparently rejected Francis's offer to become archbishop of Paris. Nevertheless, the pope made him a cardinal in 2022, and upon handing him the red biretta whispered in his ear: "Stay close to the people."

Aveline has emerged as an ecclesiastical leader in the Mediterranean basin, and is known to fully support Francis's pastoral vision of the Church, through attention to migrants and the poor, dialogue with other religions—especially Islam—and a commitment to synodality.

On April 2, he was elected president of the French Episcopal Conference in the first round of voting.[105]

His major handicap, as we have noted, is that he does not speak Italian fluently, although he can read an Italian text, as he did at the general congregations and when he delivered a homily at Mass in Italian last Sunday. We were surprised to hear from French sources that before leaving for Rome, Cardinal Aveline hinted to his friends in Marseille that he might not return home, suggesting that he could be elected. If so, he would be the first Frenchman to become pope since Gregory XI (1370–1377), the last of the Avignon popes, who returned to Rome a year before his death, thus ending the period in which the papacy was in exile.

ANOTHER VERY POPULAR CANDIDATE is Italian Cardinal Matteo Zuppi, 69, archbishop of Bologna and president of the Italian Bishops' Conference. He is the first priest of the lay community of Sant'Egidio. A humble man, he leads a simple lifestyle in a house with retired priests and is deeply committed to the poor and to dialogue with other religions. A former auxiliary bishop in Rome who commuted by bicycle, as he now often does in Bologna, Zuppi was created a cardinal by Pope Francis in 2019. Zuppi has been deeply involved in peace negotiations in Africa and elsewhere, and was appointed by Francis as his special envoy to Kyiv, Moscow, Washington DC, and Beijing to help seek paths toward peace in Ukraine and foster humanitarian initiatives.

Some cardinals have told us that they consider his membership in Sant'Egidio, an influential Catholic lay movement, his Achilles' heel. Cardinal Angelo Scola faced a similar handicap in the 2013 conclave because of his close ties to the Communion and Liberation movement.

Cardinal Zuppi is considered an alternative Italian candidate if Parolin fails to advance on the first ballot; he is expected to receive some Italian and perhaps African votes on the first ballot, but his chances appear slim.

The person campaigning for Zuppi, who invited several cardinals to dinners and lunches, is Archbishop Vincenzo Paglia, the president emeritus of the Pontifical Academy for Life and fellow Sant'Egidio community member.

---

105. "Ally of Pope Francis Elected France's Top Bishop," www.france 24.com, February 4, 2025.

ALSO MENTIONED AS *PAPABILE* is the 68-year-old Maltese cardinal Mario Grech, who served as bishop of Gozo from 2005 to 2019. Grech endorsed Pope Francis's position in the 2015 apostolic exhortation *Amoris Laetitia* on the possibility, under certain conditions, of divorced and remarried Catholics receiving communion. Francis appointed him secretary general of the Synod of Bishops in 2020 and, shortly thereafter, created him a cardinal. As secretary general of the Synod of Bishops, he became internationally known for his vigorous promotion of synodality and his central role in organizing recent synods. He could garner votes, but his support appears limited. Europe has fifty-two votes in the conclave.

Another European cardinal who is certain to receive votes, especially from those who do not share Pope Francis's synodal vision for the Church is Péter Erdő, 72, archbishop of Budapest (Hungary), the candidate from the most conservative sector. A distinguished canon lawyer, he was close to John Paul II, who ordained him bishop in St. Peter's Basilica on January 6, 2000, then appointed him archbishop of Budapest, and finally cardinal in 2003. He was elected president of the Hungarian Bishops' Conference and president of the European Bishops' Conferences in 2005, a position he held for two terms. He became known for hosting the 52nd International Eucharistic Congress in Budapest in September 2021, which Francis closed. According to *The New York Times*, some prominent American conservatives consider Cardinal Erdő "a preferable choice to be the next pope." He has the support of Hungarian Prime Minister Viktor Orbán and had the support of deceased Australian Cardinal George Pell, who passed away in 2023. "He is what we need right now," said Brian Burch, the US ambassador-designate to the Holy See, known for his anti-Francis stances. "We need someone who can teach clearly and be strong."[106]

Gerry estimates that Erdő could obtain a maximum of 30 votes in the conclave, a third of the 89 needed to be elected.

Some sectors of the Italian press, on the other hand, are promoting Franciscan Cardinal Pierbattista Pizzaballa, the Italian-born Latin patriarch of Jerusalem, who is fluent in modern Hebrew but not Arabic and is in the spotlight over the war in Gaza, as an alternative candidate if Parolin or Zuppi are unsuccessful. But since he is only 60 years old—his birthday on the day of Francis's death—many say he is

---

106. Elizabeth Dias, "Conservative Catholics Take Stage in Rome, Looking to Shape the Church," *New York Times*, May 6, 2025.

"too young" to be pope. Furthermore, his chances seem slim because he does not support a synodal Church.

IN A HEATED CLIMATE and not without its share of backstabbing, *La Bussola Quotidiana*, an ultraconservative Italian news outlet that has long denigrated Pope Francis and the "Babel synod,"[107] today published two striking articles. One attacks Tagle,[108] "the cardinal who loves casinos," and whom it evidently considers Parolin's main contender; the other takes aim at the emerging Cardinal Prevost,[109] "who should not be voted for" because of his alleged involvement in covering up sexual abuse while a bishop in Peru.

How long will the conclave last? That's the million-dollar question.

Since 1939, only two conclaves have lasted three days: the 1958 conclave, which elected John XXIII, and the 1978 conclave, which elected John Paul II. All other conclaves have elected a pope in two days.

Gerry is surprised when, on the eve of the conclave, two cardinals tell him today that they think it might take at least three days, and perhaps longer, to elect Francis's successor.

That said, a lot can change once the cardinals begin voting. If the first ballot tomorrow afternoon reveals three or four contenders with substantial votes, then the electors' eyes will turn to the second and third ballots on the morning of Thursday, May 8, which will determine whether any of them gain the momentum that will put them on the path to the papacy.

If we don't have a pope on the fifth ballot on Thursday night, this could suggest that candidates other than the favorites have come to the fore. If there is no election on the third day, then a real surprise can be expected, such as the Luxembourg Cardinal Hollerich or the Filipino Cardinal David, both polyglots and perhaps too open-minded.

We learned of the existence of a "plan B" that would aim, in this unlikely scenario of a deadlock, to turn to someone who is not among

---

107. Tommaso Viglezio, "Tagle, il cardinale che ama i casinò," *La Bussola Quotidiana*, May 6, 2025.

108. Tommaso Viglezio, "Tagle, il cardinale che ama i casinò," *La Bussola Quotidiana*, May 6, 2025.

109. Riccardo Cascioli, "Prevost e soci, i coinvolti negli abusi sessuali non vanno votati," *La Nuova Bussola Quotidiana*, June 5, 2025.

the 133 electors. Who? Capuchin Cardinal Sean O'Malley, archbishop emeritus of Boston. We know him well. He wrote the prologue to the US edition of my biography of Francis. He is a very affable figure with his white beard, brown habit, and sandals, known for his fight against the abuse scandal. He garnered 10 votes in the 2013 conclave, the most any American ever obtained. Is it science fiction? No, we have been told that O'Malley is the "plan B" for a group of conservative cardinals. But he doesn't know that.

SEVERAL CARDINALS ENTER the residences of Domus Santa Marta and the old Santa Marta, where they take possession of their rooms, which are already equipped so that nothing can interfere with the vote. In Santa Marta, the cardinals surrender all cell phones, tablets, and smart watches, which they will retrieve only after the new pope has been elected.

Cardinal Fernando Chomali, archbishop of Santiago de Chile and active on social media, says goodbye to his followers. "Today I enter the conclave without a cell phone. I face God alone to vote for who will be the pope, a responsibility that overwhelms me. In prayer, it has emerged: Lord, have mercy; long live Chile, my soul; I love the Church that showed me Jesus Christ our Lord, Light, Way, Truth, and Life," he writes, also uploading a video taken beneath Bernini's Colonnade.

Other cardinals will enter Santa Marta tomorrow morning, in time to travel from there to St. Peter's Basilica for the *pro-eligendo Pontifice* Mass, the kickoff of the election process. In St. Peter's Square, the same climate of enormous expectation is felt by cardinals and journalists. The loudspeakers have already been set up for the *"Habemus Papam"* and the burgundy curtains have been draped over the central balcony or loggia of St. Peter's Basilica, where Francis's successor will be presented to the world. It is impossible to know if he will then surprise everyone with the informal *"Buonasera"* that marked the beginning of that revolution of proximity of the first Argentine pope, arrived from the end of the world, which many want to see continue.

As is customary on the eve of a conclave, I participate in a *"totopapa"*—a survey on who will be the next pope—with Vaticanist friends (Cristina Cabrejas and Juan Vicente Bo will be the winners), and also in an office pool with the newspaper staff. We bet on three cardinals and even guess what name they'll choose: my first candidate is Pablo "Ambo" Virgilio David, who could be called Lorenzo (I spoke with an expert on Asia, and he told me he's a very popular saint in the Philippines); my second candidate is Robert Prevost, who could be called Agustín, because he's an Augustinian; and my third is the Frenchman Jean-Marc Aveline, John XXIV....

After so much stress, it's time to keep things light.

PART III

# THE CONCLAVE

MAY 7, WEDNESDAY [GERRY]
*The Hour of Truth*

IT'S A GRAY DAY, with clouds, sun, and drizzle, all mixed together. I begin what is sure to be a long day by doing an interview with the BBC's international radio service.

Immediately afterward, Betta and I go to the Vatican. The two of us will have live coverage throughout the day and will follow the *pro-eligendo Pontifice* Mass from the Press Office. We walk and have a much-needed cappuccino and *cornetto* in a bar on Via del Pellegrino. Betta is wearing a new green shirt—as she says, the color of hope—given to her by her cousin Francesca, brighter than the black or dark-colored ones she has worn so far.

Many cardinal electors who decided to sleep last night at Santa Marta should also be having breakfast. The rest arrive to take up their rooms early in the morning. A small number—sixteen—have been assigned to live in the old Santa Marta residence.

Around the world, Catholics are praying for the cardinals as they prepare to enter the conclave to elect a new pope, someone they hope will be able to touch the hearts of the people as Francis—the first Latin American and the first Jesuit pope—did during his 12-year, 39-day leadership of the Church.

At 10 AM the 133 cardinal electors and about 100 non-voting cardinals over the age of 80 enter St. Peter's Basilica in their scarlet vestments and white miters to concelebrate the Mass for the election of the pope.

As Francis had intended, 91-year-old cardinal dean, Giovanni Battista Re, presides over the ceremony. In a solemn Latin Mass accompanied by the music of beautiful choirs, Cardinal Re outlines the profile that Francis's successor should have.

"We are here to invoke the help of the Holy Spirit, to implore his light and strength, so that the pope that the Church and humanity need at this difficult, complex, and tormented moment in history may be elected," he says at the beginning of his sermon.[1]

Some Vatican experts who are with us in the Press Room—where an atmosphere on the verge of a nervous breakdown prevails—interpret this phrase as an allusion to a diplomatic candidate for a world in flames. That is, Cardinal Parolin, the favorite of those who seek a return to a more calm, formal and predictable Church. Cardinal Re, also a diplomat, goes further and, perhaps aware of the still unclear situation because no one has the 89 votes necessary to be elected, emphasizes what "the only just and necessary attitude" is in view of entering the Sistine Chapel for "an act of utmost human and ecclesial responsibility, and a decision of great importance... a human act for which one must abandon all personal considerations, and keep in mind and heart only the God of Jesus Christ, and the good of the Church and humanity," he states, referring, perhaps, to the division between those who follow Francis's path of openness and reform and those who prefer to put a stop to it.

The sermon catches my attention because Cardinal Re quotes Paul VI and John Paul II, but Francis is nowhere mentioned. This is a very suggestive omission.[2] I alert Betta, who is sitting next to me, who mentions it to Irene who is behind me.

The dean, reflecting on the day's readings, speaks of the importance of Jesus's love.

"The love that Jesus reveals knows no limits and must characterize the thoughts and actions of all his disciples, who in their conduct must always manifest authentic love and commit themselves to building a new civilization, which Paul VI called the 'civilization of love.' Love is the only force capable of changing the world," he says.

Then he emphasizes the importance of ecclesial communion and universal human brotherhood. "Among the tasks of every successor of Peter is to increase communion: the communion of all Christians with Christ; the communion of bishops with the pope; and communion among bishops. Not a self-referential communion, but one directed entirely toward communion among persons, peoples, and cultures, en-

---

1. "Santa Messa 'Pro Eligendo Romano Pontifice,'" Sala Stampa delle Santa Sede, May 7, 2025.

2. Elisabetta Piqué,"Sugestiva omisión de la figura de Francisco en la misa que marca el inicio del cónclave," *La Nación*, May 7, 2025.

suring that the Church may always be a 'home and school of communion.' There is also a strong call to maintain the unity of the Church on the path traced by Christ to the apostles. The unity of the Church is willed by Christ; a unity that does not mean uniformity, but a firm and profound communion in diversity, as long as it remains fully faithful to the Gospel," he adds, in a strong voice, in Italian.

The cardinal electors, who from this afternoon will be completely incommunicado, listen attentively. Since there is no translation—as there was at the general congregations—it is evident that there are many who do not understand what the dean is saying. Some pray and gaze at the basilica's magnificent ceiling, their faces serious, seated in the front row before Bernini's imposing Baldachin and very near Peter's tomb.

"Every pope continues to embody Peter and his mission, and in this way represents Christ on Earth; he is the rock upon which the Church is built," the cardinal dean states. "The election of the new pope is not a simple succession of persons, but is always the apostle Peter who returns.

"The cardinal electors will cast their votes in the Sistine Chapel, where—as the apostolic constitution *Universi Dominici Gregis* states—everything contributes to making the presence of God more vivid, before whom each one must one day appear to be judged."

Cardinal Re, who as vice-dean presided over the 2013 conclave that elected Jorge Bergoglio, then cites the "Roman Triptych" of Pope John Paul II—of whom he was one of the closest collaborators—which expresses "the wish that, in the hours of the great decision through voting, Michelangelo's majestic image representing Jesus the Judge would remind everyone of the great responsibility of placing the 'sovereign keys' (Dante) in the right hands.

"Let us pray, therefore, that the Holy Spirit, who in the last hundred years has given us a series of truly holy and great pontiffs, may grant us a new pope after God's heart for the good of the Church and humanity.

"Let us pray that God may grant the Church the pope who best knows how to awaken the consciences of all and the moral and spiritual forces in today's society, characterized by great technological progress, but which tends to forget God. Today's world expects much from the Church to protect those fundamental human and spiritual values without which human coexistence will not be better or bring good to future generations."

Cardinal Re concludes by asking that "the Blessed Virgin Mary, Mother of the Church, intervene with her maternal intercession, so that the Holy Spirit may enlighten the minds of the cardinal electors and bring them together in the election of the pope our time needs."

During the solemn Mass, broadcast live around the world, at the moment of the sign of peace, Re and Parolin embrace. During the embrace, Cardinal Re—who often speaks loudly because he has hearing problems—can be heard saying to Parolin: "*Doppi auguri Pietro!*" He thus wishes him "double good wishes"—widely interpreted not only as the director general of the conclave, as the highest-ranking cardinal-bishop, but also as the leading candidate.

When the solemn Mass ends, the cardinals make their way to Santa Marta for lunch before beginning their isolation and seclusion. Cardinal Prevost exits St. Peter's Basilica alone through the Porta della Preghiera, and Emilce Cuda, the secretary of the Pontifical Commission for Latin America over which he has presided the past two years, who attended the Mass with her husband Patrick Dunbar, goes to greet him. She accompanies him to the exit and as she bids farewell says, "The next time we meet I expect to see you in white."

RE'S HOMILY, which omitted Francis, is causing unrest in the "Bergoglian" camps. "Not mentioning Francis, erasing him as if he hadn't existed and as if saying 'Let's move on to something else,' was very aggressive," an indignant prelate told us quietly, recalling that at the *pro Eligendo Pontifice* Masses of 2005 and 2013, the homilies did mention John Paul II, who died on April 2, 2005, and Benedict XVI, who had resigned on February 11, 2012.

The strange thing is that the Italian media—which do mention his "*Doppi auguri, Pietro*" comment—don't seem to notice this detail, as if caught up in another dimension and gagging on anything that could be seen as unfavorable to the pro-Parolin campaign. When, at the request of Paolo Fucili, a colleague from the Sat 2000 television channel (owned by the Italian bishops), Betta goes live to comment on the Mass, she points out this striking omission of Cardinal Re. Once the broadcast is over—from that enormous post set up for the main television stations near the Press Room—Paolo is very surprised and says he hadn't noticed. But Andrea Tramontano, his cameraman, whom we have known from dozens of trips around the world with Francis, tells him that he had indeed noticed Re's absence. "Well, Betta, you did well to mention it on air," Andrea says, with his traditional pipe in his mouth.

In the Vatican Press Office, where most seem convinced that Parolin will be the next pope, some are commenting on the lead headline of the right-wing daily *Il Giornale*.[3] Probably the only Italian newspaper not campaigning for him but rather for a more conservative candidate, like Pizzaballa, *Il Giornale* reveals that Parolin confessed to a childhood friend that he was very restless. "Three days ago, I sent him a message; now he doesn't respond. I told him I didn't know what was best for him. He replied that he didn't know either and that he was a little upset," said Roberto Apo Ambrosi, a former schoolmate of Parolin's. *Il Giornale* runs an unsympathetic front-page headline: "Parolin: I'm upset."

THE CONCLAVE AREA is now under extreme surveillance. The entire Vatican area associated with the conclave has been placed off limits to the outside world, with a communications blackout, because secrecy is one of the fundamental pillars of a conclave. In Santa Marta, the windows facing outside have been duly sealed to prevent them from being opened and any indiscreet person from overhearing an inappropriate conversation. Furthermore, all the windows in the rooms of the Apostolic Palace through which the cardinals will pass on their way to or from the Sistine Chapel have been blacked out to prevent any curious outsiders from seeing anything. And yesterday, all access points to the conclave area were sealed with some eighty lead seals to ensure that no unauthorized person can enter. The Vatican has also carried out environmental sweeps aimed at identifying possible spying devices present in the Vatican. Furthermore, they have begun using signal jammers that will block cell phones and possible hidden microphones. The entire Vatican, with the Sistine Chapel in particular, has become a kind of digital bunker, impervious to any attempt at physical or electronic intrusion.[4]

The 133 cardinal electors return to their rooms where they remove their red cassocks and head to the Santa Marta dining room for

---

3. Francesco Boezi, "'Mi sento turbato.' Le voci sull'elezione e l'ansia di Parolin favorito in San Pietro," *Il Giornale*, May 7, 2025.

4. Irene Hdez Velasco, "Secreto absoluto o excomunión inmediata: la Santa Sede se blinda en vísperas del cónclave," *El Confidencial*, June 5, 2025.

lunch. Afterward, they retire to their rooms to rest, read, or pray before heading to the Pauline Chapel in the afternoon.

At 3:15 PM we learn that many cardinal electors are still sleeping! They no longer have their cell phones with them—which they use as alarm clocks and which they left in clear plastic bags upon entering confinement.... And the domestic staff at Santa Marta are forced to go door to door, knocking, to wake them up and inform them that they have to start getting ready. They must be ready by 4 PM to walk or take a bus, escorted in all cases, to the Pauline Chapel in the Apostolic Palace.

"It took me almost thirty minutes to fasten my cassock," a tall, young cardinal tells us, shaking his head and laughing.

By 4 PM everyone is ready in their ceremonial robes and waiting to be transported to the Pauline Chapel. The chapel is named after Paul III, the Farnese Pope who commissioned it between 1537 and 1540. It is located at the top of the Scala Regia, the Royal Staircase designed by Gian Lorenzo Bernini (1663–1666) to connect the Vatican Palace with St. Peter's Square and Basilica.

Upon arrival, the 133 cardinals take their seats in pre-assigned places in order of precedence. For many, it is their first time there. And while they wait for the ceremony to begin, they marvel at the two magnificent paintings by Michelangelo that adorn the walls: "The Conversion of St. Paul" (1542–1546) and "The Crucifixion of St. Peter" (1550). He painted them at the request of Pope Paul III after completing the "Last Judgment" in the Sistine Chapel.

At that moment, many thoughts run through their minds. By now, almost all the electors have decided for whom they will cast their first vote. Others, however, are still unsure which cardinal would make a good pope, so they will cast what Pope Francis once called "a wait-and-see vote." That is, they will vote for someone they esteem for their leadership or courage in certain difficult circumstances, or perhaps for a friend, in an "attitude of 'wait and see,' until the first ballot reveals who the real contenders are.

At 4:30 PM, the procession starts. It is a ceremony with an imposing setting, rich in history, ritual, and pomp, which as it begins is seen live on the screens of the Press Room and also on televisions around the world. The entire planet, or at least Catholic-majority countries, like Argentina, follows the conclave with media attention focused on the stars. Juan, one of the chiefs at Betta's *La Nación*, compares the anticipation of the *fumata* to that typically present during a World Cup!

ACCORDING TO THE *ORDO RITUUM CONCLAVIS* (Book of Rites of the Conclave),[5] the ceremony begins with a prayer. Cardinal Parolin, the highest-ranking cardinal bishop, presides over the rite and delivers a brief exhortation. The 133 cardinals from seventy countries on every continent then begin a slow procession, in order of precedence, toward the Sistine Chapel.

This is a truly global conclave, the largest and most diverse in history, with 17 electors from Africa, 23 from Asia, 52 from Europe (including 19 Italians), 23 from Latin America (including Mexico), 14 from North America (10 Americans and 4 Canadians), and 4 from Oceania. Almost all cardinals wear red, but not the Eastern rite cardinals, who wear a black habit, or the Dominicans, who wear their white habits.

The cross is carried at the head of the procession, followed by the members of the Sistine Choir, two masters of ceremonies, two sacristans, and an ecclesiastical assistant to Cardinal Parolin. Behind them are the secretary of the College of Cardinals, Brazilian Archbishop Ilson de Jesús Montanari; the Italian Capuchin Cardinal Raniero Cantalamessa, who will give the meditation to the electors; and then the 133 cardinals, who process in reverse order of hierarchical precedence and seniority in the order: first the cardinal deacons, then the cardinal priests, and lastly the cardinal bishops.

Behind them, a deacon carries the Book of the Gospels.

Cardinal Parolin, who presides over the conclave, is last in the procession, accompanied by the master of ceremonies, Archbishop Diego Ravelli, who has held this role since 2021 and is known for his rather traditionalist tendencies.

The distance between the Pauline Chapel and the Sistine Chapel is short, and as the cardinal electors slowly advance in procession, the renowned Sistine Choir accompanies them, singing in Latin: first the Litany of the Saints, and then *Veni Creator Spiritus*, the ninth-century hymn that invokes the guidance of the Holy Spirit to assist them in this momentous decision, destined to influence the life of the universal Catholic Church, with its 1.4 billion members, and the peoples of the world.

---

5. The *Ordo Rituum Conclavis*, prepared by the Office of Liturgical Celebrations of the Supreme Pontiff, describes in detail, in Latin and Italian, the entire ceremony related to the election of the pope.

The cardinals enter the Sistine Chapel two by two, beginning with the two last cardinal deacons created by Pope Francis on December 7, 2024: George J. Koovakad of India and Fabio Baggio of Italy. The cardinals walk to the center, bow in reverence before the cross, and then proceed to their pre-assigned seats on either side of the central aisle, or to the rectangular seats at the back of the chapel. Never before in history have so many electors entered this chapel to elect a pope.

For many of them, it is their first time in the Sistine Chapel. And they gaze in awe at the magnificent frescoes on the chapel walls, commissioned by Sixtus IV from a team of Renaissance artists including Botticelli, Perugino, Pinturicchio, Ghirlandaio, and Rosselli.

While they wait for all to be seated, they contemplate Michelangelo's magnificent works. The ceiling, with its scenes from the Book of Genesis, the best known of which is the Creation of Adam, depicting God reaching out to create Adam, which Michelangelo painted between 1508 and 1512 under the patronage of Julius II. And the famous painting above the altar with the haunting scene of the Last Judgment, which the same genius painted for Clement VII and Paul III between 1535 and 1541.

After the conclave, one of the electors, the Filipino Cardinal Pablo Virgilio "Ambo" David, will post on his Facebook account[6] a deeply moving personal reflection on that moment. As never before in history have so many cardinals sat for a conclave in the Sistine Chapel, the seating arrangement is new and complex: there are two long rows of tables on either side of the central aisle, and four rows of tables located at the back of the chapel, each with seven cardinals seated, perpendicular to the four main rows. The tables are covered with a burgundy cloth—the same as the chairs—at the bottom and beige at the top.

Cardinal Prevost takes a seat between Cardinal Tagle and Cardinal Louis Raphael Sako, patriarch of the Chaldeans of Iraq. They have also been together at the general congregations and appear relaxed.

The conclave is a deeply spiritual experience for everyone.

In a post-conclave interview, Washington DC Archbishop Cardinal Robert McElroy will remark that "For me, it was like a mini-re-

---

6. Reproduced with permission in *America*, May 22, 2025: "Cardinal David: How the Sistine Chapel Spoke to Me in the Conclave."

treat. I wished it had been longer. I expected it to be fascinating, but it was much more than that: it was an experience of grace. As we entered the Sistine Chapel in procession, with the choir singing the litanies of the saints, you were fully aware of being in communion with all the generations that have preceded you, all standing before the Last Judgment, which looms so powerfully on the wall. My seat was directly below the Creation of Adam, and to my right was the Last Judgment. It was a profoundly spiritual moment. At a certain point, analytical thinking ceased to be important and was overtaken by a spiritual movement: the presence of God was palpable."[7]

ON THE TABLE IN FRONT OF EACH CARDINAL are three texts: the apostolic constitution *Universi Dominici Gregis,* which governs the election process; the *Ordo Rituum Conclavis*; and a prayer book with the Liturgy of the Hours. There is also a sheet with the names of the 133 cardinals present.

Once all have taken their places, Cardinal Parolin appears tense as he recites the common formula of the solemn oath[8] that obliges the cardinals to faithfully and scrupulously observe all the norms and prescriptions of the apostolic constitution relating to papal election, and to maintain strict secrecy at all times regarding everything that occurs during the conclave. The oath obliges them to keep secret everything they see or hear during the conclave related to the election of the new pope, unless the new pope or his successor explicitly grants them special authority. It also requires them to refrain from using any audio or video equipment to record anything related to the papal election during the conclave. Finally, it requires that they not support or allow any interference or intervention by any secular authority, group of people, or individuals in the election of the pope. The penalty for breaking the oath is excommunication.

When Cardinal Parolin finishes reading the oath, each of the electors, in order of precedence, approaches the lectern located in

---

7. Gerard O'Connell, "Cardinal McElroy on Pope Leo's Missionary Past and if Trump Influenced the Conclave," *America,* May 27, 2025.

8. The text of the oath is found in no. 53 of the apostolic constitution *Universi Dominici Gregis,* promulgated by John Paul II on February 22, 1996, and amended by Benedict XVI on June 12, 2010, and February 25, 2013.

the center of the Sistine Chapel, on which lies an open copy of the Gospels. There, with their right hand on that book, they repeat a brief formula of the oath.

"I (name) promise, bind myself, and swear, so help me God and these Holy Gospels which I touch with my hand."

The cardinals read this oath in Latin, which poses a problem for many—among them, for the only Chinese cardinal present, Stephen Chow, who is fluent in the two most widely spoken languages in the world, English and Chinese, but not Latin. "I felt awkward pronouncing those words in Latin," he later confessed, emphasizing that it was "uncomfortable" for him to have to do so publicly, aware that Vatican television was broadcasting this highly symbolic moment live.[9]

This oath-taking ritual alone lasts an hour and a half. When it ends, the master of ceremonies, Archbishop Ravelli, loudly calls out the famous command *"Extra Omnes!"* ("Everyone out!"). Everyone must leave the chapel. And the world witnesses this fascinating scene: the closing of the heavy wooden doors of the Sistine Chapel, marking the end of the Vatican's live broadcast and the beginning of the world's most secret election. Two Swiss Guards, dressed in their distinctive blue, yellow, and red uniforms and holding halberds, stand guard outside.

The only ones remaining locked inside the Sistine Chapel, besides the 133 cardinal electors, are, for now, Archbishop Ravelli and Capuchin Cardinal Raniero Cantalamessa, who has been chosen to give the final meditation.

All eyes are on the charismatic, 90-year-old Italian Capuchin friar, bespectacled and bearded, former preacher of the Papal Household (1980–2024). Francis gave him the red biretta on November 28, 2020, but allowed him to keep his friar's habit instead of wearing the scarlet cardinal's robes. He also delivered the first of two meditations to the cardinals before the conclaves of 2005 and 2013. But this time, he is to give the second meditation, before the electors cast their first vote.

He was expected to preach for about fifteen minutes. But Cantalamessa goes much further, surpassing all estimates. Speaking in Italian, he delivers a meditation that lasts almost an hour.

---

9. Gerard O'Connell, "Cardinal Chow on the Conclave: 'We Voted for a Pastor for the World,'" *America*, May 19, 2025.

"It was long. But they gave us the English translation of the text, thank God, so I was able to read it and follow along. It was a good meditation," Cardinal Chow recounted.

BUT THE DELAY IS NOT JUST DUE to Cantalamessa. Once the cardinal finishes his meditation—considered by others to be "too long"—Archbishop Ravelli escorts him out of the Sistine Chapel and leaves with him. Then, in accordance with the rules of the conclave, the junior cardinal deacon George J. Koovakad of India—who in recent years had been the organizer of Pope Francis's foreign trips—is in charge of firmly and definitively closing the doors of the Sistine Chapel, leaving the electors completely alone. The Swiss Guards remain on guard outside, however.

Then another twist occurs: the voting can't begin. What's happening? Security officers warn that they're picking up a signal from the Sistine Chapel! How? Yes, they warn Cardinal Parolin that, although the isolation should be complete, it appears there's an active SIM card! A moment of total bewilderment immediately ensues, while the cardinals, incredulous, stare at each other, until one of them (one of the older ones, whose name we prefer to keep confidential) suddenly discovers he has his cell phone in his pocket. Disoriented and distressed, the cardinal hands over the forbidden instrument. After this unusual scene, unimaginable even for a film and never before seen in the history of modern conclaves, which further delays things, the proceedings move forward. Since many of the cardinals seem tired and it is almost 7 PM, Cardinal Parolin asks if they want to vote now or return to Santa Marta for dinner. By a show of hands, the cardinals leave no room for doubt: they want to vote now!

Parolin then explains the voting process in both Italian and English, as many do not understand Italian.

The first phase of the process begins with the distribution of ballots, one to each of the electors. Then, according to the rules, before voting begins, the junior cardinal elector—using wooden balls whose numbers correspond to the cardinals—randomly draws the names of three "scrutineers" (tellers) and three "reviewers" to supervise the first voting session. The chosen scrutineers are Hungarian Cardinal Péter Erdő, Swiss Cardinal Emil Paul Tscherrig, and Italian Cardinal Mario Zenari.

The second phase is the first of the secret ballots. Each cardinal has before him a rectangular ballot sheet on which the words *Eligo in Summum Pontificem* (I elect as Supreme Pontiff) are printed in Latin, and below is a space to write the name of the person for whom he wishes to cast his vote. The electors must write in such a way that their handwriting cannot be easily recognized. Once the cardinal completes his ballot, he must fold it so that the name of the person he is voting for cannot be seen.

Once all the electors have written the name of their chosen candidate and folded their ballots, each cardinal, in order of precedence, takes his ballot between his thumb and index finger and, holding it up so it can be seen, proceeds to the altar. There are the three tellers and an urn, made of silver and gilt bronze by the Italian sculptor Cecco Bonanotte, bearing an image of the Good Shepherd. The urn is covered by a similarly decorated paten to receive the ballots.

Upon reaching the altar, the cardinal elector, standing in the shadow of Michelangelo's impressive Last Judgment, pronounces the following oath in Latin, in a clear and audible voice: "I call Christ the Lord to witness, who will judge me, that I give my vote to whomever, in the presence of God, I believe ought to be elected."

He then places his ballot on the paten, which he tilts so that the ballot slips into the urn. Finally, he bows in reverence before the cross and returns to his seat. Thus, successively, the 133.

Once everyone has placed their votes in the urn, the three tellers —Cardinals Tscherrig, Zenari, and Erdő—begin the count, which is not simple. Everyone watches the ritual, rapt. The first teller shakes the ballots in an urn to mix them. The second begins counting them, removing each ballot from the first urn and transferring it to a second urn (exactly the same as the first), which is empty. The Constitution establishes that if the number of ballots cast does not exactly correspond to the number of voters present, the vote is declared void and must be repeated. (*Universi Dominici Gregis* 68.)

When it is verified that the number of ballots matches the number of voters, the process continues with the opening of the urns. The three tellers sit at the table in front of the altar. The first opens the ballot, silently reads the name, writes it down, and passes it to the second teller. The second teller does the same, then passes it to the third teller, who reads the name on the ballot and then announces it aloud to the entire assembly, after which he writes it down on a piece of paper prepared for that purpose. Cardinal Erdő—the candidate from the more conservative wing—is the third scrutineer and has to read aloud the names of those who have received votes—including his own. But his voice gets increasingly quieter as he continues to read the names, to the point where people complain that they can't hear him. Parolin stands up to position the microphone closer to him. The atmosphere is tense.

"Erdő looked very old," one cardinal will later comment. It is an impression shared by many that will also be reflected in their vote the following morning.

It is the first time the cardinals have laid their cards on the table, and it is no surprise that the votes are scattered on the first ballot. The same thing happened in the 2013 conclave, reflecting the uncertainty among many electors. In 2013, one in five of the 115 electors received at least one vote; this time, more than 30 cardinals received at least one vote, or as one cardinal will later tell us, "everyone was doing their own thing."

Cardinal Chow will comment: "We know that the first ballot is always scattered. I mean, recent history is always like this. Imagine if we had elected the pope on the first ballot.... People would have started asking questions and saying it was rigged, that everything was decided before we went in. But," he adds, "when you look at the first round of voting, you can see who the most influential candidates are."[10]

The results of the first round of voting show that more than 30 candidates got votes but only three received between 20 and 30 votes, just as happened in the 2013 conclave.[11]

*First Vote:*
Erdő
Prevost
Parolin

Aveline came in fourth with more than 10 votes but less than 20 votes, while several cardinals, including, Tagle, Farrell, Turkson, Zuppi, and Grech, got less than 10 votes. And many got just 1 or 2 votes, including Pizzaballa.

---

10. Gerard O'Connell, "Cardinal Chow on the Conclave: 'We Voted for a Pastor for the World,'" *America*, May 19, 2025.

11. Gerard O'Connell, *The Election of Pope Francis* (Orbis Books, 2019), 206.

The results of this first ballot reveal that at this stage there are three main contenders: Erdő, Prevost, Parolin. The votes are closer than anyone could have expected, with only a few votes separating the three frontrunners.

Cardinal Erdő finished first, just ahead of Prevost and Parolin. He was known to be the standard-bearer for the more theologically conservative wing of the electors in this conclave, so he had been expected to garner a considerable number of votes in the first ballot. His result shows they were well organized.

That Erdő came first is a surprise, but an even bigger one is that Prevost is second, as he had remained under the radar before the conclave and had attracted little media attention. Some electors at first had ruled him out as a possibility because he was an American. Now many are wondering how he will fare tomorrow, when the cardinals return to the Sistine Chapel.

That Cardinal Parolin came in third, just one vote behind Prevost, was another surprise. "He did far worse than you could have imagined," one elector told me, and added, "before going into the Sistine Chapel, they [Parolin's supporters] said he had 40 votes, but this didn't hold up in the first ballot."

On the eve of the conclave, the Italian press had reported that (apparently based on information from his supporters) he might have had as many as 40, 45, or more votes going into the conclave. At the time, I found it difficult to understand how they had arrived at such figures.

The big question now is whether, among the many who didn't vote for any of the three main candidates, there are cardinals who would now support one or other of them in the first ballot tomorrow morning.

A fourth candidate, Aveline, though he received far fewer than 20 votes, appears to be still in the running, though his lack of fluency in Italian is a major drawback. And although he had delivered a speech in Italian in the general congregations, he had appeared to be reading it and so wasn't convincing of his fluency in Italian, an elector told us.

Tagle, long considered one of the two front-runners and widely seen as the main challenger to Parolin, has not performed well. Sources would later attribute this to the fact that on the eve of the conclave he was the victim of numerous social media attacks in North America and Italy, which caused many of his would-be supporters to reconsider and abandon him. "He suffered from those attacks," an elector said. "He got few votes, because the Asians were divided," will lament another cardinal who supported him.

"Zuppi did not fare well given the roles he has," another elector noted, referring to the high positions held by the Italian cardinal. He is the archbishop of Bologna, president of the Italian Bishops' Conference, and Pope Francis's special envoy to try to negotiate humanitarian agreements between Ukraine and Russia. His chances have diminished greatly.

Upon seeing the results of the first ballot, a cardinal who had supported Prevost from the beginning is worried and later said, "I felt there could be a problem." His concern was that if Erdő's supporters decided to back Parolin, or vice versa, then either could gain momentum on the second or third ballot.

Since no candidate obtained a two-thirds majority in the first and only round of voting, as the ritual dictates, the ballots are collected and taken to the back of the Sistine Chapel, where, on the left-hand side, there are the two specially installed stoves, one for burning the ballots and the other to produce black or white smoke.

The stoves are joined by a flue that is connected to the chimney erected outside the chapel, a chimney that is now at the center of global media attention. The idea of using a stove dates back to the eighteenth century, when the master of ceremonies came up with a plan for communicating to the world whether a new pope had been elected by dissipating white or black smoke through the chapel chimney as the ballots and minutes were burned.[12] Centuries later, the ballots and minutes are burned in a stove that has been used at every conclave since 1939. One of the tellers fulfills this mission with the assistance of the conclave secretary, Archbishop Montanari, who is readmitted to the Sistine Chapel after the votes have been counted. As the burning begins, an electronic smoke-producing device first used in the 2005 conclave is placed in the second stove and activated. This device contains a cartridge with five types of chemical vapors that can produce black or white smoke as required. The burning and smoke-signaling operations must be completed before the cardinals leave the Sistine Chapel.

---

12. See O'Connell, *The Election of Pope Francis*, 207.

OUTSIDE, THE SUN HAS ALREADY SET over Rome, and the thousands of Romans and pilgrims present in St. Peter's Square are growing increasingly anxious and restless. Why hasn't the *fumata* yet appeared?

In the 2013 conclave, the 115 cardinal electors were also unable to make a decision on the first day, and the first sign came at 7:41 PM, when black smoke rose from the chapel's chimney.[13]

Now, experts and television commentators are beginning to wonder about the reason for this delay. Could it mean that, contrary to all expectations, the cardinals have elected a pope on the first ballot? Or are they voting for a second time, against the rules? What other explanation could there be?

Many journalists are beginning to panic and speculate, but I'm not worried. Without taking into account that no one knows how long Cardinal Cantalamessa's meditation lasted, I estimate that voting may not have started until 6:15 PM, and if each of the 133 electors takes approximately one minute to cast his vote, the voting may not be over before 8:15 PM. Then, the count could take another thirty minutes, so we would have to wait another thirty to forty-five minutes, so I estimate we can expect a result around 9:00 PM or shortly after.

And I'm not mistaken. At 9:01 PM, the long-awaited black smoke finally emerges from the Sistine Chapel chimney, signaling that no pope has been elected. Since it is already nighttime, it is difficult to see the black smoke with the naked eye. It can be seen much better on the giant screens placed in St. Peter's Square and on the Via della Conciliazione. A loud "Ohhhh!" erupts along with applause from those tens of thousands of people who have waited several hours standing, with cell phones in hand, for that first signal to come out, which everyone assumed was going to be black, but which, being the first, is still historic.[14]

I'm live with CTV's international correspondent, Adrian Ghobrial, broadcasting for Canada from a spectacular location high above the Augustinian House that overlooks St. Peter's Square. This is the building where Cardinal Prevost lived for many years when he was superior general of the Augustinian order.

---

13. See O'Connell, The Election of Pope Francis, 207.

14. Elisabetta Piqué, "Fumata negra en el primer día de cónclave: los gestos de los cardenales antes de la votación," *La Nación*, May 8, 2025.

Betta is below, in the square, in the middle of the crowd, experiencing this incredible moment alongside Clara Fontan, Mariana Capaccioli, an Argentine radio journalist, and another Paraguayan colleague, Mónica Ayala. The area is so crowded—you can see a wide variety of people, a woman with a dog, a couple with a baby in a stroller, some Filipinos excited about a pope from their homeland—that cell phones aren't working well. It's impossible to tweet with images. The crowd is so anxious that, suddenly, in the kind of atmosphere that prevails at historic moments, they begin to applaud as if to urge the cardinals to hurry....

During the long wait and at dusk, the temperature had dropped abruptly. It's cold. Betta and her colleagues don't know whether to return to the Press Room to look for a coat.... Just as Betta and Mariana decide to do so and are entering the Press Room, they hear the "Ohhh!" from the crowd, realize that the smoke has appeared, and run back to the plaza to capture the moment amidst the general excitement.

Shortly thereafter, the crowd disperses, happy to have been there and not at all disappointed because no one, in truth, really expected any color other than black.

IN THE SISTINE CHAPEL, the 133 cardinals, exhausted and hungry, sing Vespers, the Church's evening prayer, before being taken back to Santa Marta. Upon their return, they go to their rooms to change, before heading down to the dining room for dinner just after 9:30 PM. Some, however, decide to go straight to bed and skip dinner. After all, it has been a long and emotional day.

While they dine, seated at tables of no more than ten people, they discuss the results of the first ballot, which has made many things clear. While the voting revealed that Erdő, Prevost, and Parolin are the front runners, that first session also showed that Erdő, despite coming first, seems too old and tired for the demanding role of pope. His performance during his reading of the votes is likely to lose him votes.

Parolin's votes are far below expectations, and given that he is the best-known candidate, and the one that seemed to have had the best chance of succeeding Francis, his low support does not bode well for him.

Prevost's vote, on the other hand, is surprising in two ways: he received more votes than Parolin despite being considered a dark horse and having flown under the radar. Moreover, although he is not the first American to receive votes in a conclave—Cardinal Sean O'Malley received ten votes in the first ballot of the 2013 conclave[15]—he is the first to receive such a large number of votes. Nationality does not appear to be an insurmountable obstacle, but the real test will come tomorrow morning.

During dinner, in a moment of relaxation, Ghanaian Cardinal Peter Turkson doesn't hide his disappointment with that first vote and remarks, "Neither Africans nor Asians will ever be taken into account." His comment reminds me of what an African cardinal elector told me after the 2005 conclave: "I predict that we will have several popes from Latin America in the next twenty-five years, but it will be a hundred years before we have an African pope." Other comments from the cardinals during dinner relate to more earthly and eschatological issues: since there is no bathroom in the Sistine Chapel, it is very inconvenient to have to ask permission to leave the Chapel accompanied by the junior cardinal deacon George J. Koovakad. "It's like going back to kindergarten; they should think differently for the next conclave," one cardinal will tell us later.

For not a few cardinals, dinner extends almost to midnight, and over drinks they continue to reflect on the situation. When eventually the cardinals retire to their rooms, each takes with him an alarm clock that the Vatican has sent as a courtesy to ensure that they wake up on time the next morning!

Many cardinals, especially the 40 or more who are undecided, when they return to their rooms review again the biographies of the three lead candidates in more detail and pray for enlightenment in their choice. Those staying on the second floor of Santa Marta Nuova, the place where Francis lived during his twelve-year pontificate, pass by his sealed room 201, think of him, and bless themselves.

AT THE GENERAL CONGREGATIONS, the cardinals, influenced by the impact Francis had on the people—as was so evident at his funeral—had drawn up a profile of the new pope. Most of the electors said

---

15. O'Connell, *The Election of Pope Francis*, 206.

they wanted a "pastor" above all else, which is logical, given that 92 of the 133 electors are diocesan bishops, or had been until recently. Now applying that profile to the three main contenders, the "pastor" characteristic fits well with Prevost and Erdő. But it fits poorly with Parolin, a diplomat.

Although Aveline is considered a pastor, "he didn't get that many votes" on the first ballot some cardinals told us. We later learn that some of those who had voted for him in the first round concluded that he was "going nowhere," so they voted for Prevost on the second ballot.

Tagle is undoubtedly a "pastor," having governed the Archdiocese of Manila, the largest diocese in Asia, and previously a smaller diocese in the Philippines. But support for him fell far below expectations on the first ballot because of his perceived weakness in governance as president of Caritas Internationalis and in his tenure as prefect of the Vatican Dicastery for the Evangelization of Peoples. And so he is more or less ruled out. Grech was also a bishop, but because he didn't score high in this first ballot it seems he is out of the running.

As the cardinals go to sleep, the big question, not just for them but for everyone, is only one: What will happen in the first two ballots tomorrow morning?

MAY 8, THURSDAY [GERRY] _____
*White Smoke*

WITH ADRENALINE ALREADY PUMPING—will there be a pope today?—Betta and Irene and I go to the Vatican early to follow everything and to see, around noon, what we expect to be the second black smoke.

We again have a cappuccino and a *cornetto* together, this time at the Bar de Penitenzieri, a Vatican classic next to the Jesuit Curia.

At Santa Marta, the cardinals have a continental breakfast between 6:30 and 7:30 AM. Cardinal Dolan sits at a table with his jar of peanut butter that he brought from New York, and to his surprise

Prevost comes and sits next to him. "No doubt he was attracted by the peanut butter!" Dolan joked in a lecture at Fairfield University in early September. He also revealed that prior to the conclave, cardinals kept asking him, "Who is Robert Prevost?" but he confessed that at that time he didn't really know the man. Later, however, Dolan will tell the *NY Post* that as they chatted he found Prevost to be open and engaging. "We swapped some stories about my hometown of St. Louis, where he had lived during his novitiate with the Augustinian order." Dolan, whom some media mistakenly presented as a "kingmaker" said, "I came away impressed."

After breakfast the cardinals, again dressed in their scarlet robes, go to the Pauline Chapel where they concelebrate Mass. Cardinal Parolin presides and delivers the homily. They remain for a moment in silent prayer before heading to the Sistine Chapel, where they resume their assigned seats and recite Lauds, the Church's morning prayer.

Once the prayers are concluded, the second ballot begins, following exactly the same ritual as that of the previous evening. Three new tellers and three new reviewers are randomly chosen by the junior cardinal deacons using wooden balls, and two ballots are given to each voter, as two votes are expected to be held this morning.

The third teller, who will read out the names, is Robert Francis Prevost!

"It's God's sense of humor," one cardinal will comment later, noting that since Erdő was the third teller in the first ballot and had to read his own name many times, the same thing now happens to Prevost! And in the second and third ballots, he will have to read his own name "many times."

At around 9:30 AM each of the 133 cardinals writes the name of the person they have chosen to be pope on their ballot, folds it into the appropriate shape, and solemnly carries it to the altar.

Unlike the previous evening, when a livelier atmosphere reigned, not a fly can be heard flying in the Sistine Chapel now: Cardinal Parolin has expressly requested that silence be maintained during the voting.

Once the votes are cast, the tellers then mix the ballot sheets and count the votes to verify that the number of votes corresponds to the number of electors present.

They then proceed with the opening of the ballot sheets. Each teller performs his review task and the third one, Cardinal Prevost, reads the names aloud for all to hear. This must have been a bit embarrassing, because he had to read his own name repeatedly.

*Second Vote:*
Prevost
Parolin
Erdő
Aveline

The second ballot reveals a drastic change from the previous night. The undecided voted more decisively this time, and some who had voted for other candidates in the first ballot, after praying and discernment before God, change their votes.

Cardinal Prevost is the main beneficiary. He is definitely in the lead, having gained many votes. Parolin too gains some votes, but not many. Erdő has lost votes, a sign that his chances are on the decline. Contributing to this, according to our sources, is his poor performance in the reading of the votes last night.

Since no cardinal has obtained a two-thirds majority, that is, the 89 votes needed to be elected, the electors immediately proceed to the third ballot. And they use the second ballot sheet they received at the beginning of the election process this morning. The atmosphere is tense.

ONCE THE THIRD BALLOT is complete, the votes are counted. Following the same ritual, the same three tellers verify that the ballots cast match the number of electors, read the names on the ballots, and Cardinal Prevost again "sings" the names of those who have received votes loudly and clearly. The Chicago-born cardinal now has to read his own name more frequently. He is doing it well, but one wonders: What must he be feeling?

The results show that only a handful of real candidates remain, among them two leading candidates and a third still with a chance, but little hope.

*Third Vote:*
Prevost
Parolin
Aveline

After the count, the cardinals anxiously begin to chat among themselves and make comments. No cardinal has obtained the 89 votes necessary to be elected. But it is clear that Cardinal Prevost has gained the momentum, and though still lacking the two-thirds majority, it is evident to everyone that he is on the path to the papacy. It's just a question of whether he would need one or more ballots to be elected.

The other main contender is Parolin, but only a few votes are flowing in Erdő's direction. "Parolin had a block of votes that never really grew much," another elector will tell us after the conclave.

For the second time, the ballots from the two rounds of voting are gathered and taken to the stove at the back of the Sistine Chapel for burning. The appropriate chemicals are activated in the second furnace to produces a very dark smoke signal.

OUTSIDE, THE CLOCK STRIKES 11 AM, and once again thousands of Romans and pilgrims gather in St. Peter's Square and along the Via della Conciliazione awaiting the smoke. The sun is already beating down, but the most important thing is that chimney atop the Sistine Chapel, being watched directly or on the mega screens broadcasting live images to the world. There, during the waiting period, as had happened during the 2013 conclave, the protagonist becomes a seagull strolling along the ancient red tiles surrounding the chimney. Expectation soars. Will there be white smoke?

The mystery ends at 11:51, when black smoke rises. "Ohhhhhhhh!" is the reaction of the fifteen thousand people present, who take videos and photos of this extraordinary scene, which, in broad daylight, looks much better than the night before. It is fascinating, as some tourists comment, because in the advanced technological age of the twenty-first century, the Vatican continues to send news via smoke signals!

BETTA PROVIDES A MINUTE-BY-MINUTE report from the Press Room. She has coordinated with Julieta from the newspaper *La Nación* to have profiles of the favorites ready, in case there is a white smoke in the afternoon. Guille, Guillermo Idiart, the new correspondent in the United States, has already sent a note describing Robert Francis Prevost. Luisa Corradini, the correspondent in France, put together a profile of Aveline, and Betta has taken care of Parolin.

Seeing that *Corriere della Sera* has published an interview with Cardinal O'Malley—who is not participating in the conclave this time because he has already turned 80—Betta, who knows him well, asks for an interview again, as she had done a few days earlier. Minutes later, her cell phone rings. It is O'Malley, who not only grants her request but also speaks some words that will prove prophetic. When Betta asks him the meaning of the two black smokes—last night and this afternoon—and whether they reflect a "division," Cardinal O'Malley downplays the situation. "Partly it's due to the fact that there are several candidates who could be considered. On the other hand, the vast majority of the cardinals are newcomers; it's their first time participating in a conclave, and many don't speak Italian," he tells her.

When does he think we'll see the white smoke? "I don't know. The last time [in 2013] it was at night. I wouldn't be surprised if it's tonight. But since the cardinals are considering many names, it could also be tomorrow morning (Friday). I think it'll be soon; I don't think the conclave will last long," he predicts, speaking in perfect Spanish.

Asked if an American pope is possible, O'Malley, who was a *papabile* last time, assures her that this time the taboo could be broken. "I think anything is possible. The fact that we've already had popes from Poland, Germany, and Argentina makes anything possible. A pope from the United States can't be ruled out. It's true that in today's world it's more difficult for an American to be elected, but not impossible."

Which kind of pope is your dream? Betta asks. "We all dream of a pope who is perfect and who can meet all the needs of the Church, but that person doesn't exist. I hope the Holy Spirit chooses the best possible person and everyone is willing to help him. Everyone realizes the importance of the papacy, and this was made clear by the international response we saw to the death of Pope Francis. The funeral demonstrated the importance of the Petrine Ministry, which goes beyond the Church in a world where leadership is lacking and there is so much polarization. The prophetic voice of the Holy Father is fundamental because it can bring to the whole world the Gospel message of help for the least, of peace, of justice, and it is a service to humanity. And above all, Pope Francis, with his personality and desire for closeness, had an enormous impact outside the Church. I think the cardinals want that to continue with the next pope."

Betta immediately writes up the interview for *La Nación*.[16] She also will use this predictive information in an episode for CNN International just after 3 PM.

INSIDE THAT OTHER-WORLDLY CAPSULE that is the conclave, meanwhile, the 133 cardinal electors, after leaving the Sistine Chapel, return to their apartments in Santa Marta. They remove their ceremonial robes and go down to the dining room for lunch. There, the air is filled with great anticipation. Everyone knows that, barring some unexpected event, the end of the conclave is near. The waiters serving the tables notice that the atmosphere has changed: if the previous evening had been tense, this afternoon it is almost cheerful, and the electors seem more relaxed. The menu is also good: Italian pasta and steak with salad.

While they eat, many look around to see if Cardinal Prevost, having endured the stress of having to read out his name so many times at the end of the second and third ballots, will appear for lunch. Although some media outlets will say that he stayed in his room writing his introductory speech, he does come down for lunch and becomes the center of attention for many of his colleagues. "It was already clear then that we could complete [our mission] by the end of the day. How many more votes it would take, I didn't know. But it was very clear that we were moving in a direction that was probably unstoppable," Cardinal Blase Cupich of Chicago would later say.[17]

Cardinal Chow would tell us: "When you look at the results of the first ballot, you can see which candidates carry the most weight," and then, when the cardinals vote on the second and third ballots, "there is more clarity; individually, there is more clarity. It's truly discernment," he adds, highlighting the spiritual perspective. "Discernment consists of going in with some data, contemplating it, praying about it, and following the Holy Spirit. The Holy Spirit moves your heart, and you can choose to respond or not. You can choose to focus on your own preference. Or you listen. And then you see people gradually come to an

---

16. Elisabetta Piqué, "El cardenal O'Malley, sobre el cónclave: 'No me sorprendería si esta noche hay fumata blanca,'" *La Nación*, May 8, 2025.

17. Gerard O'Connell, "Interview: Chicago's Cardinal Cupich on Why the Cardinals Chose Pope Leo XIV," *America*, May 11, 2025.

agreement. It's truly the Holy Spirit, if you listen, who unites us. Our hearts were moved by the Holy Spirit, and we responded."[18]

The day after the conclave, the Italian media would report that "during lunch, Parolin saw that the writing was on the wall" and suggested to his supporters that they support Prevost. But several voters told us that this was not the case. One of them said: "It is false that Parolin took a step back and asked his supporters to vote for Prevost, as the Italian media says."

AFTER LUNCH, with everyone sensing that these will be the last hours of their confinement, the cardinals retire to their rooms. Some to rest—even to take a nap—others to read or pray. Cardinal Prevost also retires to his room. But this former mathematics graduate from Villanova University, aware that he could in all likelihood be elected in the afternoon session, decides to jot down what he might say from the loggia of the Vatican Basilica, the central balcony of St. Peter's, that same day. Unlike Cardinal Bergoglio, who felt comfortable speaking spontaneously and did not prepare a text for the 2013 conclave, Cardinal Prevost—who is of a different age, a different style, a different personality—prefers not to improvise and to have a prepared text.

At 3:30 PM, the cardinals are once again dressed in their blood-red cardinal's robes, ready, almost eager, to be led back to the Pauline Chapel under escort. The sky is blue, the sun is shining, and an Italian Carabinieri helicopter is hovering overhead. Outside, the crowd is growing in St. Peter's Square and on the Via della Conciliazione, as if people are strongly sensing that a new pope will be elected this afternoon.

The cardinals gather again in the Pauline Chapel and head for the Sistine Chapel at 4:45 PM, aware that they will cross the Atlantic for the second time in this first quarter of the twenty-first century to elect the next pope.

When they take their preassigned seats in the Sistine Chapel, under the presidency of Cardinal Parolin, they follow the well-known and well-oiled procedure established by the apostolic constitution. This time, three new tellers are chosen at random. They are Cardinals Timothy Radcliffe, Reinhard Marx, and Fernando Filoni, who will

---

18. Gerard O'Connell, "Cardinal Chow on the Conclave: 'We Voted for a Pastor for the World,'" *America*, May 19, 2025.

read out the names. Two ballots sheets are again given to each cardinal elector. Each one writes the name of his chosen candidate, folds the paper, takes it to the altar, and casts his vote.

Incredibly, the same thing happens today as in the fifth ballot of the 2013 conclave, which I reported in my book *The Election of Pope Francis*.[19] When the tellers count the ballots, something doesn't add up: there should be 133 ballots, but instead there are 134! The third teller, Cardinal Filoni, verifies this and informs the other cardinals of the error. Cardinal Parolin then, following the constitution,[20] declares the count void without reading any of the names on the ballots sheets which will be burned unopened at the end of the afternoon vote.

As happened in 2013, two ballots were stuck together.

This time we know the "culprit": Spanish Cardinal Carlos Osoro Sierra, archbishop emeritus of Madrid—who would turn 80 just eight days later—publicly admits that he made a mistake by accidentally placing one of his ballots on top of the other. Deeply embarrassed, he apologizes to the other cardinals and asks for two new ballots.

In an atmosphere of great expectation, the cardinals repeat the fourth round of voting. They write the name of their chosen candidate on the ballot, fold it, and take it to the altar where they place it, following the same pre-established ritual.

"At the time of the final vote, everyone knew what was coming. You approached with your ballot in hand, placed it on the paten, then slid it into the urn. People were radiant with joy. Even those who had been planning to vote for others smiled, moved by the clarity of what was emerging. It was a profound spiritual gift for all of us," Cardinal McElroy will recount.[21]

The count begins, and the tension is suddenly loosened by a hilarious scene. The third teller is tasked not only with reading aloud the name of the cardinal voted for but also with writing the name on the tally sheet. He must then pierce each counted ballot sheet with a needle through the word "Eligo" and place it on a thread for safekeeping.[22]

---

19. O'Connell, *The Election of Pope Francis*, 225.

20. *Universi Dominici Gregis*, 28.

21. Gerard O'Connell, "Cardinal McElroy on Pope Leo's Missionary Past and if Trump Influenced the Conclave," *America*, May 27, 2025.

22. *Universi Dominici Gregis*, 69.

Filoni had problems with threading the ballot sheets and asked Radcliffe if he could do it, but the British cardinal said no, since it was not his task, and then a South American cardinal offered to do it.

"Tagle sat next to Prevost while the votes were being counted, supporting and encouraging him," recalled Cardinal Chow, who sat opposite the future pope. "Tagle even offered him a Halls candy as the situation was becoming tense," other firsthand witnesses of the moment noted. Cardinal Sako, patriarch of the Chaldeans and the first Iraqi to vote in a conclave, sat on the other side of Prevost, also encouraging him.

"I was amazed at how much he seemed at peace, even as the votes were being counted," an elector told me.

"Each cardinal had a notebook with all the names, to keep track, which we had to hand over at the end, but throughout the process, we all knew when the threshold was approaching. It wasn't a surprise. We applauded when the eighty-ninth vote was confirmed, but the reality had already been building before then," McElroy explained.

The applause lasted about five minutes, according to several sources, and then Cardinal Parolin intervened to remind them that the tellers had not finished counting the votes. In fact, the cardinals would hear Cardinal Filoni read Prevost's name aloud many more times. When the tellers finished counting and the third teller announced that Cardinal Prevost had received 108 votes, applause erupted again.

*Fourth Vote:*
Prevost
Parolin

The apostolic constitution clearly lays down the steps to be taken once the conclave reaches this stage.[23] All are scrupulously followed.

First, the junior cardinal deacon, George Jacob Koovakad, summons the secretary of the College of Cardinals, Archbishop Ilson de Jesús Montanari, and the master of Papal Liturgical Celebrations, Archbishop Diego Ravelli, as well as two other masters of ceremonies, to the Sistine Chapel. Then comes the time to ask Cardinal Prevost if he accepts his election.

---

23. *Universi Dominici Gregis*, 87–89.

In the apostolic constitution, Pope John Paul II says the following: "I also ask whoever is elected not to renounce the ministry to which he is called for fear of its burden, but to humbly submit to the plan of the divine will. Indeed, God, in imposing this burden upon him, will hold him with his hand so that he may carry it; in conferring upon him such a burdensome task, he will also give him the help to carry it out, and, in giving him the dignity, he will grant him the strength not to be overwhelmed by the weight of his office."[24]

Cardinal Parolin, who presides over the conclave, is responsible for asking in Latin—with Prevost, standing before him—on behalf of the entire college of electors: "Do you accept the canonical election as Supreme Pontiff?"

"I accept!" Prevost replies in Latin.

Argentine Cardinal Ángel Rossi will later disclose, "From where I was sitting, I could see his face, which was a gentle face. And when he was asked [if he accepted], he was smiling, but not as if saying 'I won,' but with a confirmation of peace in his heart."[25]

The apostolic constitution establishes that "after his acceptance, the elected person, if he has already received episcopal consecration, is immediately Bishop of the Church of Rome, true Pope and Head of the College of Bishops. He thus acquires and can exercise full and supreme power over the universal Church."[26] It further declares that "the conclave ends immediately after the new Supreme Pontiff assents to his election, unless he determines otherwise."[27]

As soon as Prevost gives his assent, Cardinal Parolin asks him a second question: "How do you wish to be called?"

The new pope replies: "Leone."

The cardinals look at each other, surprised by this decision linked to Pope Leo XIII, the pope famous for the first "social" encyclical, *Rerum Novarum*.

"I very much appreciate the name and the obvious reference to *Rerum Novarum*," Cardinal Czerny tells us later in an interview. "I don't know if there is an issue of greater and more inclusive concern

---

24. *Universi Dominici Gregis*, 86.

25. Elisabetta Piqué, "El cardenal argentino Ángel Rossi: 'León XIV tiene una forma más "tradicional," pero no es un dinosaurio,'" *La Nación*, May 13, 2025.

26. *Universi Dominici Gregis*, 88.

27. *Universi Dominici Gregis*, 91.

for the vast majority of people on the planet than work, which is so threatened not only by artificial intelligence and the market model that Francis criticized so much, but also by climate change, by war and violence, and by human rights violations. You could say that work is the central issue today. I am very grateful that he has quietly stated that our Church will accompany the People of God, all the people, in this fundamental concern that everyone have a good job."[28]

After the acceptance and choice of name, the master of ceremonies, Monsignor Ravelli, following the ritual and "acting as a notary and having two masters of ceremonies as witnesses," drafts "a document certifying the acceptance of the new pope and the name he has taken."

In the apostolic constitution, John Paul II also decrees: "At the end of the election, the cardinal *camerlengo* of the Holy Roman Church will draft a document, to be approved by the three Cardinal Assistants, declaring the result of the vote at each session. This document will be delivered to the Pope and, thereafter, will be kept in a designated archive, inside a sealed envelope, which no one may open unless the Supreme Pontiff gives his explicit permission."[29]

After accepting the election and declaring his new name, Pope Leo XIV leaves the Sistine Chapel and heads to the so-called "Room of Tears," the small dressing room located at the top left of the Sistine Chapel, where the new pope removes his cardinal's robes and puts on the white cassock that popes began wearing in the thirteenth century.[30] This place is called the "Room of Tears" because of the strong emotions felt by the newly elected pope, which can sometimes lead to tears. Leo enters with Archbishop Ravelli, who closes the door.

In the room there are three sets of papal robes in three different sizes (small, medium, and large), consisting of a white woolen vestment, a short red ermine cape called a *mozzetta*, and some accessories: a gold cord for the cross, a white belt with gold tassels that will later bear the new pope's coat of arms, and red leather shoes.

---

28. Gerard O'Connell, "Cardinal Czerny on if Pope Leo Is a New Francis, a New Benedict—or Something Else," *America*, May 23, 2025.

29. *Universi Dominici Gregis*, 71.

30. Innocent V, elected in the first conclave in history in 1276, was the first member of the Order of Preachers to be elected pope. Since he decided to continue wearing his white Dominican habit as pope, he is often cited as the pope who started the tradition of popes wearing white cassocks.

The curious thing is that, because of the "spending review" initiated by Francis in the Vatican to eliminate unnecessary expenses, only one new set of robes has been created: the medium-sized one. The other two, the small and the large, have been recycled! They are the same ones from the 2013 election (when the Argentine pope was elected after Benedict XVI's resignation), and were not used at the time by Bergoglio. With great reserve, the Italian ecclesiastical tailor, Ety Cicioni, in his Borgo Pio laboratory has made only size M. He has aired out and ironed sizes S and L, something that is necessary after they've been wrapped in cellophane for twelve years.

Probably unaware that these are "low-cost habits," as the newspaper *Il Messaggero*[31] defined them, Leo opts for size M.

Unlike Francis, he decides to follow tradition by wearing the *mozzetta*. But, like Francis, he chooses to continue wearing his own black shoes, not the red ones that had been specially made. When he finishes changing, he returns to the Sistine Chapel and is again greeted by the cardinals with warm applause.

While Leo changes, the scrutineers collect the ballots from both rounds of voting (including those that had been spoiled because they were stuck together), take them to the stove at the back of the chapel to be burned, and add the appropriate chemical into the second stove to make the smoke white.

AT THAT MOMENT, Via della Conciliazione is packed with people, and St. Peter's Square is jammed. Betta and I had covered the conclaves in 2005 and 2013; we knew that atmosphere of excitement, but we have never seen such a large crowd at this time on the second day.

After lunch with Juampy, who has also been working since the morning helping with interviews for CNN, and after being interviewed by SKY News and Chilean and Portuguese newspapers, I head back up to the rooftop terrace of the Augustinian House to join the CTV team. Drones and helicopters hover in the sunny blue sky, also waiting in anticipation.

Betta and Irene are just leaving the Press Room to try and get something to eat, figuring, like everyone else, that since no *fumata* has

---

31. Franca Giansoldati, "Abiti low cost per il nuovo Papa, tre taglie a disposizione. Il Vaticano: 'Ricicliamo quelli di Bergoglio del 2013,'" *Il Messaggero*, May 9, 2025.

been released, the votes in the fourth ballot have not yet been collected, and there is still time for a coffee.

They haven't had lunch, and at the bar on Via della Conciliazione, a block from the Sala Stampa, people are waiting in line. Crossing to the other side of the street is impossible, so they try Via dei Corridori, which has been fenced off due to the crush of people who keep arriving. At that moment, another "Ohhhhhh!" is heard, but it's a false alarm: on the giant screens on Via della Conciliazione, the "star" seagull, the one that hovers around the chimney of the Sistine Chapel, suddenly appears with her little chick, her gray-feathered baby, which she is feeding through her beak. "Ohhhhhhh," exclaims the crowd, celebrating this tender scene. Many take photos in front of this image, which Betta also films and later tweets.

Two minutes later, at 6:07 PM, there's not an "Ohhhhhhh!" but something much louder, like a scream: "Yes!" It's white smoke!

"*Abbiamo il Papa!*" (We have a pope!), everyone exults, and they start filming the white smoke that begins to rise in the distance, first timidly, then forcefully, from the most closely watched chimney in the world. Some people dance with joy, others hug, take selfies, and start running to get closer to the basilica, a scene Betta captures and posts on X.[32]

A minute later, as if to make it clear that yes, it's true, there is a new pope, the six bells of St. Peter's Basilica begin to ring in celebration. The atmosphere is euphoric.

THE NEWS IMMEDIATELY HITS social media and television screens across the world. Vatican officials from the Secretariat of State, upon hearing the news, like the Romans who begin to head toward the Vatican, also run to see the smoke. Everyone is convinced that such a rapid result—only four votes—can mean only one thing: Parolin has been elected pope. Almost everyone in the Press Room thinks exactly the same. "It's Parolin, for sure, it's Parolin," people say. And Vatican media leaders share that opinion: their support for Parolin is no secret. We're even told that there's an edition of *L'Osservatore Romano*, the Vatican newspaper, ready to roll off the press.

Betta and Irene, as well as Juampy, who are in the square talking to the people, sense that almost everyone there also believes the new pope is Parolin.

---

32. Elisabetta Piqué on X, "Fumata blanca," May 8, 2025.

When the white smoke clears, things immediately begin to change in the area in front of St. Peter's Basilica: various members of the Italian armed forces—the Army, the Air Force, and the Navy—arrive, as if on a military parade, with their bands. So too do the Vatican Gendarmerie and the Swiss Guard, all ready to stand at attention to salute the new pope with all due honors. At 7:14 PM, an hour and a few minutes after the white smoke erupted, following a tradition dating back to 1484, the senior cardinal deacon of the College of Cardinals, the 73-year-old French cardinal of Moroccan origin Dominique Mamberti, appears on the central balcony of St. Peter's Basilica to announce the name of the new pope to the world. The windows open, the large burgundy curtains open, and now the atmosphere is beyond electric. Mamberti steps forward and stands there for a moment while the crowd festively roars. He remains silent until the noise subsides, and then he makes the famous announcement in Latin: "*Annuntio vobis gaudium magnum: Habemus Papam!*" ("I announce to you great joy: We have a pope!"). The human tide erupts into another mighty roar. Mamberti has to wait. Then, breaking the suspense, he pronounces, in Latin: "*Eminentissimum ac reverendissimum Dominum, Dominum Robertum Franciscum, Sanctae Romanae Ecclesiae Cardinalem Prevost.*"

Another impressive ovation then erupts, which is, in truth, a bit subdued, followed by much perplexity: few know who he is! Even among several foreign journalists there is bewilderment, but Juampy immediately recognizes the name and alerts them that this is the man who, until Pope Francis's death, ran the Dicastery for Bishops.

Betta does the same, explaining to everyone around her in the square —very many of whom are speechless, surprised, almost disappointed—that the new pope is American, but also Peruvian, and that he is very good, that he is in line with Francis.

Elisabetta and I know him, and we are delighted. Besides, I have spoken with him several times, and at length, in private on some occasions, so I know him a little better than Betta, although in no way as well as we knew Cardinal Bergoglio when he stepped out onto that same balcony on the evening of March 13, 2013.

Cardinal Mamberti then announces the name the new Pope has chosen: Leo XIV. The crowd erupts in thunderous excitement at the name, chanting the resonant "Leooooo-ne" in the full-throated style of enraptured Italian soccer fans. On a terrace of the Apostolic Palace where officials of the Roman Curia who were ready to celebrate the election of Parolin have gathered, the climate is totally different. Everyone is stunned, frozen, defeated. But a monsignor tries to react positively: *"Lo faremo uno di noi"* (We will make him one of us)," he remarks, trying to raise their spirits.

SHORTLY AFTER THIS, the first American-born pope, Leo XIV, steps onto the balcony. Although few know him, the euphoria is immense, and he is greeted with applause and cheers. Overwhelmed by emotion, he remains silent for a few minutes, bowing, surrounded by a few cardinal electors, including Parolin, who wears a forced smile. This is logical. Prevost's election represents a severe blow to that lobby of Italian cardinals who dreamed of reconquering the papacy and stemming the tide of novelty brought about by Francis. The conclave dared to break the taboo that there could be no pontiff from the United States, one of the world's superpowers. With that audacity that Francis always lauded, it has chosen Prevost, the first American pope, but with a Latin American and—especially—Peruvian heart, as he himself will make clear when he presents himself to the world and speaks not just in Italian, but at the end also in Spanish, though not in English.

Amid a jubilant St. Peter's Square packed with people waving the flags of various countries and holding cell phones to record the moment, the new pope not only immediately says "thank you" to Francis—a phrase that triggers another round of heartfelt applause—but also makes it clear that he will follow in his footsteps in favor of a Church that is open to all: synodal, missionary, and working for peace.

He also makes clear that he will do so in his own style, without being a carbon copy of Francis. In fact, everyone instantly notices that he has decided to wear the red *mozzetta* over his white cassock that his predecessor Jorge Bergoglio had intentionally eschewed.

"Peace be with you all,"[33] are his first words in a soaring voice, which once again sends St. Peter's Square into a jubilation. "Dear sisters and brothers, this is the first greeting of the Risen Christ, the Good Shepherd who gave his life for God's flock," Prevost introduces

---

33. Bendición Apostólica "Urbi Et Orbi," Primer Saludo Del Santo Padre León XIV, www.vatican.va.

himself, speaking fluently in Italian, with a bit of a South American accent that is anything but North American.

"I also hope that this greeting of peace enters your hearts, reaches your families, all people, wherever they may be, all nations, and the whole earth." Then he adds, "Peace be with you. This is the peace of the Risen Christ, an unarmed peace and a disarming peace, humble and persevering," he continues, using the same words Jesus used after Easter.

"[This peace] comes from God, God who loves us all unconditionally," he says, recalling words often repeated by his Argentine predecessor, whom he immediately mentions. "We still hear in our ears that weak but always courageous voice of Pope Francis blessing Rome!" he exclaims, alluding to the superhuman effort his predecessor made on his last outing, on Sunday, April 20, Easter Sunday, the day before his death.

"The pope who blessed Rome gave his blessing to the world, to the whole world, that Easter morning. Let me continue that same blessing: God loves us, God loves you all, and evil will not prevail," he asserts, offering the same message of hope as Francis. "We are all in God's hands. Therefore, without fear, united hand in hand with God and with one another, we move forward. We are disciples of Christ with God, and we move forward with one another. Christ precedes us. The world needs his light. Humanity needs him as a bridge to be reached by God and by his love," he affirms, appearing very spiritual, yet concrete.

"Help us too, together, to build bridges, through dialogue, through encounter, uniting all of us to be one people always at peace," he asks, reflecting, once again, another point in common with his predecessor, who tirelessly called for a culture of dialogue and encounter and to build bridges, not walls.

"Thank you, Pope Francis!" he reiterates, also thanking all "the brother cardinals who have chosen me to be the successor of Peter and to walk alongside you, as a united Church, always seeking peace, justice, always seeking to work as men and women faithful to Jesus Christ, without fear, to proclaim the Gospel, to be missionaries," he adds, reading from the text he prepared after lunch.

In a square where few know who he is, the pope also makes it known that he is an Augustinian, "a son of Saint Augustine," who said, he recalls: "with you I am a Christian and for you a bishop." The new pope then adds that "In this sense, we can all walk together toward that homeland that God has prepared for us."

As the new bishop of Rome, Prevost then expressly greets the Church of the Eternal City. "We must seek together to be a missionary Church, a Church that builds bridges, dialogue, always open to welcome like this square with open arms," he declares. "All, all those who need our charity, our presence, dialogue, and love," he adds, visibly moved.

Immediately after this, the new pope, who has a Peruvian passport and was not only a missionary there for twenty years but also a bishop, shifts to speaking in Spanish, his second language.

"And if you allow me, a word, a greeting to all those, and in particular to my beloved diocese of Chiclayo, in Peru, where a faithful people have accompanied their bishop, shared their faith, and given so much, so much to continue being the faithful Church of Jesus Christ," he says, captivating the thousands of Latin Americans present, including many Argentines with flags.

"To all of you, brothers and sisters of Rome, of Italy, and throughout the world, we want to be a synodal Church, a Church that journeys, a Church that always seeks peace, that always seeks charity, that always seeks to be close, especially to those who suffer," he continues, leaving no doubt that his election was the great gamble of those cardinals who were looking for someone to follow in the footsteps of Francis.

Leo XIV, who proves to be, like his predecessor, another devotee of the Virgin Mary, concludes by recalling that "today is the feast day of Our Lady of Pompeii. Our Mother Mary always wants to journey with us, to be close, to help us with her intercession and her love. So I would like to pray with you. Let us pray together for this new mission, for the whole Church, for peace in the world, and let us ask this special grace of Mary, our Mother," he says, as he then, along with thousands of people, recites the Hail Mary in Italian.

Then the square vibrates again, and many feel a thrill similar to when, on March 13, 2013, Francis requested that all pray an Our Father, a Hail Mary, and a Glory Be.

On Argentine social media, many note that today, May 8, also marks the feast of Our Lady of Luján, patroness of Argentina. "I didn't know that," Leo would confess a few days later to the Argentine priest Mariano Fazio, number two of Opus Dei, when he received him in audience with his superior (called "the Prelate") in the study adjacent to the Paul VI Hall, where an image of Our Lady of Luján still hangs. "You'll have to travel to Argentina to meet her," Mariano would suggest.

Finally, the newly appointed pope imparts his first *Urbi et Orbi* blessing to the city and the world, deeply moved but unshaken.

When he finishes, the Swiss Guard, the Gendarmerie, and the Italian Armed Forces pay him full honors and their bands play. Pope Leo greets them in gratitude and leaves the balcony.

Once inside, he is driven by car to Santa Marta, where he again joins the other cardinals for a festive dinner. According to one cardinal, he eats little: like a good shepherd—or like a bride and groom at a wedding—he spends his time going around the tables and greeting his former companions from a historic and surprising conclave that ultimately lasted less than twenty-four hours.

DEMONSTRATING GREAT INNER FREEDOM, that night Leo returns to his own Vatican apartment in the Palazzo della Doctrina della Fe, formerly known as the Holy Office. From there, he responds online to some of the many messages he has received, including a key question: Which Chicago baseball team does he support? The Chicago Cubs or the White Sox? "Sox!" he replies immediately, in a single word.

From the moment the white smoke rises until 10:30, neither Elisabetta, nor Irene, nor I have had a moment's respite. Betta remains writing in the Press Room, where shortly before 9:00 PM Matteo Bruni appears with some information.

"The choice of the name Leo XIV is a clear reference to the modern Social Doctrine of the Church, which began with *Rerum Novarum*, the encyclical of Pope Leo XIII (Gioacchino Vincenzo Raffaele Luigi) Pecci," he explains. "It is also clearly a non-accidental reference to men and women and their work in an age of artificial intelligence," he adds. Bruni also reports that, in what will be his official debut, tomorrow at 11 AM local time, the new pope will celebrate his first Mass alongside the cardinals in the Sistine Chapel. On Sunday, however, he will reappear on the central balcony of St. Peter's Basilica for the Marian prayer, the Regina Caeli. On Monday, in line with tradition, he will have an audience in the Paul VI Hall with the four thousand journalists who came from around the world to cover a conclave that ultimately proved to be Francis's last surprise.

Bruni, who throughout these months has been exemplary for his enormous patience and kindness, leaves to the applause of the journalists, who are exhausted but relieved that the all-consuming suspense is finally over....

Later, Betta is forced to call him because a loudspeaker announces that the Press Room is about to close. "Matteo, they elected the new pope. There are journalists from all over the world who need to work—they can't close!" she says, in a move that is applauded by several journalists standing next to her, frantically busy with work. Gracious as ever, Matteo resolves the problem by ordering that the hours be extended at least one more hour.

From the "*Habemus Papam,*" I spend the next four hours, almost nonstop, commenting on the election of the first American pope with Adrian Ghobrial on CTV—for Canadian national and regional channels—along with Neil McCarthy, spokesperson for the Canadian Conference of Catholic Bishops. As we stand on the rooftop terrace of the Augustinian House, we learn that, below our feet, the friars are celebrating the election of their brother "Bob," their former prior general, who is now the first Augustinian pope in history.

In my commentary, I highlight the fact that 133 cardinals from seventy countries, many of whom barely knew each other two weeks ago, were able to elect a new pope in less than twenty-four hours. I say this is a truly extraordinary testimony of unity in a world at war, deeply divided and polarized. That such a diverse group of cardinals from every continent and of different nationalities, cultures, and languages could vote without coercion, and in total freedom, for the first American missionary pope in the two-thousand-year-year history of the Church is something beyond human machinations, I emphasize. It is undoubtedly a sign that the Spirit of God was at work in the conclave. How else can it be explained? It is the clearest sign to date that the cardinals are united and a powerful message of encouragement for the world's 1.4 billion Catholics. With all this, I conclude that Pope Leo XIV knows he has the entire Catholic Church behind him as he faces the challenge of providing moral leadership to people in this polarized, war-torn world in the changing climate of the twenty-first century.

Just as we finish broadcasting, exhausted, around 10:30 PM on the Roman night, I receive a telephone call from a British television channel asking me how well I know the new pope given—they inform me—that I am one of the eighty-seven persons that Cardinal Prevost (now Leo XIV) follows on his Twitter—now X—account. This is news to me. I had no idea that he followed me on X. I knew that, unlike Francis, he has a smartphone, is active on social media, uses X and WhatsApp, and is very modern in this way. But the phone call from

London also showed me clearly how every aspect of Leo's personal life is being scrutinized. He no longer has any privacy.

On my way home, on foot, I meet up with my friend Rodney Leung, producer and coordinator of Chinese programming for Salt and Light TV, Canada, along with a group of Chinese Catholics from Hong Kong, and chat with them for a while.

Betta and Irene, also returning on foot, make part of the journey with our friend Nicole Winfield of AP, who lives a few blocks from us and makes no secret of her complete astonishment at the election of a fellow countryman. Betta tells her she understands because she's been through it before....

Juan Pablo also returns late, and we all have dinner together, almost at midnight, with some delicious *polpette al sugo* (meatballs with tomato sauce) that Teresa, our home help, had left us. There are also mashed potatoes, which we reheat. And with a much-needed red wine, we toast the new Pope, Leo, who now takes the baton from Francis—our friend in heaven—to lead the Catholic Church in the second quarter of the twenty-first century.

# Part IV

# A MISSIONARY POPE

MAY 9, FRIDAY [BETTA] ────────────────────────
*The Day After*

WE WAKE UP EARLY, with the same adrenaline rush as usual, although now more relaxed: there's a pope. As always, we read the newspapers: "The American Pope" is the headline of most of them.[1] Some, though, like *La Stampa*, go with *"Il Papa dei due mondi"*[2]—"the Pope of two worlds."

Confirming that he already has his own style, Vatican News reports that Leo XIV spent his first night as pontiff in the Palazzo del Sant'Uffizio, where he has lived until now.[3] When he arrived by car at the courtyard of the building, he was greeted by applause and shook hands with well-wishers. He spoke in Spanish with some faithful from Mexico and Venezuela.

French nun Nathalie Becquart, undersecretary of the Synod of Bishops, is a neighbor in the same building and posted a photo on X: "I am happy to meet and congratulate our new Synodal Pope who returns to our Palazzo where he lives."[4]

Then a little girl named Michele approached to ask him to bless and sign a Bible. The new American-Peruvian Pope promptly agreed, with a sense of humor: "I still have to practice that signature; the old one doesn't work anymore," he commented humbly. After asking the girl to spell her name, he surprised everyone by asking, "What day is it today? May 8th?"

---

1. *Corriere Della Sera, La Repubblica, Il Messagero.*

2. *La Stampa*, front page, May 9, 2025.

3. "Grazie a voi!" la prima uscita di Leone XIV nel Palazzo del Sant' Uffizio," www.vaticannews.va, May 9, 2025.

4. Sr. Nathalie Becquart on X, "So glad to meet and congratulate our new synodal Pope...," May 8, 2025.

It is surely a dramatic change in the life of someone who, in just a few hours, goes from being a cardinal—known to those very few who make up the Dicastery for Bishops and the Latin America Commission, but unknown to the world, except in Peru—to becoming the supreme leader of the Catholic Church.

Beyond the shock, Prevost was aware of the speculation about him as a *papabile*, as he told some people after the election. But "I didn't expect to be pope. I never thought the cardinals would elect an American pope."

When Elise Ann Allen asked Leo in the interview for her biography of him if he had in any way suspected he could be elected pope, he answered: "Honestly, no. I mean, I tried not to think about it, because then I probably wouldn't have slept. But the night before I entered the conclave, I was able to sleep because I said to myself, 'They're never going to elect an American as pope.' It was like leaning into that, like a kind of 'Just relax. Don't let this go to your head.' Because obviously during the congregation, in the pre-conclave meetings, I had heard a couple of things. There were some rumors. But I also thought about the case you asked me about earlier [that of the allegations in Chiclayo], which was a concern for some of the other cardinals, if this issue of sexual abuse was going to be a problem, and about the other reasons, the experience, the short time as a bishop, as a cardinal. And then that's when I thought about the old, famous adage that people just said, 'There's not going to be an American pope.' Cardinal [Blase] Cupich was quoted in one of the Chicago newspapers just days before the conclave. They asked him who was going to be the next pope, and he said, 'I'll tell you what, he's not going to be an American.' So I said to myself, well, that's good news, because I wasn't looking for it, honestly. And in any case, things were as they were."

He is not the only American cardinal who thought this way. His compatriot, Robert McElroy, before becoming archbishop of Washington, had told me in an interview with *La Nación* that he considered it "impossible to have an American pope."[5] After the conclave, Gerry and I sat down with him, and we asked him again: How was it possible?

"I always thought it would be impossible to have an American pope because the United States has such tremendous military, eco-

---

5. Elisabetta Piqué, "Robert McElroy: 'Es imposible que haya un papa norteamericano,'" *La Nación*, August 26, 2022.

nomic, and cultural power in the world that there would be resistance to the Church being seen as American, even symbolically. But once inside the conclave, that ceased to be an impediment for several reasons," McElroy told us.[6]

"One of them is that Pope Leo has spent much of his life outside the United States: in Latin America, around the world with his Augustinian community, and now here in Rome. But the most important thing is his way of being and serving the Church in general, especially through his identity as a missionary," he added.

"The prism through which the cardinal electors viewed him was not nationality, but missionary identity. When the electors evaluated the various candidates and their qualities, his nationality was not what defined him. They didn't see him as an American or a Peruvian, but as a missionary. That was the central lens through which most of the electors understood his life, his priesthood, and his ministry. And that identity resonates particularly in continuity with the teaching of Francis, in which missionary discipleship is the central core of identity for all Catholics. So I think that was the lens that lessened much of the resistance that his American identity might have provoked in another context."

Cardinal Chow of Hong Kong asserts that they had voted for a pastoral pope, that it was not a matter of nationality. "I think it's pretty clear that Francis was a pastoral pope, because we could see at his funeral, four hundred thousand people came in just a few days.... After his death, the world turned out, not just the Church, to mourn and say goodbye. Then it became very clear that we weren't electing a pope just for the Church, but also for the world. And we could see how Francis has influenced the world, has impressed the world as a pastor, a pastor of the world."[7]

Speaking to the Catholic newspaper *Avvenire*, in which he also expressed great satisfaction, Luxembourg Cardinal Jean-Claude Hollerich said, "We have not elected a pope who is anti-Trump. We have elected a man of prayer, a disciple of Jesus, a helmsman who knows how to guide the Church through the waves of history. The fact that he is an American citizen is a coincidence. Also, Donald Trump will fade

---

6. Gerard O'Connell, "Cardinal McElroy on Pope Leo's Missionary Past and if Trump Influenced the Conclave," *America,* May 27, 2025.

7. Gerard O'Connell, "Cardinal Chow on the Conclave," *America*, May 19, 2025.

away, while Leo's pontificate will last a long time. It will be a pontificate in continuity with the teachings of Pope Francis, and that is why I am very happy. It is what the majority of the cardinals wanted."[8]

The Brazilian Franciscan cardinal of German origin Leonardo Ulrich Steiner, 74, agreed that nationality was not an issue during the conclave. In 2019 Pope Francis appointed this staunch defender of the Indigenous peoples of the Amazon and their cultures archbishop of Manaus in the Amazon region, a diocese with more than two million inhabitants, and made him a cardinal in 2022. Steiner emphasized that, beyond being born in Chicago, Prevost had the qualities to be pope "because he is a man who knows how to listen, and when he speaks, he speaks with precision."[9] "He never interrupts you. He is always very affable when he speaks, and he does so thoughtfully seeking the truth. I think the others noticed that too," he says, adding that he met him during the last Synod on Synodality because they had been on the same working group.

"Then what impressed me most was the fact that he was a missionary bishop who had worked in Peru. He was there for ten years as a bishop, was elected vice president of the Peruvian Episcopal Conference, and was present at some meetings of the Latin American bishops, although he wasn't so well known at the time.

"Think about it! A North American Augustinian who was a missionary bishop and was called by the pope [to work at the Vatican's Dicastery for Bishops]. I heard that it was very difficult for him to accept that assignment," he added. "I think that in the conclave, it was this missionary spirit, what Jesus says at the end of the Synoptic Gospels, that was emphasized more than anything else.

One of Asia's most prestigious prelates, Cardinal Oswald Gracias, archbishop emeritus of Bombay, former president of the Federation of Asian Bishops' Conferences and member of C9 (the council of cardinals from all continents created by Pope Francis), tells Gerry in an interview after the conclave that he too welcomes the election of Leo XIV.

Cardinal Gracias was ineligible to vote in the conclave because he is over 80 years old. Asked if he was surprised by Prevost's election, he answers: "I am delighted. I am surprised because he was not on

---

8. Giacomo Gambassi, "Il cardinale Hollerich: 'Non abbiamo eletto un Papa anti-Trump. Durerà molto di più,'" *Avvenire*, May 10, 2025.

9. Gerard O'Connell, "Cardinal Steiner on How Pope Leo Will Follow Pope Francis," *America*, May 29, 2025.

the lists mentioned in the media or in the debates, but he had a low profile and was an ideally prepared person. So for me it was a moment of ecstasy, of joy.

"Once again, my faith is strengthened. The Holy Spirit is with the Church and made his presence felt strongly in this conclave. I was at the last conclave. I felt it then, and I see it very clearly this time as well." He observes that "it would not have been possible without the intervention of the Holy Spirit for 133 Church leaders to agree and in twenty-four hours achieve a two-thirds majority for one candidate.

"I knew Leo before he became pope. He is so well prepared, so authentic, so much so that I feel it is a response from God. The Holy Spirit has given us a pope that we need, that the Church needs, and that the world needs at this moment in history. I believe the pope should be a leader of the world, a moral leader of the world. It is a very smooth transition, and I believe it is God's will. Looking around, I can honestly say that there was no one as well prepared as he was, no one more suitable than he was [to be elected Pope]. So, for me, it is a moment of faith, a moment of joy, a moment of true expectation and hope, and of looking forward. Asia wants to collaborate with him to the fullest."

Cardinal Gracias continues: "I have had meetings with him, we've had serious conversations about issues I was studying, and I found it a pleasure to talk with him. I found him to be very intelligent. He gets straight to the point. He's observant. He's not a big talker; you have to ask him questions, and then he's very open. I discovered that he is a man who knows what he thinks, a man who sees the problem, a man who loves the Church very much, a man who truly has the spirituality of a religious man who is so committed to the Church—perhaps it is the Augustinian spirit. He has a profound inner strength to face difficulties. That is what I felt. Perhaps it is his life of prayer, a spirituality with profound inner strength.

"He is not Francis II; he is Leo XIV. That's very clear from his personality, from my conversation with him, and yet he's totally in line with Pope Francis, in priorities, in the direction of the Church, in theology, in political life, in ethics, in economics. I think he is the ideal man for the Church [at this moment in history]. I truly thank the Holy Spirit for having made his presence strongly felt in the conclave."[10]

---

10. Gerard O'Connell, "Cardinal Gracias: 'Pope Leo Is the Ideal Man to Lead the Church at This Time,'" *America*, May 28, 2025.

Italian Cardinal Gianfranco Ravasi, an 82-year-old biblical scholar and theologian, who was also aged out of the conclave,[11] notes that the new pope "is a very simple person, with an intense humanity. Along the lines of Francis, but less sharp-edged (*spigoloso*). Very tactful. More than once I had the opportunity to walk with him, talk, and exchange books. He's a man who creates spontaneity, which unites him and differentiates him from Bergoglio. He's gentler," Ravasi says. "In a world full of shouts, he's a delicate North American who represents the entire continent, including South America. He's not the American Yankee. He took charge of an important dicastery like the Bishops' Office and therefore has an international outlook, but he preferred to take a low profile, not hiding the fact that he did not expect to be elected. The speed [of the elections] was surprising, but during the congregations, some signs had emerged."

Another cardinal who is delighted with the result of the conclave is Juan José Omella, archbishop of Barcelona and president of the Spanish Bishops' Conference (2020–2024). In a long interview with Spain's COPE radio,[12] he says he considers Leo a pope for this moment of the twenty-first century. "Always the Church, the Holy Spirit, gives the pope we need at every moment. I think this is the one we needed. I don't know if we had thought much about him—everyone knows who they were voting for—but the Holy Spirit has led us to him."

Cardinal Omella has known him since they were together in the Dicastery for Bishops—first as members, and then when he became prefect. "We've had almost four or five years together," he said. "I see him as a very simple man, very humble, very intellectually prepared, with a vision of the world, because he has also been a general of the order, has visited their houses as superior general, and has been able to see the reality of the churches where the Augustinians are all over the world, knowing the world, and at the same time, a man who has been pastor of a diocese in Peru, in Chiclayo, apart from the fact that he was a missionary, but already with responsibility as a pastor, as a bishop, he is a man with the smell of the sheep, I would say in the language of Pope Francis." Omella describes him as "a prepared man, a

---

11. Gian Guido Vecchi, "Nel programma di Papa Leone XIV i temi di Bergoglio. Ma lui è più dolce," *Corriere della Sera*, May 9, 2025.

12. "El cardenal Omella desvela cómo ha vivido el cónclave y qué le ha sorprendido del papa león xiv," podcast, www.youtube.com, May 9, 2025.

simple man, and then, with a virtue that has surprised me a lot: he knows how to listen. He listens a lot, and in the end responds, talks, but also cares a lot about your opinion. Not 'I know everything,' no. 'What do you think?' And he has his say. 'Is this okay with you? I think this could be a solution.' A man who listens, who dialogues, and who shares opinions.

"Moreover," he says, "Leo comes from a religious order and brings that experience with him. Religious have the experience of community life. They have the experience of shared government, because the superior general always has a council of generals who vote for him from the different nations where they work. In a way, this also points to the fact that a superior general, being pope, will have to have a council of cardinals, or some governing council, to help him govern. It is not so easy to govern a universal Church such as the Catholic Church."

Cardinal Omella concludes by saying, "Having heard him speak from the central balcony of St. Peter's after his election and after listening to his homily to the cardinals this morning, I think we have got it right. This man gives hope, opens paths, and I believe that he will lead us to the right place."

Yet another European cardinal who greatly rejoices at the election of Prevost is Cardinal Vincent Nichols, archbishop of Westminster and president of the Catholic Bishops' Conference of England and Wales, who like Omella has also worked with him in the Dicastery for Bishops and feels the cardinals in conclave had little difficulty in reaching their decision in less than twenty-four hours. Cardinal Nichols says, "I think it was a short conclave in part because Pope Francis left us a good legacy. He left a college of cardinals who were dedicated, who had this desire for the Church to be more missionary, and that actually led us very, very easily to the decision we made."[13]

His fellow Englishman, Arthur Roche, prefect of the Dicastery for Divine Worship and the Discipline of the Sacraments, the Vatican's office for liturgy, agrees. "It's clear from the speed with which Pope Leo's election was made that Pope Francis has left the Church more united than critics would give him credit for," he says in a CNN

---

13. Holly Cole, "Cardinal Reveals What It Was Like to Be Part of Conclave,"www.bbc.com, May 10, 2025.

interview,[14] adding: "No organization would have been able to elect a world leader so quickly otherwise."

Two African cardinals (who don't want to be identified) also rejoiced at Prevost's election, even though he seems not to have been on their radar when they entered the Sistine Chapel. "We didn't know each other so well when we entered the conclave, but the Holy Spirit worked well, and the one whom we thought would be pope when we went in didn't become pope, but another did."

BEYOND THE CARDINALS' COMMENTS, John Prevost, one of the new pontiff's two brothers, recounts in an NBC Chicago interview that on the eve of the conclave, they had a simple phone conversation which included jokes and everyday references. As on other occasions, they shared online word games, such as Words with Friends or Wordle, a way to stay connected despite the responsibilities Robert faced.

"I asked him if he had seen the movie *Conclave*, to see if he at least had an idea of how to behave," reveals John Prevost, who received a "yes" in response. He explained that his goal was to distract his brother and ease the tension of what was coming.

During that conversation, neither Robert nor his family believed that the outcome of the conclave would result in his being elected. Although his brother had "a vague feeling" about the final outcome, there was a general consensus that an American pope was unlikely, for both political and cultural reasons. "I didn't believe it, and neither did Rob. I have to say that Pope Leo didn't believe it at all, because the attitude was that there wasn't going to be an American pope. I don't know how true that is, but one of the priests at Providence, up in New Lenox, told me, 'In Las Vegas, the odds of your brother getting it are eighteen to one,'" he recalls.[15]

In another interview, John says that his younger brother 'Rob' "has a great desire to help the oppressed and the disenfranchised, the people who are ignored." He predicts that his brother will continue the legacy of his predecessor Pope Francis. "The best way I could de-

---

14. "Pope Leo XIV Calls on Priesthood to Show Humility in First Mass as Pontiff," www.cnn.com, May 9, 2025.

15. "Pope Leo's Brother Reveals Their Last Conversation Night before Conclave," www.nbcchicago.com, May 8, 2025.

scribe it right now is that he will follow in Francis's footsteps. They were very good friends. They knew each other before he was pope, even before my brother was a bishop," he adds.[16]

AMID THESE REFLECTIONS, at 11 AM Leo XIV makes his debut as the new pontiff, which Gerry and Irene and I follow from the Vatican Press Room.

In a solemn Mass, as is traditional, he presides with the cardinals in the same place where he was elected. Leo XIV does not hide his emotion when, before giving his first homily as the 267th pontiff, he speaks for the first time in English, his mother tongue, aware that most of the cardinals who elected him do not speak Italian.

"I begin in English, then I will continue in Italian," he says. "I want to repeat the words of the responsorial psalm: I am happy to be here with you, dear brothers, so that the wonders of the Lord continue to come upon us. I have been called to carry a cross, and blessed with this mission, I want you also to walk with me because we are a community, a Church that must proclaim the good news, and I can count on you in proclaiming the Gospel," he states, confirming that he will seek mediation, beyond the internal divisions between progressives and conservatives, to preserve the unity of the Catholic Church in turbulent times around the world.

The Latin Mass is accompanied by beautiful choirs and includes two readings, in English and Spanish, read by consecrated women. In his first homily as successor of Peter, Leo XIV reflects on the figure of the first apostle, who accepted God's gift, and the path one must follow to allow oneself to be transformed.

"God, in a special way, by calling me through your vote to succeed the first of the apostles, entrusts this treasure to me, so that, with your help, I may be its faithful steward for the entire mystical body of the Church; so that this may increasingly be the city set on a hill, the ark of salvation that navigates the tides of history, the beacon that lights the nights of the world," he says. "And this is not so much thanks to the magnificence of its structures and the grandeur of its buildings — like the monuments we find ourselves in — but to the holiness of its

---

16. Robert Chiarito and Mitch Smith, "'I Was Stunned': Watching from Illinois, Pope's Brother Reflects on History," *New York Times,* May 8, 2025.

members, of that 'people acquired to proclaim the wonders of him who called them out of darkness into his marvelous light.'"[17]

In line with Francis and always reflecting on Peter, the new pope emphasizes that, beyond the profession of faith, "another important aspect of our ministry" is "the reality in which we live, with its limits and its potential, its questions and its convictions."

He then warns against "a world that considers Jesus a person of utterly no importance, at most a curious figure, who can arouse astonishment with his unusual way of speaking and acting. And so, when his presence becomes bothersome because of the demands for honesty and the moral demands he makes, this world will not hesitate to reject and eliminate him."

However, he recalls that in the Gospel for the common people, "the Nazarene is not a charlatan; he is an upright man, a courageous man, who speaks well and says just things, like other great prophets in the history of Israel.

"That is why they follow him," the pope says, "at least as far as they can without too much risk and inconvenience. But they consider him only a man, and that is why, at the moment of danger, during the Passion, they too abandon him and leave, disillusioned. The relevance of these two attitudes is striking. Both embody ideas that we can easily find — perhaps expressed in different language, but identical in substance — in the mouths of many men and women of our time."

Dressed in white and gold vestments, he warns that "today, too, there are many contexts in which the Christian faith is considered absurd, something for weak and unintelligent people, contexts in which other securities are preferred, such as technology, money, success, power, or pleasure.

"We are talking about environments where it is not easy to bear witness to and proclaim the Gospel, and where those who believe are ridiculed, hindered, and scorned, or, at most, tolerated and pitied. And yet, precisely for this reason, these are places where the mission is more urgent, because the lack of faith often brings with it tragedies such as the loss of the meaning of life, the neglect of mercy, the violation of human dignity in its most dramatic forms, the crisis of the family, and so many other wounds that bring no small amount of suffering to our society.

---

17. Holy Mass of His Holiness Leo XIV with the College of Cardinals, "Homily of the Holy Father," Holy See Press Office, May 9, 2025.

"There are also contexts in which Jesus, although appreciated as a man, is reduced to nothing more than a kind of charismatic leader or superman, and this is not only among non-believers, but even among many baptized people, who thus end up living, in this context, a de facto atheism.

"This is the world entrusted to us, and in which, as Pope Francis often taught, we are called to bear witness to the joyful faith in Jesus the Savior. For this reason, for us too, it is essential to repeat: 'You are the Messiah, the Son of the living God.' It is fundamental to do this first and foremost in our personal relationship with the Lord, in our commitment to a daily journey of conversion. But also, as a Church, living together our belonging to the Lord and bringing the Good News to all," he continues.

"I say this first of all for myself, as Successor of Peter, as I begin my mission as bishop of the Church in Rome, called to preside over the universal Church in charity, according to the famous expression of St. Ignatius of Antioch. He, while being led in chains to this city, the place of his imminent sacrifice, wrote to the Christians there: 'At that moment I will truly be a disciple of Christ, when the world will no longer see my body.' He was referring to being devoured by the beasts of the circus—and so it happened—but his words evoke in a more general sense an irrevocable commitment for anyone who exercises a ministry of authority in the Church: to disappear so that Christ may remain, to make himself small so that he may be known and glorified (cf. John 3:30), spending himself to the end so that no one may lack the opportunity to know and love him."

The pope ends his homily be saying, "May God grant me this grace, today and always, with the help of the tender intercession of Mary, Mother of the Church."

AFTER THE MASS we write and send our articles. In a new flurry of news, the Vatican has announced that Leo XIV will formally assume office on Sunday, May 18, in a ceremony once again attended by heads of state and government, crowned heads, and representatives of the international community.

Just as on the day after the election of Benedict XVI and of Francis, the Vatican also announces that the new pontiff has decided to provisionally confirm all the highest positions in the Roman Curia, the central administration of the Catholic Church. "His Holiness, Leo

XIV, has expressed his wish that the heads and members of the institutions of the Roman Curia, as well as the secretaries and the president of the Pontifical Commission for Vatican City State, continue provisionally in their respective positions *'donec aliter providuatur'* (until otherwise arranged)," the Holy See Press Office says in a statement, adding that "the Holy Father wishes, in fact, to reserve some time for reflection, prayer, and dialogue before any final appointment or confirmation."

Meanwhile, the House of the Pontifical Prefecture announces the agenda for the coming days. Tomorrow, the new pope will meet with the cardinals, and the day after, on his first Sunday as supreme leader of the Catholic Church, he will appear on the central balcony of St. Peter's Basilica to lead the Marian prayer, the Regina Caeli—which substitutes for the Angelus during Eastertide.

On Monday in the Paul VI Audience Hall he will have his first audience with the four thousand journalists arrived from around the world to cover the *sede vacante* and the conclave that elected him, . Meanwhile, the pope concerned about a world in flames, whose first word upon presenting himself to the world was "peace," will receive the heads of mission of the diplomatic corps accredited to the Holy See on Friday, May 16.

I MAKE SEVERAL STANDUPS for LN+ while Gerry lunches with an old friend, 87-year-old British Cardinal Michael Fitzgerald, a member of the Missionaries of Africa and an expert on Islam and Christian-Muslim relations. Created a cardinal by Francis in 2019 in what he called "an act of justice," Cardinal Fitzgerald was the only one of the four British cardinals ineligible to enter the conclave. But he participated in the general congregations and makes no secret of his delight at the election of Leo XIV. Like many others, he never thought he would see an American in the Chair of Peter in his lifetime.

After lunch, Gerry does another podcast for *America* magazine with Sam Sawyer, editor-in-chief, and hosted by Colleen Dulle, on "What Does the Rapid Election of Pope Leo Mean for the Catholic Church?"[18]

---

18. "What Pope Leo XIV's Speedy Election Means for the Catholic Church," podcast, www.youtube.com, May 9, 2025.

Afterward, we meet in St. Peter's Square and hurry together to a press conference with several American cardinals at the North American College (NAC) of Rome on the Janiculum Hill.[19]

In a very relaxed atmosphere and with classic Yankee humor suggesting that almost everyone supported Prevost, his compatriots confirm that, as Gerry and I had heard, Cardinal Prevost didn't exactly shine when he spoke to the assembly at the general congregations. Cardinal Wilton Gregory, archbishop emeritus of Washington, acknowledges that he "didn't have a great intervention." But he counters that he did have an impact and was very "effective" in small groups during lunches and coffee breaks. "It's not like he stood up and gave an overwhelmingly convincing speech."

Also participating in the press conference is the French Cardinal Christophe Pierre, nuncio to the United States. In keeping with the relaxed atmosphere, Pierre, a diplomat who joked about the French origin of the new pontiff's surname, also provides clues about what happened within the *cum clave* confinement in the Sistine Chapel.

After quoting the French poet Charles Péguy, who said, "Everything begins in mysticism and ends in politics," he says that "in the conclave, what began politically ended mystically. No one told us where to go; the only method was the human method of talking to one another, listening to one another, and in the end, things became clear. The conclave is a moment of discernment. We are in prayer, and we knew we could solve the problems of diversity. The Holy Spirit had to help us; He didn't float up in the air, but helped us act," he explained. "At one point, I said to the Holy Spirit: What do I do?"

Cardinal Joseph William Tobin, archbishop of Newark, who has known Leo for thirty years, reveals that the long meditation given by the preacher of the Papal Household, Raniero Cantalamessa, after the doors of the Sistine Chapel had closed was key. The 90-year-old Capuchin friar had said to them: "Be yourselves."[20]

---

19. Those participating were Blase Cupich (Chicago), Daniel Di Nardo (emeritus of Galveston-Houston), Timothy Dolan (New York), Robert McElroy (Washington), Joseph Tobin (Newark), Wilton Gregory (emeritus of Washington) and the apostolic nuncio (Vatican ambassador) to the United States, Christophe Pierre, who resided at the college before the conclave.

20. Elisabetta Piqué, "Los votos que consagraron a León XIV en un cónclave que dejó un gran derrotado y el nombre que ya es un programa," *La Nación*, May 9, 2025.

In a true indication that not everything is so secret in a conclave, while the American cardinals were giving their impressions in public, about a fifteen-minute walk away, the three Canadian cardinal electors, Gerald Cyprian Lacroix, archbishop of Quebec; Thomas Collins, archbishop emeritus of Toronto, who also participated in the 2013 conclave; and his successor in Toronto, Frank Leo—all of whom Gerry knows—were also holding their press conferences at the Canadian College. Neil McCarthy, a spokesman for the archdiocese of Toronto, who was with Gerry on CTV, conducts the conference, and Sebastian Gomes covers it for *America* magazine.

"We elected a pope in less than twenty-four hours. That says something! It's a great statement of how we were able to listen together to the will of God, to the Holy Spirit, and use our intelligence based on what we heard to make a decision and come together," said Lacroix, 67. "I'm very grateful. And I'm happy to share this with you because if you hear certain things in movies or in the media, or from people on the outside, you can't capture the beauty of how we experience this inside. It's like looking at a church: if you look at the stained-glass windows from the outside, it's all dark, but if you're inside and the light comes in, it's beautiful. That's how I would describe the conclave for me. From the inside, it was a beautiful experience, and I thank God for having had this opportunity once in my life," he says.[21]

TOWARD THE END of another exhausting day, Irene and I interview our friend, American Jesuit Father James Martin, author of religious bestsellers, a media star, and one of the most influential voices in the progressive Catholic world in the United States. Editor at large of *America* magazine, in recent years he has become a leading figure in pastorally accompanying and defending the LGBT community.

Martin—who has always enjoyed the support of Pope Francis in his ministry and traveled to Rome to comment on the conclave for the American television network ABC News—joins the general enthusiasm for the new pope.

He says he knows him because he sat at his table at the Synod. "I thought he was a great person. He's very humble, modest, and reserved; he speaks softly, but he is very intelligent, organized, and

---

21. "Three Canadian Cardinal Electors Speak after Election of New Pope," podcast, www.youtube.com, May 9, 2025.

hardworking. I think he's someone with a great personality, sensible and direct. I think he will be a great pope. I have a feeling he will be a pope with his own style. But since when he stepped out onto the central balcony of St. Peter's Basilica after being elected, he mentioned synodality and spoke of building bridges, it seems to me he is interested in continuing the legacy of Pope Francis. Furthermore, his adoption of the name Leo XIV indicates that he's also interested in the great tradition of Catholic social teaching."

Martin says that it's "difficult to know" whether Leo will have the same openness as Francis toward the LGBT community. In this regard, some media outlets predict, based on prior statements, that Leo XIV will be more traditional when it comes to the concept of family. "His last comment on the matter seems to date back to 2012, and a long time has passed since then. I have the feeling that the new pope is very open to listening, dialogue, and building bridges, which is part of synodality. We must also keep in mind that what a person says and does as a cardinal may be different from what he says and does as pope."

What does he think the relationship between Leo XIV and Donald Trump will be like? He answers that "in the past, Prevost has indicated his support for migrants and refugees; just look at his X account to see that. Of course, now that he is pope, he could act differently. But I think he will continue preaching the Gospel, even if it has political implications."

Trump reacted diplomatically to the election: "Congratulations to Cardinal Robert Francis Prevost, who has just been named Pope. It is a great honor to know that he is the first American Pope. What a thrill and what a great honor for our country! I look forward to meeting Pope Leo XIV. It will be a very significant moment!" he wrote, in a message on Truth Social, later republished by the White House on X along with photographs of Prevost.

Everyone knows, however, that the controversial president's preferred candidate was Cardinal Dolan, archbishop of New York, whose apparently pro-Trump stance created a stir in the polarized American Church.

I write up the interview with Jim Martin[22] and another note from the conclave based on anecdotes from the NAC press conference.

---

22. Elisabetta Piqué, "James Martin, sacerdote norteamericano: 'Tengo la sensación de que el papa León XIV está muy abierto a escuchar y dialogar,'" *La Nación*, May 9, 2025.

When we're all home, Gerry, Juan Pablo, Carolina, Irene, and I eat a delicious baked chicken with potatoes prepared by Teresa. Cristina Taquini also comes over for dinner. The conversation at the table has only one topic: Leo.

MAY 10, SATURDAY [BETTA]

*Accepting a Yoke*

THE URGENT EDGE IN THE AIR has eased, and the rhythm is less frenetic.

Because of the Jubilee of Bands and Popular Entertainment, Rome is filled with the music of all kinds of bands—military, institutional, amateur, folk, town, sports, schools—as well as performances by groups from all over the world. A party climate is in full swing today and will be tomorrow.

It is a sunny day. Irene and Cristina visit Francis's tomb in the Basilica of Saint Mary Major, something they have not yet been able to do. Two weeks after his funeral—although with the vertigo of the last days it seems that years have passed—there is still an immensely long line of people—many of them young—paying tribute to him. They wait about two hours. There are also volunteers distributing bottles of water.

Gail Scriven, top editor at *La Nación* and a friend, sends me a Whats App congratulating me on "the Great Work." She tells me to advise her if I need anything. The only thing I need is time to sleep.

The most striking item in today's newspapers is the exclusive article written by Cardinal Parolin in *Il Giornale di Vicenza*,[23] the city in the Veneto region where he was born and where many were hoping he would be elected to the Chair of Peter.

The paper's editor says, "Parolin has sent us a reflection on these frenetic days in the Vatican, in which he refers both to the significance of the election and the support of the people of Vicenza in his favor."

---

23. "Parolin e la lettera al GdV. 'Vi racconto Papa Leone XIV. Guiderà la Chiesa con serenità,'" *Il Giornale di Vicenza*, May 10, 2025.

He acknowledges that the locals would have understandably yearned for their native son's election but says that disappointment "must be overcome according to a different logic, of faith and church."

He writes: "Still 'fresh' from the strong and engaging experience of the conclave, I gladly respond to the request of the *Giornale di Vicenza* to write a commentary on the election of Pope Leo XIV, Cardinal Robert Francis Prevost, OSA. I allow myself to offer a brief testimony, beginning with the joy that in such a short time the universal Church has rediscovered its shepherd, the successor of Peter and of Pope Francis, who had the patience of retaining me as his secretary of state for almost twelve years," continues Parolin, known for his diplomatic skills and his great kindness. All Italy sincerely believed he could become the new Italian Pope.

"We firmly believe that, through the action of the cardinal electors —also through their humanity—it is the Holy Spirit who chooses the man destined to direct the Church. Technically, it is an election, but what happens in the Sistine Chapel under the gaze of Christ the Judge renews what happened at the beginning of the Church, when the apostolic college was reconstituted after the painful desertion of Judas Iscariot. The apostles prayed so that the Lord, who knows the heart of each one, would show them who was the chosen one.

"This mystery has been repeated in recent days, and we are immensely grateful to the Lord who does not abandon the Church, his beloved bride, but provides her with shepherds according to his heart. And we are immensely grateful to Pope Leo XIV for having accepted the call of the Lord to love him 'more than these' and to follow him, tending his sheep and lambs as Jesus asked Peter in the Gospel passage that we read last Sunday.

"I believe it is no secret that I reveal in writing when I say that a long and warm applause followed that 'I accept' that made him the 267th pope of the Catholic Church.

"What impressed me most about him was the serenity that shone through his face in such intense and, in a certain sense, 'dramatic' moments, because they totally change a man's life. He never lost his gentle smile, although, I imagine, in the lively awareness of the many and not simple problems that the Church of today is facing."

Continuing to praise the American pope, Cardinal Parolin adds, "We have discussed these at length during the congregations of cardinals that preceded the conclave, where each of the participants—

cardinal electors and non-electors—were able to present the face of Catholicism in their respective countries, the challenges that await, the prospects for the future.

"And since the Church, following her Lord, is profoundly incarnate in the history of men and women of every time and every latitude, the new pope is well aware of the problems of today's world, as he demonstrated with his first words from the loggia of St. Peter's, referring immediately to 'disarmed and disarming peace.'

"Since meeting him at the beginning of my service as secretary of state regarding a difficult situation having to do with the Church in Peru, where he was a bishop of the Diocese of Chiclayo, I have always experienced this serenity in Cardinal Prevost.

"I had the opportunity to collaborate directly with him over the last two years, after Pope Francis called him to Rome and appointed him head of the Dicastery for Bishops. I have experienced in him understanding of situations and people, serenity in his arguments, balance by proposing solutions, respect, attention, and love for all."

Cardinal Parolin concludes: "I believe that Pope Leo XIV, in addition obviously to the grace of the Lord, will find in his extensive experience as a religious and pastor, as well as in the example, teaching, and spirituality of the great Father Augustine—whom he mentioned in his opening words—the resources for the effective performance of the ministry that the Lord has entrusted to him, for the good of the Church and of all humanity.

"We are close to him with our affection, our obedience, and our prayers."

MEANWHILE, ON HIS SECOND DAY as pope, in the traditional address to the College of Cardinals behind closed doors in the Synod Hall, Leo XIV makes clear that his governing priorities are in line with the "precious legacy" of his predecessor.[24]

He opens these important remarks with gratitude for the cardinals' presence and support and sadness over the recent loss of Pope Francis. He reminds them of their mission to support the papacy, and says: "You, dear Cardinals, are the closest collaborators with the pope. This has proved a great comfort to me in accepting a yoke

---

24. Address of His Holiness Pope Leo XIV to the College of Cardinals, May 10, 2025, www.vatican.va.

clearly far beyond my own limited powers, as it would be for any of us. Your presence reminds me that the Lord, who has entrusted me with this mission, will not leave me alone in bearing its responsibility. I know, before all else, that I can always count on his help, the help of the Lord, and through his grace and providence, on your closeness and that of so many of our brothers and sisters throughout the world who believe in God, love the Church and support the Vicar of Christ by their prayers and good works."

He then thanks the dean of the College of Cardinals, Cardinal Re, and the cardinal *camerlengo* Farrell. Some eyebrows may have been raised when he omits to mention Cardinal Parolin.

"I thank the dean of the College of Cardinals, Cardinal Giovanni Battista Re—who deserves applause, at least once, if not more—whose wisdom, the fruit of a long life and many years of faithful service to the Apostolic See, has helped us greatly during this time. I thank the *camerlengo* of the Holy Roman Church, Cardinal Kevin Joseph Farrell—I believe he is present today—for the important and demanding work that he has done throughout the period of the Vacant See and for the convocation of the conclave. My thoughts also go to our brother cardinals who, for reasons of health, were unable to be present, and I join you in embracing them in communion of affection and prayer."

He asks them to see Francis's passing in the context of Easter and encourages them to follow his legacy: "At this moment, both sad and joyful, providentially bathed in the light of Easter, I would like all of us to see the passing of our beloved Holy Father Pope Francis and the conclave as a paschal event, a stage in that long exodus through which the Lord continues to guide us toward the fullness of life. In this perspective, we entrust to the 'merciful Father and God of all consolation' the soul of the late pontiff and also the future of the Church.

"Beginning with Saint Peter and up to myself, his unworthy successor, the pope has been a humble servant of God and of his brothers and sisters, and nothing more than this. It has been clearly seen in the example of so many of my predecessors, and most recently by Pope Francis himself, with his example of complete dedication to service and to sober simplicity of life, his abandonment to God throughout his ministry, and his serene trust at the moment of his return to the Father's house. Let us take up this precious legacy and continue on the journey, inspired by the same hope that is born of faith."

Then, arriving to the core of the address, his call on all cardinals to renew full adherence to the open path initiated by the Vatican

Council II (1962–1965) is unequivocal and includes "the return to the primacy of Christ in proclamation; the missionary conversion of the entire Christian community; growth in collegiality and synodality; attention to the *sensus fidei*, especially in its most authentic and inclusive forms, such as popular piety; loving care for the least and the rejected; courageous and trusting dialogue with the contemporary world in its various components and realities."

Finally, departing from the traditional ritual, he asks the cardinals to remain in silence for some minutes and then speak with those nearest them before asking questions. He then opens the floor to questions. Many cardinals pose questions, and the topic of improving communication between them and the supreme pontiff and the possibility of holding a meeting once a year is discussed. Cardinals who, because of time limitations, are not able to ask questions are invited to do so in writing. Unfortunately, the wrong email address is given and the emails bounce. Things that happen during times of transition.

INDIAN CARDINAL OSWALD GRACIAS tells Gerry, "The meeting was a message for the cardinals: 'You are important to me, I will need your help, your assistance to direct the Church.' I think Leo had already heard almost everything they said, so he did not need to take notes. Once again he laid out his priorities: follow the Second Vatican Council and assure that the Church continues advancing in the line of Francis—synodality."[25]

Brazilian cardinal elector Leonardo Ulrich Steiner says, "What struck me about this was that in the general congregations we had asked that the new pope bring the cardinals together at least once a year, so that we could meet with each other, but also so that we could support him. And after his election, Leo immediately gathered all the cardinals."[26]

IN HIS SPEECH TO THE CARDINALS, Leo XIV lists as one of the fundamental milestones in his pontifical road map "growth in collegiality and

---

25. Gerard O'Connell, "Cardinal Gracias: Pope Leo 'Is the Ideal Man to Lead the Church at This Time,'" *America*, May 28, 2025.

26. Gerard O'Connell, "Cardinal Steiner on How Pope Leo Will Follow Pope Francis—and How He'll Chart His Own Path," *America*, May 29, 2025.

synodality," two important themes that he will repeat in several talks during the first weeks of his pontificate.

Before entering the conclave, many of the sixty-one electors who participated in the Synods on Synodality of October 2023 and October 2024—"For a synodal church: communion, participation, mission"—had told us that they wanted a new pope who would continue this process initiated by Pope Francis.

In his first address to the city of Rome and the world—*Urbi et Orbi*—on the night of his election, Leo XIV clearly expressed his intention to continue in this direction, building a synodal and missionary Church: "We want to be a synodal Church, a Church that journeys, a Church that always seeks peace, that always seeks charity, that always seeks to be close, especially to those who suffer."

His determination to continue the synodal process will be demonstrated by his decision to convene a meeting of the Synodal Council on June 26 and 27. The meeting had initially been planned by Pope Francis for those dates, but many expected it to be postponed until October because of the papal transition. However, Leo decides it is important to move the implementation process forward and not waste time.

He will attend the meeting at the Synod Secretariat and spend over an hour with the council members on June 26, confirming his full commitment to the process. Then, when he is subjected to a barrage of questions, Leo will surprise everyone by saying: "I am not the Lone Ranger. This is supposed to be a synodal process, and I have come to listen."

ON HIS FIRST SATURDAY AFTERNOON as pope, Leo makes a surprise private visit to the Augustinian shrine of Our Lady of Good Counsel in Genazzano, fifty kilometers southeast of Rome.

At the Shrine of Genazzano, the pope has his first encounter with the crowds awaiting him in the square. He then prays before the ancient icon of Our Lady of Good Counsel, much beloved by the Augustinian Order: it is an image of the Virgin Mary and the Child Jesus, brought from Albania in 1467 and kept in the ancient church administered by the Augustinians since 1356.

It is a cherished image, especially by Robert Francis Prevost, who visited this place at key moments in his life: when he was elected superior general of the Augustinian Order in 2001, when he was created a cardinal by Pope Francis in 2023, and now after his election as pope.

"I have greatly desired to come here in these first days of the new ministry that the Church has entrusted to me, to carry out this mission as successor of Peter." Recalling the visit following his election as prior general of the Order of Saint Augustine and his decision to "offer his life to the Church," the pope reiterated his "trust in the Mother of Good Counsel," a companion "of light and wisdom," with the words Mary addressed to the servants at the wedding at Cana, recounted in the Gospel of John: "Do whatever he tells you."[27]

Proving once again that he has his own style, rather than use the white Fiat 500L that Francis used to get around, he travels in another vehicle: a black six-seat hybrid Volkswagen Multivan.

Upon returning to Rome, Leo surprises everyone again: he visits the Basilica of Saint Mary Major to venerate the simple white marble tomb of his predecessor. The appearance of the new pontiff, who is acclaimed by those present, animates the ancient basilica. Leo leaves a white rose on Francis's tomb. Moved, he kneels to pray. The image soon goes around the world and is worth a thousand words.

TODAY I INTERVIEW A CURIAL OFFICIAL, Argentine moral theologian and friend Emilce Cuda, whom some have dubbed "the lady of two popes" since the white smoke emerged from the Sistine Chapel's chimney. In June 2021, Pope Francis summoned her to the Roman Curia as the first woman secretary of the Pontifical Commission for Latin America (PCAL). Bishop Robert Prevost became her direct boss when he assumed the PCAL presidency from Cardinal Ouellet in January 2023.

The first woman to earn a sacred theology doctorate in social moral theology from the Catholic University of Argentina (UCA), and who has taught for decades at universities in the United States, she is always considered the woman who best understands Pope Francis's thought, as she was a disciple of Jesuit Father Juan Carlos Scannone—a theorist of the theology of the people and mentor to Bergoglio—and is the author of the book *Para leer a Francisco* (To Read Francis), which explores the intellectual background of Pope Francis's thought.

Married to an American and the mother of two children living in the United States, she mirrors Pope Leo's Latin American/North

---

27. "El Papa León XIV visita el santuario de la Madre del Buen Consejo de Genazzano," www.vaticannews.va, May 10, 2025.

American cultural synthesis. She relates what it has been like to work for two years side by side with Prevost, the largely unknown new pontiff. "He is a very pleasant person. He is very quiet, it's true; when you speak, he listens, listens, listens. I know this from experience. When you finish giving your report and he is silent, you say, 'Okay, that's it, I'm leaving.' He says, 'No, no.' And then he starts talking. He is not a person who doesn't speak; he is a person who listens first and then gives answers. He is a person who, I know, on two very important occasions in particular, has made a critical decision and has taken responsibility for the consequences of that decision. In other words, he didn't use someone else to make the decision and then remain on the sidelines. Something that, as a woman working in the Church, having a man support me in that way, has been very important to me, and he did so while being a cardinal."[28]

How would she differentiate between the two popes? "That's a great question. I believe that we must first understand Cardinal Prevost, now Pope Leo XIV, as a process, because that is how Pope Francis defined it. I think he will not be the same as Pope Francis; he will be distinct. Distinct, not different. And that will guarantee the consolidation of processes that have been initiated, but at the same time, he will confront other realities. He is of a different generation; he handles other types of technology, for example, and has a different worldview simply because he is younger [he is 69] and because he has lived in various parts of the world and in both Americas. He knows the success of capitalism, of the American middle class, and at the same time, he knows the misery of Latin America, which isn't learned by taking a three-day trip or in one year. He chose the poor. He made the choice for the poor at age 20 and was then brought to the Curia by Francis only two years ago. This is unique," she says, "and I think that's a big difference with Pope Francis."

"Pope Francis was familiar with the political and economic reality of the east coast of Latin America, a coast where there was advanced industrial development, where there was worker organization. But the west coast of Latin America is a different reality: it's a rural reality, a fragmented reality. Francis wasn't familiar with that reality; his successor is. But, at the same time, let's not forget that he was born in Chicago, the city where American unionism was born, an organized

---

28. Elisabetta Piqué, "Emilce Cuda: 'Hay un saber de León XIV en su cultura de los dos mundos que Francisco no tenía,'" *La Nación*, May 10, 2025.

city, a society that understands politics. So there is a cultural understanding of both worlds that Francis did not possess."

She believes Prevost had massive support from the Latin American cardinals during the conclave. "Absolutely. I am amazed at how these publicity campaigns claiming [to know who] would be the winner became established.... Based on my feminine intuition, it was he, Prevost, who entered the conclave as the winner. And not because I had information from any cardinal but because I have spoken with every cardinal from Latin America and the United States, not just because of the conclave, but previously. This was a task Pope Francis entrusted to me. In the Commission's Building Bridges program, we unite not only universities, unions, and business leaders, but also cardinals, archbishops, dioceses. The profile of Latin America was a profile that would support Prevost in leading the Church. And in that, there was truly unity among the Latin American cardinals. This is significant because the media said, 'It cannot be another cardinal from Latin America,' as if Pope Francis had done things poorly, when, in truth, he gave dignity to Latin America. He gave it the dignity it didn't have, because outsiders think that in Latin America we are... 'Everyone is ignorant.'... But we have now had two popes who have shown determination. Politics as a decision is not a minor issue," she opines with her trademark fervor.

How does she think Leo XIV will deal with Donald Trump? "I believe that the Church at every historical moment chooses the person who has the capacity to dialogue with whoever holds power at that moment. At one time, with the threat of communism in Poland and the Soviet bloc, we had John Paul II. And today, when we are witnessing a "neo-feudalism" concentrated in the United States, I believe we must have a person—like Pope Leo XIV—capable of understanding the categories of that culture in order to engage in dialogue."

Finally, she does not hesitate to affirm that Prevost was Jorge Bergoglio's choice for successor: "Absolutely. As prefect of the Dicastery for Bishops Prevost had weekly contact with Pope Francis; he met with him every Saturday. The pope loved him very much. He expressed this to me specifically on several occasions."

WE END THE DAY BY GOING TO DINNER with the entire *America* magazine team at Le Cave di San Ignazio, one of our favorite restaurants, located in Piazza di San Ignazio, one of the most beautiful in Rome's historic center, across from the church of the same name. Irene joins us, and we recall that we always used to eat outside there when the kids were little, because they could get up from the table to run around and play in the square, safely and within our sight. We have some delicious homemade appetizers, a variety of focaccia, and exquisite spaghetti *alle vongole*.

Again, the theme is always the same: Leo. Since almost all the diners —except for Gerry, Irene, and me—are Americans, we speak English. As we walk home through the wonderful little streets of Rome, passing the Pantheon, Irene observes that Leo is pronounced in English exactly like the Spanish word *lío*, which means trouble or mess. Pope Francis famously exhorted the millions of young people at Rio's 2013 Youth Day: "*Hagan lío!*"—which means "Go and stir things up!" The Argentine idiom expresses not disorder but rather boldness, social engagement, and youthful energy—in this case disruption for the cause of justice, truth or the Gospel. Maybe a new *lío* begins with the youthful Leo.

MAY 11, SUNDAY [GERRY]

## Never Again War

AFTER TWO SUNDAYS WITHOUT A POPE—although it seems like many more—this is the first Sunday with a new pope. Betta and I go to the Vatican to watch his debut live before the crowds, where he will recite his first Marian prayer before hundreds of thousands of people.

It's a clear day, and thousands of people have been arriving since early to the Vatican area, which is barricaded as on important occasions. The entire area of Via della Conciliazione and its surroundings have been fenced off, and several giant screens are set up to allow viewing even to those unable to reach the piazza, even up to Castel Sant'Angelo. In addition to security control points with agents checking bags and using metal detectors, there are personnel from the Red Cross, the Carabinieri, and Civil Defense.

Because he is the first American and Peruvian pontiff, students from Marymount School and the Peruvian community have arrived early in the square, proud of "their" first pope, unfurling the red and white flag of the Andean country and the Stars and Stripes of the United States.

A festive atmosphere reigns, as bands of ninety countries from around the world parade into the square with their music and colorful traditional costumes, celebrating their Jubilee, which has coincided with the election of Peter's successor.

At noon sharp, he appears dressed in his white cassock on the central balcony of St. Peter's Basilica—the same one where he presented himself to the world last Thursday after the white smoke appeared—and the square erupts in a great roar of jubilation.

"Dear brothers and sisters, happy Sunday!" he greets them, prompting more applause and joy in a square packed with people, both Romans and pilgrims from around the world. "I consider it a gift from God that the first Sunday of my service as bishop of Rome is the Sunday of the Good Shepherd, the fourth Sunday of Easter," Leo says, noting that on this Sunday, during Mass, the reading from the tenth chapter of the Gospel of John is always proclaimed, "in which Jesus reveals himself as the true Shepherd, who knows, loves, and gives his life for his sheep.

"On this Sunday, for sixty-two years, the World Day of Prayer for Vocations has been celebrated. And," he adds, "Rome today hosts the Jubilee of Bands and Popular Entertainment," speaking in Italian with that strange accent that is neither Latin American nor American.

"I greet all the pilgrims with affection, and thank them, because with their music and performances they bring joy to the feast, the feast of Christ the Good Shepherd; yes, it is he who guides the Church through his Holy Spirit.

"In the Gospel, Jesus affirms that he knows his sheep, and that they hear his voice and follow him. Indeed, as Pope Saint Gregory the Great teaches, people 'respond to the love of those who love them.' Today, therefore, brothers and sisters, I have the joy of praying with you and with all the People of God for vocations, especially to the priesthood and religious life. The Church needs you!" he exclaims. "And it is important that young people on their vocational journey find in our communities welcome, listening, encouragement, and that they can count on credible models of generous dedication to God and their brothers and sisters.

"Let us make our own the invitation that Pope Francis left us in his message for this day, in which he asked us to welcome and accompany young people. Let us pray to the Heavenly Father that we may be, for one another, each according to his state, shepherds 'according to his heart,' capable of helping one another walk in love and truth." Then, departing from his prepared speech and recalling Saint John Paul II he announces, "And to young people I say: 'Do not be afraid! Accept the invitation of the Church and of Christ the Lord!'

"May the Virgin Mary, whose life was a complete response to the Lord's call, always accompany us in following Jesus," he prays. Immediately afterwards, demonstrating his own style, he surprises everyone by singing—and very well intoning—the Regina Caeli. His Argentine predecessor did not usually sing. He then recites the corresponding prayer in Latin and imparts the blessing.

After the prayer, in the part that often touches on political situations or crises in the world, Leo recalls that eighty years ago, on May 8, the "immense tragedy of the Second World War ended, after having claimed sixty million victims. In the current dramatic scenario of a piecemeal Third World War, as Pope Francis stated on more than one occasion, I too address the world's leaders, repeating the ever-present call: 'Never again war!'" which generates applause from the hundreds of thousands of people present.

"I carry in my heart the suffering of the beloved Ukrainian people: may everything be done to achieve a true, just, and lasting peace as soon as possible!" he prays, also demanding the release of all prisoners and the return of deported children to their families. "I am deeply saddened by what is happening in the Gaza Strip: let there be a ceasefire immediately!" he urges, also demanding "that humanitarian aid be provided to the exhausted civilian population and that all hostages be released."

In his first remarks relating to a major crisis in Asia that erupted during the conclave he also notes that he has received "with satisfaction the announcement of a ceasefire between India and Pakistan," and hopes that, "through the upcoming negotiations, a lasting agreement can soon be reached.

"But how many other conflicts there are in the world!" he exclaims, adding that "I entrust this heartfelt appeal to the Queen of Peace, so that she may present it to the Lord Jesus that he may grant us the miracle of peace," which prompts a standing ovation.[29]

---

29. Elisabetta Piqué, "'Nunca más la guerra!', el grito de León XIV en su primera aparición dominical ante 100.000 fieles e inmenso entusiasmo," *La Nación*, May 11, 2025.

The new pope then greets all those present, groups from very many countries, and congratulates all mothers, "with a prayer for them and also those who are already in heaven," recalling that Mother's Day is being celebrated today in Italy and many other countries around the world. "Happy Mother's Day to all the mothers!" he proclaims. "Thank you all, and happy Sunday to all!" he concludes, excitedly waving his hands to the crowd that chants "Leone! Leone! Leone!"

"We arrived at 9:30 AM and there were already quite a few people here," says Felicitas Lanusse, Betta's goddaughter, who is on vacation in Italy with her husband, Manuel Soria, and didn't want to miss this first public appearance by Francis's successor. "We had tickets for a train to Florence this morning, but we changed them so that we could be here to see Leo XIV's first Regina Caeli," she says. "There was a very good energy with Spaniards, Mexicans, Peruvians, and Argentinians singing and celebrating," they report enthusiastically.

THE VATICAN INFORMS US that the new pope celebrated Holy Mass in the Vatican Grottoes near the tomb of St. Peter this morning. Alejandro Moral Antón, prior general of the Order of St. Augustine, concelebrated with him. His sermon—which was initially in English and later in Italian—revolves around the figure of the Good Shepherd and speaks of Mother's Day and of the need for courage in proclaiming the Gospel.

"Take courage! Without fear! Many times in the Gospel Jesus says: 'Do not be afraid.' We need to be courageous in the witness we give, with the world and above all with life: giving life, serving, sometimes with great sacrifices in order to live out this very mission.

"I saw a little reflection that made me think a lot, because it also comes out in the Gospel. In the reflection, someone asks: 'When you think about your life, how do you explain where you have arrived?' The answer given is in a certain sense mine too, with the verb 'to listen.' How important it is to listen! Jesus says, 'My sheep listen to my voice.' And I think it is important for all of us to learn how to listen more, to enter into dialogue. First and foremost, with the Lord: always listen to the Word of God. Then also listen to others, to know how to build bridges, to know how to listen without judging, not closing the doors thinking that we have all the truth and no one else can tell us anything. It is very important to listen to the voice of the

Lord, to listen to it, in this dialogue, and to see what the Lord is calling us toward.

"Walking together in the Church, let us ask the Lord to give us this grace of being able to listen to his Word, to serve all his people."[30]

The Vatican reports that "at the end of the Mass, the pope paused in prayer before the tombs of his predecessors and in front of the niche of the pallium."

The Press Office also reports that after the Regina Caeli prayer, accompanied by the *camerlengo*, the American Cardinal Kevin Farrell; the secretary of state Cardinal Pietro Parolin; the substitute, the Venezuelan Archbishop Edgar Peña Parra; the chancellor, British Archbishop Paul Gallagher; and the regent of the Papal Household Monsignor Leonardo Sapienza, Leo reopened the papal apartment in the Apostolic Palace, removing the seals placed there on the afternoon of April 21 following the death of Pope Francis. This is customary practice. It is believed that here is where the new pope will live, resuming a tradition after Francis's hiatus, which startled everyone at the beginning of his pontificate with his decision to live in Santa Marta "for psychiatric reasons," as he often jokingly explained.

WE HAVE LUNCH WITH CARDINAL BLASE CUPICH, who was just interviewed by Martha Raddatz of ABC News.[31] The Jubilee of the Bands has packed all the restaurants in Borgo Pio, and there is a carnival atmosphere, very joyful, with music, people clapping, and videos being made everywhere. We finally find a table at Marcantonio Restaurant. And while we wait for our food—luckily, it takes a while—we interview the eloquent and friendly archbishop.

"Prevost met all the requirements" of the profile drawn up by the cardinals at the general congregations, the archbishop of Chicago tells us, while discussing the conclave without revealing its secrets. "I think the qualities the cardinals saw in him—at least the ones I considered important to know if he was the right person—were, first of all, as I said, that he's a tireless worker, that he speaks several languages, that he understands different cultures. He's lived on three continents. He's

---

30. "Homily of the Holy Father Leo XIV in the Crypt of Saint Peter's Basilica," May 11, 2025, www.vatican.va.

31. "Pope Leo XIV May Call for a Fix to the U.S.' 'broken immigration system': Cupich," May 11, 2025, www.abcnews.go.com.

a pastor and has a strong record of administration, as he demonstrated while serving as prior general of the Augustinians. Those are some of the qualities I think the cardinals identified when talking with each other, either at the general congregations or afterward, and that were important for us moving forward," he says. "It was also very clear that we wanted someone to continue the work of Pope Francis. There was no interest in moving away from that or going in another direction. There was a great appreciation for Pope Francis that we all brought to our conversations."[32]

Asked about the reaction in Chicago, the city where Leo XIV was born in 1955, Cupich reports that everyone is "very excited," adding, "I have received messages from several political leaders and other people in the city. My team told me that the churches were packed this weekend; people came to Mass because they wanted to hear him mentioned in the Eucharistic Prayer for the first time. So it was—and continues to be—very exciting."

The cardinal, considered one of Prevost's "king-makers" (election strategists), says he has known him for about six years since he was appointed, like Prevost, to the Dicastery for Bishops. "And we worked together there, but even more closely in the last two years, when he became prefect. So it's a relationship that has developed over time in these last six years," he says.

What was his reaction at seeing that the conclave was electing him? "I couldn't see him from where I was sitting; he was at the other end. Others could see him. Cardinal Tobin, when casting his vote, commented that he saw him with his head in his hands. I didn't look at him or any of the candidates because I didn't want to make them uncomfortable."

When Betta mentions the great paradox implicit in the fact that, while during the twelve years and thirty-nine days of Francis's papacy, many of the harshest attacks came precisely from the ultra-conservative wing of the United States, we now have an American pope, and asks whether he believes Leo will be able to calm this polarization of the Church in his country, Cupich sets the record straight.

"First of all, I don't think it was Pope Francis's responsibility to calm people down. It's not up to any pope to calm others down, be-

---

32. Gerard O'Connell, "Interview: Chicago's Cardinal Cupich on Why the Cardinals Chose Pope Leo XIV," *America*, May 11, 2025.

cause people will take their positions no matter what a pope does; they already have their ideas. So I wouldn't put that burden on the new pope. There's nothing Pope Francis did wrong to justify that opposition. People had their own agenda. And now we'll see if those people will continue to oppose the reforms Francis initiated. What I did notice, listening to commentators of different stripes—both right and left—is that they are willing to give the new pope some leeway. I'm glad about that. But I wouldn't be surprised if they criticize some of his decisions, especially if he doesn't radically distance himself from Pope Francis, which I don't think will happen," he says.

What does he think about some attacks from right-wing groups accusing Prevost of mishandling certain abuse cases? "Before the conclave, we were already hearing people say things about certain candidates, without any proof. And everything I have seen about how he has handled these issues, whether in Rome or in Peru, shows me that he is committed to creating safe environments for minors and promoting healing. When he has faced cases, he has done the right thing: he's visited the victims, removed the priest, initiated an investigation, informed the police, and notified Rome. Those are the steps required by *Vos estis lux mundis* and also by the statute we have in the United States, which many other countries have adopted. So, based on what I have seen, he has followed all the correct procedures. And those who make these accusations present no evidence," he answers without hesitation, calling all of this fake news.

What kind of relationship does he think Pope Leo XIV will have with Donald Trump? "I think he will treat him with respect, like any elected leader of a country. He will do that with all leaders, because he wants to build bridges. I think he will speak his mind—as Pope Francis did—but he will continue the agenda that Francis promoted and that the Holy See has maintained for decades. We have the oldest diplomatic corps in the world. We know how to do diplomacy. And I think he will rely on the professionals at the Vatican Secretariat of State to guide him in those conversations."

Asked if it's an advantage to have a Pope who speaks English and doesn't need interpreters, he clarifies that, in truth, "another advantage is having an American who speaks as an American to the American people. It's an opportunity for the Church to have a new platform from which to speak about the social Gospel, perhaps in a way that Catholics in the United States have not heard before. And that will give him the opportunity to present the Gospel in a new way, which I hope touches hearts and minds."

Does he think that, as an American, he will be able to attract the money needed in the Vatican, given the Holy See's worrying deficit situation? "I think we need to make sure we don't treat the United States like an ATM from which you can withdraw money. Whoever the pope is, he needs to call on all Catholics, regardless of their income level or country, to join this effort. And I think he's capable of doing that. But there also needs to be transparency and accountability, something that has always been important to donors. So the ideal would be for everyone to participate. The United States will certainly have an important role, but," he adds, "I hope everyone will join in."

Asked whether he thinks he'll travel soon to the United States, the cardinal remains somewhat skeptical. "I would love for him, if he visits the United States, to have his first stop be Chicago. Even so, I think he is aware of the need to stay in Rome to deal with very serious issues. He will travel, yes, but first he will have to address the most urgent reform issues. That will be a priority before traveling."

And of all those issues, which does he find most worrying? "I think it is the ongoing reform of the Curia, which includes finances, but also everything related to personnel, retirement funds, the number of employees in Vatican offices.... Also the management of the Holy See's assets. We know there is room for improvement there. And he, Leo XIV, has the ability to surround himself with the right people to carry it forward."

BETTA RECOUNTS AT LUNCH that the night of Leo's election she stayed up past 3 AM reading articles that had appeared in *La Nación*.[33] They reveal the relationship Robert Francis Prevost had with Argentina. He traveled there at least three times as prior general of the Augustinians and met his papal predecessor, who was then the archbishop of Buenos Aires. Once, when he traveled for a conference on the founder of his order, he even concelebrated Mass with him at the Buenos Aires

---

33. "Los días del nuevo papa en la Argentina y las misas a las que asistió en Buenos Aires y La Plata," *La Nación*, May 8, 2025.

Church of St. Augustine in 2006. The photo of that Mass, in which the two future popes—much younger—appear together, is extraordinary!

The person who discloses all this is the auxiliary bishop of La Plata, Alberto Bochatey, an Augustinian priest the same age as Prevost, an old friend who lived with him at the Agustinianum—the headquarters of the Order of Saint Augustine, just meters from the Vatican—while they were studying, thirty years ago. When Bochatey, who lived in Rome for sixteen years, was appointed bishop by Benedict XVI in December 2012—one of Joseph Ratzinger's last appointments —Prevost, then superior of the order, traveled to Argentina to accompany him at his episcopal ordination on March 9, 2013. By then, the See of Peter was vacant: the German pope had resigned, and the conclave was about to elect Jorge Bergoglio, the archbishop of Buenos Aires, who had already taken note of the Augustinian missionary in Peru during his visits to the capital as superior of the order. As he acknowledges in the aforementioned video from the Peruvian Episcopal Conference,[34] on those youthful trips to Buenos Aires, Prevost had had disagreements with Bergoglio—so much so that he confessed that when Bergoglio was elected pope in 2013, he had thought he would never become a bishop.

What were their differences? "These are the tensions that always exist," Bochatey explains to Betta in an interview in which he emphasizes that, beyond the disagreements, Bergoglio clearly had his eye on Prevost.[35]

"They met afterward, and Francis discovered him, let's say, as a personality. He made him a bishop in 2014, then brought him to Rome and made him a cardinal. I remember that shortly after Pope Francis made Robert a bishop in Peru (Chiclayo), I came to Rome and said, 'Thank you for appointing another Augustinian bishop, and besides, you weren't wrong because Robert is fantastic.' And Francis looked at me with one of his looks and praised him highly, telling me he was an exceptional man and that he would do very well in Peru," he recalls. "Francis gave him two of those complicated dioceses in

---

34. Conferencia Episcopal Peruana, "Papa León XIV (Robert Prevost) recibe la Medalla 'Santo Toribio de Mogrovejo' del Episcopado Peruano," youtube.com, May 10, 2025.

35. Elisabetta Piqué, "El gran desafío es que la gente acepte que es León XIV y no Francisco II," *La Nación*, May 20, 2025.

Peru to administer, and after having done so, he first made him a member of the Dicastery for Bishops, then brought him in as prefect, made him a cardinal, and made him cardinal-bishop, the top shelf. It is like he was pointing to him in a way. He was one of the cardinals he saw with hope, I think."

What was Prevost like when he met him? "He was always the best in his studies, always brilliant. When we were students here in Rome, he had already spent a year as a missionary in Peru. We were already priests, so we were around thirty years old. And we saw that he was a special man who was going to make it big because he was studious, a good listener, a good companion, and a good athlete. He did well in everything he took on. He was one of those classmates who stood out, and he was also a good friend: you could chat with him, go out for pizza, too. In other words, he was a normal guy, not boring just because he was serious or a man of few words. No, not at all. In other words, he's a very balanced, thoughtful man who knows how to command."

Bochatey began to cry like a baby when his Augustinian brother was elected pope. What does he dream of Leo XIV doing now? "I think he will undoubtedly follow the main lines proposed by Francis, who set the Church on a path necessary for the twenty-first century, which is a bit like what he said, taking the name of Leo XIV from Leo XIII, who was the one who brought the world into the twentieth century, into modernity. So, the dream is that he can continue pushing into the twenty-first century, with the certainty that he has already lived this [style of] Church.

"In what sense? When Francis spoke to us about an outgoing Church, he, Robert, had already left his native United States and spent twenty years as a missionary in Peru. When Francis said that the poor must be at the center, Robert had already argued with Fujimori and denounced Trump's policies, and he was with the poorest of the poor in Peru. When Francis spoke to us about the synodal Church, Prevost had already for years been a promoter of dialogue, of joint journeys within the Order of Saint Augustine, which involves sitting down to listen in meetings, drafting documents together. All of this was an immense experience: he already lived a synodal life within the Order. I know there are several characteristics that Francis proposed to the world that, when you look at the life of Leo XIV, he was already living them. He understood. And I think he will continue like this, evidently adding his own style, his own attitude, as the Spanish would say, since he is a more serene man. We won't see him drinking *mate* in the plaza; he will be less disruptive, but that doesn't mean he will go backwards."

For Bochatey, the pope's great challenge now will be, as a Church, to "ground Francis's ideas more deeply. Francis opened many fronts, opened many initiatives, the entire synodal path, which is a great explosion, but it must be grounded. There are still many people who don't fully understand how it's done or where all this is leading. In addition, there is the whole issue of how to organize or work for peace in the world, plus other issues to be dealt with now, such as artificial intelligence. These are very big challenges, but I think the great challenge is also for people to accept that he is Leo XIV and not Francis II. But he has his personality, his style, and great respect and affection for Francis. We mustn't forget that over the last two years he worked hand-in-hand with Francis. They met every Saturday, talking about bishops, of all things. This is a key issue in the life and governance of the Church. And between one thing and another, I'm sure they exchanged ideas and talked about many other topics, beyond the technical aspects of episcopal affairs. And Francis gave him tremendous support. He always considered him one of his hopes."

WE RETURN HOME AND, without stopping for a minute, we write up the interview with Cardinal Cupich, which is very juicy and which we will publish immediately in our respective media outlets in Buenos Aires and New York.

Betta goes to the supermarket with Irene, who wants to buy Parmigiano Reggiano and mortadella to take to Manuel. Irene was supposed to return to Madrid today, but we convinced her to change her ticket and stay an extra day so as not to miss tomorrow's audience with Leo and the four thousand journalists accredited for the conclave, which will be another historic event.

We have a farewell dinner with her, and enjoy the usual Sunday pizzas we pick up at Monte Carlo. Cristina, who will leave for Buenos Aires tomorrow, also joins us for the farewell dinner.

MAY 12, MONDAY [GERRY]
*Meeting the Press*

WE ALL GET UP EARLY. We have to be on time for Pope Leo's audience with the thousands of journalists from around the world who have come to Rome to cover his election.

We—Betta, Juan Pablo, Irene and I—take a bus because there are no taxis at the Piazza San Pantaleo stop. There are long lines to go through security at the Vatican, but luckily there's a special line for those with permanent accreditation from the Holy See Press Office.

The "Pope of the Americas" arrives at 11 AM at the immense Paul VI Hall—also called the Nervi Hall, named after the famous Italian architect Pier Luigi Nervi, who designed it in the 1960s—and is warmly applauded by the three thousand media professionals still in Rome. Many others have returned to their countries.

Once the applause ends, he greets everyone, saying: "Good morning, and thank you very much for this wonderful welcome!

"They say that when you applaud at the beginning, it doesn't mean much. But if you're still awake at the end and still want to applaud, I'm very grateful," he adds in English, breaking the ice and provoking laughter and more applause.

Then, he reads the speech he has prepared in Italian—while an English translation is displayed on large screens in the room. He begins by thanking media representatives from around the world "for the work they have done and are doing in this time, which for the Church is essentially a time of grace."[36]

He then evokes the Sermon on the Mount, where Jesus proclaims "those who work for peace" blessed, a challenge that directly addresses journalism.

"This is a Beatitude that challenges all of us, but it is particularly relevant to you, calling each one of you to strive for a different kind of communication, one that does not seek consensus at all costs, does not use aggressive words, does not follow the culture of competition

---

36. Address of the Holy Father Leo XIV to Representatives of the Media, May 12, 2025, www.vatican.va.

and never separates the search for truth from the love with which we must humbly seek it.

"Peace begins with each one of us: in the way we look at others, listen to others, and speak about others. In this sense, the way we communicate is of fundamental importance: we must say 'no' to the war of words and images, we must reject the paradigm of war.

"Let me, therefore, reiterate today the Church's solidarity with journalists who are imprisoned for seeking to report the truth, and with these words I also ask for the release of these imprisoned journalists. The Church recognizes in these witnesses—I am thinking of those who report on war even at the cost of their lives—the courage of those who defend dignity, justice, and the right of people to be informed, because only informed individuals can make free choices. The suffering of these imprisoned journalists challenges the conscience of nations and the international community, calling on all of us to safeguard the precious gift of free speech and of the press," he declares, provoking an eruption of impassioned applause from the journalists, among whom are some who have been threatened for their work.

According to the Committee to Protect Journalists, 361 journalists were in prison in different countries on December 1, 2024, for their media work, and 2,232 were imprisoned between 1992 and 2023,[37] not to mention the 1,633 journalists killed between 1992 and 2024, at least 160 of whom have been killed in the Gaza Strip since October 7, 2023.[38]

Leo refers to the information/media vertigo of the past few days:

"Thank you, dear friends, for your service to the truth. You have been in Rome these past few weeks to report on the Church, its diversity and, at the same time, its unity. You were present during the liturgies of Holy Week and then reported on the sorrow felt over the death of Pope Francis, which nevertheless took place in the light of Easter. That same Easter faith drew us into the spirit of the conclave, during which you worked long and tiring days. Yet, even on this occasion, you managed to recount the beauty of Christ's love that unites and makes us one people, guided by the Good Shepherd."

---

37. Ann Fleck, "Number of Jailed Journalists Remains High," April 25, 2025, www.statista.com.

38. Brit McDandless Farmer, "Record Number of Journalists Dead in Gaza War," 60 Minutes Overtime, www.cbsnews.com, January 12, 2025.

The pope goes on to note that "We are living in times that are both difficult to navigate and to recount" and says, "They present a challenge for all of us, but it is one that we should not run away from. On the contrary, they demand that each one of us, in our different roles and services, never give in to mediocrity."

He tells the journalists, "The Church must face the challenges posed by the times. In the same way, communication and journalism do not exist outside of time and history. Saint Augustine reminded of this when he said, 'Let us live well and the times will be good. We are the times.'

"Thank you, therefore, for what you have done to move beyond the stereotypes and clichés through which we often interpret Christian life and the life of the Church itself. Thank you because you have captured the essence of who we are and conveyed it to the whole world through every form of media possible," he says.

He alerts them to the fact that "today, one of the most important challenges is to promote communication that can bring us out of the 'Tower of Babel' in which we sometimes find ourselves, out of the confusion of loveless language that is often ideological or partisan." He tells them, "Therefore, your service, with the words you use and the style you adopt, is crucial. As you know, communication is not only the transmission of information, but it is also the creation of a culture, of human and digital environments that become spaces for dialogue and discussion."

He notes that "In looking at how technology is developing, this mission becomes ever more necessary" and adds, "I am thinking in particular of artificial intelligence, with its immense potential, which nevertheless requires responsibility and discernment in order to ensure that it can be used for the good of all, so that it can benefit all of humanity."

Addressing the media personnel as "dear friends," he says, "We will get to know each other better over time. We have experienced—we can say together—truly special days. We have shared them through every form of media: TV, radio, internet, and social media. I sincerely hope that each of us can say that these days unveiled a little bit of the mystery of our humanity and left us with a desire for love and peace."

The pope closes by quoting again the invitation that Pope Francis made in his last message for this year's Day of Social Communications: "Let us disarm communication of all prejudice and resentment, fanaticism and even hatred; let us free it from aggression. We do not need loud, forceful communication, but rather communication that is capable of listening and of gathering the voices of the weak who have no voice. Let us disarm words and we will help to disarm the world. Disarmed and disarming communication allows us to share a different view of the world and to act in a manner consistent with our human dignity."

He ends by saying, "Thank you all and may God bless you!"

Then he imparts a solemn blessing, in Latin to all those present, marking a difference with Francis, who, in that first audience with journalists on March 16, 2013, had surprised everyone with a silent blessing out of respect for journalists of other religions, or nonbelievers. In that first audience, Francis had not only revealed details of the conclave but had also made headlines by exclaiming, off the cuff, "How I wish for a poor Church for the poor!"[39]

LEO XIV THEN STEPPED FORWARD to greet several of the journalists permanently accredited to the Vatican, including Betta and me, who are seated in the front rows.

In a relaxed moment, when it was our turn, knowing that the new pope is passionate about tennis, Betta humorously suggests playing a doubles match with our friend Eva Fernández, correspondent for the Cope network, who is right next to us. The pontiff smiles and responds modestly: "I play, but I'm not that good."

Other colleagues also take the opportunity to exchange a few words, get an autograph, or sign a baseball (like a good American, he also is a fan of this sport). "I told him I was the little prioress of the Vaticanist community and that we wanted to be his allies and traveling companions, and that if one day he wanted, we would like him to listen to us," says our friend Valentina Alazraki, dean of the Vaticanists press corps, who has covered the Vatican for fifty years and has made 162 papal trips with John Paul II, Benedict XVI, and Francis.

Another colleague and friend of ours, Joshua McElwee, the Reuters correspondent, wore a Chicago Blackhawks ice-hockey-team

---

39. Audience with Representatives of the Communications Media, "Address of the Holy Father Pope Francis," March 16, 2013, www.vatican.va.

cap as he greeted the pope, and told him that he too is from the Windy City and with his family had lived just a ten-minute car-drive away from where Prevost's family lived.

In response to questions from some colleagues, Leo confirms that he wishes to make the trip to Turkey that Pope Francis would have liked to have made to commemorate the seventeen-hundredth anniversary of the Council of Nicaea. "Yes, we are preparing for it," he says. He dismisses, however, the possibility of making a trip to his mother country, the United States, "soon." But he does not rule out a trip to his adopted country, Peru. When a Peruvian journalist he knows well, Paola Ugaz, gives him a colorful Andean alpaca scarf woven by women from a very poor community, he puts it on immediately—to the delight of the photographers. Leo bids her farewell, saying, "Expect to hear from me soon in Peru."

"I'm learning," the new Pope humbly comments, admitting that he doesn't quite know who to pass things to when someone gives him something or an envelope. And after shaking hands and receiving a standing ovation, he leaves with a big smile, a brisk walk, and in very good physical shape.

ELISABETTA QUICKLY RETURNS to the Press Room to write a report on that first audience with us, the communicators.

When she goes to buy a small bottle of water from a vending machine in the back of the room, she runs into a French journalist we have known for decades, who surprises her with the question: "Did the pope thank you for the favor you did for him?"

Clearly he is referring to her April 30 article in which she reported on Parolin's weaknesses, which had a significant impact. Betta replies that, in the brief exchange with Leo, she merely suggested they play doubles tennis.

And the colleague goes further: "You know, I was with Parolin yesterday, and he told me that he is feeling deeply hurt."

"Look, I did my journalistic work," Betta replies.

I too receive a rebuke from an Italian friend and colleague for our articles on Cardinal Stella and Parolin: "You two influenced the conclave," he charged. Like Betta, I respond that we did our work honestly, and said it was Stella, not we, who damaged Parolin.

CHANGING THE SUBJECT, journalists were not aware that before this audience with the media, the pope had privately received Egyptian judge Mohamed Abdelsalam, secretary general of the Muslim Council of Elders that is chaired by the Grand Imam of Al-Azhar.

Judge Abdelsalam, whom we know well, thus becomes the first Muslim leader to be received by the new pope. He told me later that the pope confirmed his intention to continue Pope Francis's good relations with Muslims and made clear his support for the "Document on Human Fraternity for World Peace and Living Together," which Pope Francis and the Grand Imam of Al-Azhar wrote together and presented in Abu Dhabi on February 4, 2019. No pope in history had forged such a close relationship with Muslims as the Argentine Pope.

The judge told me he had urged Pope Leo to contact the Grand Imam of Al-Azhar, Ahmed el-Tayeb, and provided him with his phone number. The Grand Imam is considered by most Muslims to be the highest authority on Sunni Islamic thought and jurisprudence. Sunnis represent about 85 percent of the world's Muslim population.

The judge also told me that Leo called the Grand Imam two days later, and in that conversation, he said, he advocated the need for ethics in artificial intelligence and was pleased to see Leo's great receptiveness. The two religious leaders also agreed to continue along the path of the Document on Human Fraternity.

He added that they discussed the inhumane situation in Gaza and the need to do something to resolve it.

Judge Abdelsalam has been a close advisor to the Grand Imam of Al-Azhar for many years and represented him at Pope Francis's funeral. He did the same at the inaugural Mass, as the Grand Imam is unable to travel because of health problems. However, the Grand Imam sent a message of condolences to the Vatican on the passing of his friend, the pope, with whom he had met on numerous occasions. He also sent a message of congratulations to Leo on his election as pope. Elisabetta and I have known the judge for many years, and through him we also had a private meeting with the Grand Imam in October 2018. When I met the judge on May 19, 2025, the afternoon of the day after the inauguration of Pope Leo, he told me that he had a second, brief visit with Leo that morning, when the pope received two hundred representatives of other Christian denominations and major world religions, including Judaism and Islam.

AROUND MIDDAY, I record a video podcast[40] discussing the papal audience with the media and the first days of this new papacy with Sebastian Gomes, a Canadian and director of multimedia operations at *America* magazine; Ashley McKinless, executive editor; and the invaluable production assistance of Kevin Christopher Robles. It is the last in a series of podcasts we have been doing, as they return to New York tomorrow. Irene has already departed this afternoon.

We meet with Betta—who is scheduled to appear on LN+ with María Laura Santillán—at the Jesuit Curia, where we interview Argentine Cardinal Ángel Rossi, archbishop of Córdoba. He says he suggested to Leo that he travel to Argentina, Francis's unfinished business. "When we chatted a bit during some nice, short encounters, of course I suggested a trip to León XIV. 'You know we're waiting for you in Córdoba, in my case, and in Argentina,' I told him, and he replied, 'I'll keep that in mind.'"

The pontiff confirms that he will travel to Argentina in 2026, when he receives Argentine President Javier Milei in audience on June 7.[41] During that trip, he is also expected to visit Uruguay and, of course, his adopted country, Peru.

Always affable, Rossi confidently expresses his satisfaction with the outcome of the conclave. "Pope Leo is the confirmation of a gift from God because I truly believe this is the man the Church needs, the world needs at this moment, as far as one can see. We are not infallible, but one already realizes that he is a gift. And I say this out of the affection I have had, and still have, for our Francis, who, let's say, is buried, but not in our hearts. There are many who are happy and continue to bury him, but for us, he is alive," he says, alluding to those conservative sectors who would have preferred a pontiff who would put a stop to the processes initiated by the Argentine pope.

"Pope Leo, without in any way intending to imitate Francis, which would be bad because he's not a carbon copy; he is someone who follows that path. It would have been very sad to have squandered all the paths opened by Pope Francis. And I believe that in that sense, this Pope Leo respects the path. He follows that same path.

---

40. "What Pope Leo's First Days Tell Us about His Priorities," podcast, www.youtube.com, May 12, 2025.

41. Elisabetta Piqué, "Javier Milei se reunió por 45 minutos con el papa León XIV," *La Nación*, June 7, 2025.

Like many other cardinals, Rossi had met Prevost at the two sessions of the Synod of Synodality, in October 2023 and 2024.

"He didn't sit at the tables for English speakers, but at those for Spanish speakers. So, in the two years, we shared the table several times," Rossi says. "What qualities did I see in him? I noticed a silent man, not a mute one, a listener and very articulate person who didn't waste words. I noticed a good man in the deepest sense of the word, not in the disdainful sense, and at the same time, not at all naive in the bad sense of the word, but someone with a universal perspective. He is the son of immigrants, so he knows the reality of migrants and has had his feet in the mud. That's how he loved his people, and his people loved him, which is also very significant."

Rossi reveals that last Saturday he was praying at Saint Mary Major, where Francis's tomb is located, when Leo XIV suddenly appeared, unannounced. Then he noticed how, despite his shy appearance, the new pope immediately empathized with the people. "I was struck, seeing the faces of the people, the closeness, and the unforced rapport that emerged. Just as you often notice when that rapport is forced in some priests, some leaders of any kind. It seemed very natural to me, which is no small feat," he comments.

When Betta asks him about those on social media who say Leo is not a continuation of Francis, whether because he offered his blessing in Latin, or because he will probably live in the Apostolic Palace, or because he wore a red cape, Rossi answers using one of his very amusing metaphors. "Perhaps, on the outside, in certain ways he has a more 'traditional' manner, but he's not a dinosaur, nor does he seek to go backwards. And when you listen to him, when he speaks and expresses himself very clearly without losing his originality, he doesn't depart from the essence of Francis. That essence, it seems to me, is within him, it is in his words, which is very obvious...not to mention the fact that he refers to Pope Francis several times a day. And it does seem to me that his words and his actions speak volumes."

WE DINE WITH OUR FRIEND, Inés San Martín, a Vatican expert and former Crux correspondent who works for the Pontifical Mission Societies in the United States. She was also covering the conclave. She is about to return to her home in Florida, and we didn't get to see each other properly during the conclave. We met this morning at Leo's audience with journalists, and she, a tennis enthusiast also, suggested organizing a charity tennis match to benefit the missions.

We eat at Baires, the classic Argentine restaurant in Rome on Corso Rinascimento, behind Piazza Navona, which Betta and Inés love. Juan Pablo joins us. We have empanadas, *provoleta*, and *morcilla* as a starter, followed by a spectacular Argentine beef dish, all washed down with Argentine Malbec wine.

MAY 13, TUESDAY [BETTA]
@*Pontifex*

FIRST NIGHT I'VE SLEPT! I still get up early to go rowing on the Tiber, my passion and morning sporting routine for several years now, which I've been forced to abandon recently.... What a pleasure to be rowing again!

Gerry and I are seriously starting to think we have enough material to write a book. We contact our old publishers, and they immediately express interest. Incredibly, Irene was right. I call my brothers, Enrico and Giacomo, who have recently been abandoned—we haven't even had time to breathe—and tell them about the joint book project. Will it be grounds for divorce?

Belatedly, I complete last month's accounts for the newspaper—almost everything has been put on hold—and then I start writing up an interview with a cardinal, a task that I've been putting aside.

We have lunch with our kids Juan Pablo and Carolina, something we haven't done in weeks!

LEO XIV ALSO GOES TO LUNCH with his "family." Shortly before noon, and as he often did until recently, he appears at Via Paolo VI 25, the Augustinian headquarters, just meters from Bernini's famous colonnade, in what becomes a historic private visit. According to Vatican News, after presiding over a Mass that he concelebrated with his Augustinian brothers on the very day the Church commemorates the

Blessed Virgin Mary of Fatima, he has lunch with them, something he used to do almost daily as a cardinal.

Leo feels at home there, and it's only natural. He lived in the General Curia of the Augustinians for twelve years, from 2001 to 2013, the two consecutive terms during which he was prior general.

"He used to come here regularly to eat, and he wanted to thank the community for it. He came to celebrate the Eucharist and eat with us. It was a family visit, a thanksgiving visit. We spent very familiar and pleasant moments together. He knows everyone, and we all know him, and that's why it's so beautiful," the current prior general, Spanish Father Alejandro Moral, tells Vatican media. "Other people also came to greet him, the employees who work with us, the cooks," Moral explains, emphasizing that it was an unforgettable moment of conviviality.

"It was his first visit as pope, and we were all very happy."

What did he tell them? "That we should always be close to one another, living, as Saint Augustine asks, in communion," he answers.

"It was difficult for us to recognize him as pope, because his proximity, his closeness, made us feel like he was still Father Robert," comments Father Gabriele Pedicino, prior provincial of the Augustinians of Italy. Pedicino emphasizes that the new pope even told them how he felt about being elected. "Until now, we've told journalists about the Augustinians' feelings, and now we've also heard a bit about the pope's. But out of respect, we're keeping what he said as a gift he wanted to give only to his brothers, because it's true that he's our brother, but now he's the pope."

Monsignor Lizardo Estrada Herrera, also a member of the Augustinian family, auxiliary bishop of Cuzco, Peru, and secretary general of CELAM (Latin American and Caribbean Episcopal Council), also expresses his gratitude for the visit and for this "normal moment of community life, because he always came here and was with this community," although "now he is the Holy Father."

Estrada reveals that, like his predecessor, the new pontiff also asked them to pray for him. "Pope Leo XIV asked us for prayers, thanked us, and encouraged us to continue being good Augustinians, to make Saint Augustine known. We are grateful to have experienced this moment of joy. We greatly enjoyed being with him."

Needless to say, when Leo left the Curia, news of his visit to his "family" having already spread like wildfire, hundreds of people had gathered outside to take photos, greet him, and cheer him with cries of "Long live the Pope!"

ANOTHER SURPRISE OF THE DAY is that the chief rabbi of Rome and the American Jewish Committee (AJC) issued a press release revealing that Pope Leo had sent personal messages on May 8, the day of his election, pledging to strengthen good relations between the Catholic Church and the Jewish community. The news was also published on the website of the United States Conference of Catholic Bishops.[42]

The Jewish community of Rome released a statement saying that following Pope Leo's election at last week's conclave he sent a message to Rome's chief rabbi, Riccardo Di Segni, pledging to strengthen ties between the Catholic Church and Jews. According to ANSA, Leo informed Di Segni of his election and pledged to "continue and strengthen the Church's dialogue and cooperation with the Jewish people in the spirit of the Second Vatican Council's declaration *Nostra Aetate*." It added that the rabbi "received with satisfaction and gratitude the words addressed to him by the new pope" and announced that he would attend Leo's investiture on May 18.

The AJC published a similar statement on its X account, according to which Pope Leo XIV on May 8 sent virtually the same message to Rabbi Noam Marans, AJC's director of interreligious affairs, which read: "Trusting in the help of the Almighty, I pledge to continue and strengthen the Church's dialogue and cooperation with the Jewish people, in the spirit of the Second Vatican Council's declaration *Nostra Aetate*." The AJC published a copy of the letter, but it was not signed.

These messages are not found on the Vatican website, which archives all of Leo XIV's letters, speeches, and homilies, as of July 7, 2025. This is strange; who sent them?

The letters seem to indicate that the Vatican wants to strengthen relations with the Jewish community following recent tensions, after Israeli Prime Minister Benjamin Netanyahu observed three days of silence before his office conveyed Israel's condolences to the Catholic world over the death of Pope Francis. Netanyahu then decided to send a low-level delegation to the Argentine pope's funeral, led by Israel's ambassador to the Holy See, Yaron Sideman. This low-level representation was seen as a reaction by the Israeli government to Pope Francis's strong denunciation of the dramatic situation in Gaza, where more than 50,000 Palestinians, including more than 16,000 children—and the number is rising—have been killed in Israel's retaliation for

---

42. Justin McLellen, "Pope Pledges Strengthened Dialogue with Jewish Community," usccbnews.org/news, May 13, 2025.

the brutal Hamas attack of October 7, 2023, which killed some 1,200 Israelis and took 250 hostages. In interviews with major Italian newspapers Israel's ambassador to the Holy See attempted to downplay his government's silence and to highlight the fact that he was representing the State of Israel at the funeral on Shabbat, the Jewish holy day of rest.[43]

AWARE OF THE HORROR EXPERIENCED in Gaza, an area so devastated by bombing that it has become unlivable and the International Red Cross has described it as "a living hell," Pope Francis called daily, while he had the strength to do so, the Argentine priest Gabriel Romanelli, pastor of the only Catholic church in the Strip.

At the head of the Church of the Holy Family, Father Romanelli—of the Institute of the Incarnate Word, born in Villa Luro, Buenos Aires, fifty-five years ago and a resident of the Middle East for almost three decades—told me a few days ago that, to remember those moving calls and the encouragement that Pope Francis gave his community until the end, he began ringing the bells every day at 8:00 PM, the hour at which they received that joy.[44]

"We ring the bells with a hymn to the Virgin, since he chose to rest in the Church of Saint Mary Major in Rome," he told me in a telephone conversation. "There is no special prayer; some make the sign of the cross, as is customary here in the Middle East, while others continue with their activities. However, everyone knows that we are remembering the pope's call. It is a way to remember him, to pray for him, and also to keep his words and his encouragement alive. For more than a year and a half, more than five hundred times, he gave us his support, asking us to protect the children, to help everyone, thanking us for our prayers and blessing us. He thanked us for the service provided to the thousands of civilians in the area."[45]

---

43. Maurizio Caprara, "Da Israele c'è grande rispetto. Papa Francesco era contro l'antisemitismo," *Corriere della Serra,* April 25, 2025.

44. Elisabetta Piqué on X, "Las campanas de la parroquia de #Gaza suenan ahora todos los días a las 8 de la noche (7 de Italia) para recordar los llamados diarios que durante un año y medio les hizo el papa Francisco," April 28, 2025.

45. Elisabetta Piqué, "El último cumpleaños del Papa, celebrado en Gaza a través de una conmovedora llamada," *La Nación,* April 28, 2025.

On the grounds of the only Catholic church in the Palestinian enclave, located in the Zeitun neighborhood—the oldest in the Strip, now surrounded by rubble and ruins—about five hundred people have been sheltering since October 7, 2023, including the elderly and children, some disabled and sick people, and not only Christians but also Muslims.

I was in that church at the end of 2012, during one of the many wars I covered in Gaza. I remember that when I traveled to Argentina for Christmas and, as always, Gerry and I went to lunch with Father Jorge at the archbishopric, I had told him about that church—then headed by another Argentine priest—where the shock wave of the bombing had blown out the church windows. There, in that church property, they gave shelter and assistance to their neighbors, sharing bread, water, and food with the neighborhood. I remember having shown him photos and videos of a Mass celebrated in Arabic and also photos of the horror and the destruction—minimal in comparison to the present situation—of that war in the Palestinian enclave.

When was Pope Francis's last call to Gaza? "He called us the last time on Holy Saturday. We all knew that 'the Pope's hour,' as we called it here, was 8 PM in Gaza, 7 PM in Rome, but that day Father Yussef sent him a message saying, 'Holy Father, look, we'll be in church at 8 PM. We'll be at the Easter Vigil, which is long, about three hours.' And then that last time he called earlier, at 7:20 PM. We were already in church praying the rosary when Father Yussef's phone rang. This time it wasn't a video call, but a simple, brief but clear call. He asked us how we were, thanked us for our prayers, as always, asked about the children and everyone, and said, 'I'm praying for you and sending you my blessing.' Father Yussef greeted him, and I did too, along with Sister Maravillas de Jesús and some families who were present. And that was the last call.

"He didn't call us on Easter Sunday, but we had seen online that he was in St. Peter's Square and had delivered this very consistent message calling for peace for all, an end to the war, and with all the conditions, the release of the hostages, the consistent entry of humanitarian aid, peace for both Palestinians and Israelis—in other words, the Easter message. And he didn't call us that Sunday, but we said, well, he is probably tired, he won't be able to. And so, on Monday, the sad news came, which we received right in the Orthodox Church. We had gone to greet the Greek Orthodox community for Easter, and we did not have internet here, but they did. They gave us the news. People started offering their condolences, the Orthodox, the Catholics, the Muslim neighbors in the neighborhood," he said.

Do they feel like orphans now? "People are very sad, very moved, and at the same time very comforted. They see the death of Francis around [the feast of] the Resurrection, during the Octave of Easter, as a sign of divine predilection, of divine goodness. It's a mixture of sadness and a kind of serenity. In short, everyone knows that the Church is always close to those in need and that, as cardinal patriarch of Jerusalem Pierbattista Pizzaballa has often stated, the Church will always be there for her children to help them. On the one hand, yes, the pope's voice at eight o'clock at night will not be heard, but his legacy remains."

On July 17, 2025, in an Israeli attack on his church, later ruled an accident, three people were killed and Father Romanelli's leg was slightly injured. "Certainly nothing major," he later told me,[46] always very measured, when he specified that among the most seriously injured was "a young man who wants to consecrate himself to God; he had been preparing for several years. He was supposed to go to Italy to attend the IVE seminary in 2023, but the war started and he wasn't able to leave." Commenting on the famine, he said that what was happening in Gaza was "something truly inhuman."

CONFIRMING THAT, beyond the developments of the transition, the climate of intrigue is an ever-present ingredient in Vatican affairs, Benedict XVI's former private secretary, German Archbishop Georg Gänswein, breaks a silence he has maintained for months with words that do not hide a certain resentment.

"Now that a new phase is beginning, I sense a certain diffuse relief. The era of arbitrariness is over. We can count on a papacy that can guarantee stability and that relies on existing structures without overturning or upsetting them," says Gänswein, in an interview with *Corriere della Sera* that may resonate with some.[47]

---

46. Elisabetta Piqué, Gabriel Romanelli, sacerdote argentino en Gaza: "Lo que está sucediendo en la Franja es deshumano," *La Nación*, July 24, 2025.

47. Massimo Franco, "Monsignor Georg Gaenswein: 'È finita la stagione dell'arbitrarietà. Il passato confuso deve essere superato,'" *Corriere della Sera*, May 25, 2025; Elisabetta Piqué, "El exsecretario de Benedicto que tuvo una turbulenta relación con Francisco rompió el silencio," *La Nación*, May 13, 2025.

"When I saw him come out onto the balcony and he had a text in his hand, I said to myself: it has started well. Leo XIV will build bridges like his predecessor, but in a context and with a style different from that of Francis. There are great tensions in the Church today, and there are terrible conflicts outside. I think doctrinal clarity is needed now. The confusion of recent years must be overcome. And the instruments to use are the structures that already exist: the Church's institutions are neither leprosy nor a threat to the pope. They are there to help the pontiffs, who must allow themselves to be helped. You cannot govern alone, distrusting your own institutions," he says, alluding to the Argentine pope's harsh criticism of the Roman Curia.

As is well known, Benedict's former private secretary, a 68-year-old conservative, had a turbulent relationship with Francis, especially after publishing a venomous memoir immediately following the German pope's death. Despite this, Francis had shown great generosity by deciding to send him last year as nuncio to Lithuania, Latvia, and Estonia.

AFTER SEVERAL DAYS OF SILENCE, the pope finally returns to social media this Tuesday. Pope Leo XIV "will continue to maintain an active presence on social media through official papal accounts on X and Instagram," the Vatican Dicastery for Communication reports.[48]

The popes' presence on social media dates back to December 12, 2012, when Pope Benedict XVI launched the @Pontifex account on what was then Twitter; a few months later, it was revived by Pope Francis. On March 19, 2016, the official Instagram account, called @Franciscus, was added.

Pope Leo XIV thus "inherits the legacy of the X @Pontifex accounts used by Pope Francis and, before him, Benedict XVI, which, publishing in nine languages (English, Spanish, Portuguese, Italian, French, German, Polish, Arabic, and Latin), have a total of fifty-two million followers."

The name of the papal X accounts will remain the same: @Pontifex. On Instagram, in continuity with Pope Francis's account, @Franciscus, "the new pope's account is called @Pontifex–Pope Leo XIV, and

---

48. "Pope Leo XIV Will Maintain an Active Social Media Presence," www. vaticannews.va, May13, 2025.

is the only official account of the Holy Father on that platform," the Vatican explained, emphasizing that "the content published on the @Franciscus account will continue to be accessible as an Ad Memoriam commemorative archive."

Pope Francis's activity on social media was significant: a total of some fifty thousand posts, published on the nine @Pontifex accounts and on @Franciscus. The pope communicated almost every day of his pontificate with brief evangelical messages or exhortations for peace, social justice, and care for creation; and he achieved great engagement, especially during difficult times, such as, for example, in 2020, a year of exceptional numbers due to the pandemic, when his messages were viewed twenty-seven billion times.

LEO DEBUTED ON INSTAGRAM with the same words with which he introduced himself to the world on May 8, after his election: "Peace be with you all! This is the first greeting from the risen Christ, the Good Shepherd. I too would like this greeting of peace to enter your hearts, to reach your families, to all people, wherever they are, to all nations, to the whole earth." Tomorrow, he will write the same thing on his X accounts.

Prevost, as cardinal, had an account on X (@drprevost) that he managed by himself. And he used it, as the international media were quick to report soon after his election, pointing to re-tweets of articles. Among these re-tweets was one, on February 13, by Sam Sawyer, SJ, editor-in-chief of *America* Media, on "Pope Francis's letter, JD Vance's '*ordo amoris*' and what the Gospel asks of all of us on immigration."[49]

In other words, Leo XIV knows the world of social media and how to use it, which is a great difference from his predecessor, who always recognized that he was "more than primitive" in this respect. Francis never wanted to have, nor had, a cellular phone, we recall, as Gerry, Juampy, Caro and I have dinner together, late as usual.

---

49. Sam Sawyer, SJ, "Pope Francis' Letter, JD Vance's '*ordo amoris*' and What the Gospel Asks of All of Us on Immigration," *America*, published on February12 and retweeted by Cardinal Prevost on February 13. He also retweeted Kat Armasm National Catholic Reporter online op-ed that said "JD Vance Is Wrong, Jesus Doesn't Ask Us to Rank Our Love for Others," NCRonline, February 1, 2025.

## MAY 14, WEDNESDAY [GERRY]
*Peace a Priority*

On his sixth day as pope, Leo XIV receives in audience the five thousand participants in the Jubilee of the Eastern Churches that are present in war-torn regions of the world such as Ukraine, the Middle East, the Horn of Africa, and India, among several other countries where the Christian minority is persecuted and forced to flee their land.

In the Paul VI Auditorium, one can see the flags of Ukraine, yellow and light blue, but also of Lebanon, Egypt, Iraq, India, Canada, and even one of Jerusalem. Listening attentively are the faithful and leaders of the twenty-three Eastern Churches around the world, which have a membership of eighteen million: Maronites, Italian-Albanians, Chaldeans, Syro-Malabars, Armenians, Copts, Ethiopians, Melkites, Greek Catholics, and others. The pope gives another key speech[50] in which, just as he did when he presented himself to the public after his election, he will reiterate that his top priority will be peace.

He reminds the political leaders conducting the conflicts that "the Holy See is always ready to help bring enemies together, face to face, to talk to one another, so that peoples everywhere may once more find hope and recover the dignity they deserve, the dignity of peace."

"The peoples of our world desire peace," he states. Addressing these leaders he says, "I appeal with all my heart: let us meet, let us talk, let us negotiate! War is never inevitable. Weapons can and must be silenced, for they do not resolve problems but only increase them.

"Those who make history are the peacemakers, not those who sow seeds of suffering. Our neighbors are not first our enemies, but our fellow human beings; not criminals to be hated, but other men and women with whom we can speak. Let us reject the Manichean notions so typical of that mindset of violence that divides the world into those who are good and those who are evil," Leo concludes, drawing vigorous applause.

---

50. Address of the Holy Father Leo XIV to Participants in the Jubilee of Oriental Churches, www.vatican.va, May 14, 2025.

"Let us pray for this peace, which is reconciliation, forgiveness, and the courage to turn the page and start anew," he urges, adding "Who, better than you, can sing a song of hope even amid the abyss of violence? Who, better than you, who have experienced the horrors of war so closely that Pope Francis referred to you as 'martyr Churches.'"

One and a half million Christians have left the Middle East since 2003 due to the war in Iraq. There used to be one and a half million Christians in that country alone when the conflict began; today, the number is estimated at around three hundred thousand, as Iraqi Cardinal Sako has repeatedly reported in the press, and also to his brother cardinals.

We saw the difficulties firsthand when we accompanied Pope Francis on his courageous trip to Iraq in the midst of the pandemic in March 2021 (thanks to which we obtained one of the first available COVID-19 vaccines), to the Holy Land (2014), to Egypt (2017); and before that, with John Paul II to Lebanon in 1997 and to Syria in 2000; and with Benedict XVI to Lebanon in 2012.

"From the Holy Land to Ukraine, from Lebanon to Syria, from the Middle East to Tigray and the Caucasus, how much violence do we see! Rising up from this horror, from the slaughter of so many young people, which ought to provoke outrage because lives are being sacrificed in the name of military conquest, there resounds an appeal: the appeal not so much of the pope, but of Christ himself, who says, 'Peace be with you!' and adds: 'Peace I leave you; my peace I give to you. I do not give it to you as the world gives it,'" Pope Leo exclaims, quoting the words of Jesus, which he also used last Thursday when he presented himself to the world for the first time after his election, on the balcony of St. Peter's Basilica.

"Christ's peace is not the sepulchral silence that reigns after conflict; it is not the fruit of oppression, but rather a gift that is meant for all, a gift that brings new life," he tells them in a speech interrupted many times by applause.

He thanks God for all those who, "in silence, in prayer, in offering, weave threads of peace." Addressing "the Christians—Oriental and Latin—who, especially in the Middle East, persevere and resist in their lands, stronger than the temptation to abandon them," he states that "Christians must be given the opportunity, not just in words, to remain in their lands with all the rights necessary for a secure existence. Please, let us work to achieve this!" he exhorts, evoking more applause.

He prays for them: "May your churches be an example, and may their pastors appropriately promote communion, especially in the Synods of Bishops, so that they may be places of collegiality and authentic co-responsibility." He continues by requesting "transparency in the management of goods" and "a witness of humble and total dedication to the holy People of God, without attachment to honors, worldly powers, and one's own image."

From the beginning of his speech, Leo XIV emphasizes the immense importance of these churches and tells those present, "I am happy to meet you and to dedicate one of the first meetings of my pontificate to the Eastern faithful. You are precious!"

He recalls "the variety of their origins, their glorious history, and the bitter sufferings" that many of their communities have endured or are enduring. He reiterates what Pope Francis said about the Eastern Churches: "They are Churches to be loved: they preserve unique spiritual and wisdom traditions, and have much to tell us about Christian life, synodality, and liturgy." He also mentions the ancient Fathers, the Councils, and monasticism, which he calls "inestimable treasures for the Church."

The new pope mentions Leo XIII (1878–1903), the first pontiff to dedicate a specific document to the dignity of these churches (*Orientalium dignitas*, 1894). He also recalls that John Paul II, in an apostolic letter, affirmed that they have "a unique and privileged role, as the original context of the nascent Church" (*Orientale lumen*, 1995).

Pope Leo XIV highlights that some of their liturgies still use the language of Jesus (Aramaic), and says the concern expressed at the end of the nineteenth century by Leo XIII that all this wealth could be lost remains valid and more relevant than ever. "Today, many Eastern brothers and sisters, including many of you, are forced to flee their native lands due to war, persecution, instability, and poverty, and run the risk, upon reaching the West, of losing not only their homeland but also their religious identity. And so, with the passing of generations, the priceless heritage of the Eastern Churches is lost," he laments.

He reiterates Leo XIII's call to safeguard and promote the Christian East, and specifically asks the Dicastery for the Eastern Churches—headed by the Italian Cardinal Claudio Gugerotti—to help define principles, norms, and guidelines through which Latin pastors can concretely support Eastern Catholics in the diaspora to preserve their living traditions and, with their unique characteristics, enrich the contexts in which they live.

"The Church needs you," Leo XIV assures them, highlighting the great contribution that the Eastern Churches can make, especially through "that sense of mystery, so alive in your liturgies, which involve the total human person."

"You sing the beauty of salvation and inspire wonder at the divine greatness that embraces human smallness!" he affirms. "And how important it is to rediscover, even in the Christian West, the sense of the primacy of God."[51]

After the speech, which is delivered in Italian—but which could be read, translated into English, on the giant screens in the hall—Leo XIV, with a smile, greets the leaders of the various Eastern Churches present in the front row, among whom is Sviatoslav Shevchuk, head of the Ukrainian Greek Catholics (who told us that he was on a "death list" when Russia invaded Ukraine in February 2022).

Then Leo receives various gifts, such as a golden cape, which he at one point places over his white robe, to the joy of the photographers and thousands of attendees, who cheer him on, even shouting "USA! USA! USA!"

After an hour-long audience, the pope leaves the Paul VI Hall, waving to the hundreds of faithful gathered at the barriers along the central corridor, who, cell phones in hand, ask him to bless a rosary or deliver a letter. Amid an atmosphere of euphoria and jubilation for the new pope, he stops only to bless a baby.

---

"IT'S TRUE, WE ARE RESISTING, despite the heavy difficulties," Cardinal Pizzaballa, Latin patriarch of Jerusalem, later comments, highlighting the new pope's gratitude to Christians who refuse to abandon lands as difficult as those of the Middle East. "And it's not just the small community in Gaza that has become one of the symbols of the horrors of war, but also those in the West Bank that are burdened by all kinds of burdens. Visiting the patriarchate's parishes, I certainly notice

---

51. Gerard O'Connell, "Pope Leo XIV Promises Eastern Catholics He Will Work for Peace in Their War-torn Countries," *America*, May 14, 2025; Elisabetta Piqué, "León XIV reiteró que la prioridad de su papado será la paz: 'Haré todo el esfuerzo posible,'" *La Nación*, May 14, 2025.

fatigue, but also a great deal of commitment and desire to move forward," he states. "Of course, Jerusalem is a kind of paradigm of what's happening on the planet from a religious, political, social, and I would say energy perspective.... Peace is sorely missing here, not only in our cities and in everyday life, but also in our thinking."[52]

AT THE SAME AUDIENCE, 36-year-old Peruvian priest Edgard Iván Rimaycun makes his first public appearance as Leo XIV's personal secretary. Although the news of his appointment is not official, the Peruvian priest will be the new pontiff's secretary and can be seen sitting next to him during the audience, according to the EFE news agency.[53]

Rimaycun has long been at Robert Prevost's side in Chiclayo, Peru, where he served as bishop. They later met again at the Vatican when he was appointed by Francis in 2023 as prefect of the Dicastery for Bishops.

In 2006, Rimaycun, then aspiring to become a priest and having entered the Santo Toribio de Mogrovejo Major Seminary in Chiclayo, first met Prevost, whom everyone then called "Padre Roberto." He became his spiritual father and wanted Rimaycun to work with him when he was ordained bishop at the Cathedral of Santa María de Chiclayo. He had already been seen during Pope Leo XIV's first visits outside the Vatican walls, but he had not been present at Monday's audience with journalists. So today was his first official appearance, arriving at the audience with the pope, positioning the microphone correctly, passing him the pages of his speech, and sitting next to him.

Those who knew Cardinal Prevost well say it was clear that the Peruvian priest would continue as secretary during his pontificate, given the strong bond that unites them. Rimaycun, who is originally from Chiclayo, wrote in 2023 when Prevost was ordained cardinal: "Thank you very much, Monsignor Robert Prevost, for everything, for allowing me to work by your side, but above all for your friendship and trust. To my Bishop, my Friend. Safe journey and a big hug!

---

52. Giacomo Gambassi, Cardinale Pizzaballa, "Il futuro della pace passa da Gerusalemme," Avvenire, May 15, 2025.

53. "El secretario de León XIV, el peruano Edgard Iván Rimaycun, hace su primera aparición," www.swissinfo.ch, May 14, 2025.

*Oremus ad invicem*!" After being summoned to Rome, Rimaycun stated: "I left Chiclayo with nostalgia, but with the consolation of knowing that a friend awaits me with whom I will continue working for the good of the Church."

ON THE SIXTH DAY after his election, Leo XIV writes his first tweet, still focused on the theme of peace and with the words he used when he first appeared before the faithful.[54]

His busy schedule includes audiences with American Cardinal Sean O'Malley, archbishop emeritus of Boston; the Spanish Monsignor Fernando Ocáriz Braña, prelate of Opus Dei, and his deputy, the Argentine Mariano Fazio; and Italian Archbishop Salvatore Fisichella, organizer of the current Jubilee 2025, only the second jubilee in history to have been opened by one pontiff and closed by another.[55]

PRIVATELY, AND BECAUSE OF HIS PASSION for tennis, he also receives the Italian number-one tennis player, Yannik Sinner, along with the president of the Italian Tennis Federation, Alberto Binaghi, and their respective families. Just as when the Argentine pope would receive a soccer star, this meeting has a huge impact: in a relaxed setting, Sinner gives him a racket, and the pope jokes about playing at Wimbledon, as seen in the images released. However, the meeting also draws criticism, such as that of Codacons (the Italian consumer protection association), which, in a statement, calls the meeting "inappropriate" because "at a time of war and geopolitical tensions, tennis cannot be the pope's priority." Indeed, the photo with Sinner would end up on the front pages of newspapers around the world the next day, eclipsing his important words about the urgent need to silence the guns.

---

54. Pope Leo XIV on X, "¡La paz esté con todos ustedes!" x.com/Pontifex, May 14, 2025.

55. Gerard O'Connell, "What Is a Jubilee Year? The History and Meaning behind a Centuries-old Tradition," *America,*' February 23, 2025.

MAY 15, THURSDAY [GERRY]
*An Unknown Past*

ALTHOUGH ONLY A WEEK HAS PASSED since his election, it is already clear that Leo XIV has a very different style from that of his Argentine predecessor, who upon being elected had caused a stir with his informality and little adherence to protocol.

In the speeches he delivers at the audiences he inherited from Francis, Leo almost never improvises, but rather adheres rigorously to the prepared text. We see this again this morning when he receives the Christian Brothers Schools—founded by Saint John Baptist de La Salle (1651–1719)—in the Clementine Hall.

In his speech,[56] Leo emphasizes La Salle's ability to respond creatively to the many difficulties of his time and to venture "down new and often unexplored paths." It was this French saint and educator who launched the "pedagogical revolution," which not only meant teaching directed at classes rather than individual students. It also involved, Leo recalls, the adoption of French as the language of instruction instead of Latin, making it accessible to all; Sunday classes, which young people forced to work during the week could also attend; and the participation of families in school programs, according to the principle of the "educational triangle," still valid today.

"All this can but make us think, and it also raises useful questions. What, in the world of youth today, are the most urgent challenges to be faced? What values are to be promoted? What resources can be counted on?" he asks.

"Young people of our time, like those of every age, are a volcano of life, energy, sentiments and ideas. It can be seen from the wonderful things they are able to do, in so many fields. However," he adds, "they also need help in order for this great wealth to grow in harmony, and to overcome what, albeit in a different way from the past, can still hinder their healthy development.

---

56. Address of the Holy Father Leo XIV to the Brothers of the Christian Schools, May 15, 2025, www.vatican.va.

"While, for example, in the seventeenth century the use of the Latin language was an insuperable barrier to communication for many people, today there are other obstacles to be faced." He mentions "the isolation caused by rampant relational models increasingly marked by superficiality, individualism, and emotional instability; the spread of patterns of thought weakened by relativism; and the prevalence of rhythms and lifestyles in which there is not enough room for listening, reflection, and dialogue, at school, in the family, and sometimes among peers themselves, with consequent loneliness."

He describes these as "demanding challenges," and says, "we too, like Saint John Baptist de La Salle, can turn them into springboards to explore ways, develop tools, and adopt new languages to continue to touch the hearts of pupils, helping them and spurring them on to face every obstacle with courage in order to give the best of themselves in life, according to God's plans. In this sense, the attention you pay, in your schools, to the training of teachers and to the creation of educating communities in which the teaching effort is enriched by the contribution of all is commendable. I encourage you to continue along these paths."

His speeches are being scrutinized by Vatican experts who, although it is still too early, are beginning to draw some conclusions.

Our Mexican friend Valentina Alazraki, dean of Vaticanists, shares her thoughts with us:

"The first thing that struck me after his election was his inner freedom, in the sense that it was very difficult to be Francis's successor, because we were all wondering what the new pope would do when he appeared from the central loggia of the basilica, how he would dress, what car he would get into, would he go to Santa Marta or would he return to the Palace—a whole series of symbols that had marked Pope Francis's pontificate. And seeing him appear dressed as his predecessors dressed, that immediately made me think that he is a free man, a man who doesn't feel obligated to imitate, so to speak, or necessarily to follow in the footsteps of his predecessor."

She adds, "And I noticed the same freedom when he didn't go to Santa Marta; he stayed in the apartment he was occupying at the Holy Office the night of his election."

"Since his election," she says, "we've heard many comments from people who want to see in him total continuity with Francis, others who want to see total discontinuity, those who say he's reminiscent of John Paul II, or reminiscent of Benedict XVI, for various reasons, or of

Pope Francis himself. I think that, if he had wanted to follow completely in the footsteps of one of his predecessors, he would have called himself John Paul III, or Benedict XVII, or Francis II," she adds. "But he chose a totally different name, from a pope who is remembered above all for the encyclical *Rerum Novarum*, which was the basis of the Church's social doctrine. So, as far as this social vision is concerned, it's obviously a very broad vision in the wake of Pope Francis's social sensitivity, albeit with different nuances due to different life experiences, because he was a missionary in Peru, in completely abandoned areas, and he has great sensitivity in that sense."

PREPARATIONS ARE IN FULL SWING for next Sunday's inaugural Mass, which will once again transform Rome into the *caput mundi*, the capital of the world, as delegations from around the world will once again be present. This afternoon Betta goes to the Press Office, which now looks empty compared to a week ago.

There, she interviews Paola Ugaz, the Peruvian journalist who earned notice last Monday by placing a colorful Andean alpaca scarf on Pope Leo XIV and smilingly taking a photo with him during his first audience with the international press.

Paola has known "Robert," as she often calls Prevost, since 2018, when he was bishop of Chiclayo, but above all, vice president of the Peruvian Episcopal Conference and president of the commission for victims of abuse. In that position, he quietly helped dozens of survivors of abuse perpetrated by the Sodalitium Vida Cristiana, a conservative Peruvian Catholic religious group that was similar to a cult and had been founded by layman Luis Fernando Figari in 1971. It was investigated and then suppressed by Pope Francis shortly before his death.

Paola, 51, is the author of *Half Monks, Half Soldiers*, written together with Pedro Salinas, a survivor of SVC abuse. The book uncovered that abuse and marked the beginning of the organization's downfall. After writing the book, she and her colleague began receiving threats and even accusations before the Peruvian courts for trumped-up crimes. But "Robert," along with Peruvian cardinals Pedro Barreto, SJ, and Carlos Castillo, spoke out in 2018 to support them, and they changed the course of history.

"At the time, Prevost was vice president of the Episcopal Conference, and rebelling against the Sodalitium was extremely complicated because of its immense economic and business power," Paola says.[57] Then, after their book was published, new cases and more victims emerged, and "Robert" hit a wall: the president of the Peruvian Episcopal Conference, Miguel Cabrejos. "But Robert isn't a person who grabs a match and burns down the building. He seeks out paths and finds another way to help. What do I mean? In the film *Spotlight*, you see when they publish the denunciation of abuse and more cases, more abuses appear. But when we published the book in 2015, we were just a couple of freelance journalists. We didn't have the *Boston Globe* behind us, and all the victims were calling us with desperate cases. We're talking about 2018. We didn't know what to do with so many stories. And we spontaneously organized help. A psychoanalyst friend who has passed away put together a team of psychologists to provide pro bono care to desperate victims. And at that moment, spontaneously, Robert became the person who individually helped truly broken victims.

"He became the bridge between the Sodalitium and very complicated victims, securing financial settlements, medicines, and psychologists. I had forgotten about this, but I just saw it again in my email these days. And he supported the so-called 'Figari slaves,' who are people who lived with Figari for twenty to thirty years, whose lives are shattered and who needed immediate settlements because they had suicidal tendencies," she adds.

"Figari's slaves lived at his disposal twenty-four hours a day, preparing his meals, passing him the remote control when he watched movies. Figari would ask them, 'Who is capable of taking out and showing their penis on the table?' Absurd orders. Because what he had said was that he who obeys is never wrong," Paola recalls.

"Prevost did all his helping privately until 2020, when all the lawsuits against us began," she says, explaining that she started to be accused by the Sodalitium of leading a money-laundering network. The same thing happened to her colleague, Salinas, who was actually sentenced for defamation and ordered to pay astronomical sums.

"In Peru, they fabricate cases and accusations. But it's not just a mudslinging machine; they also file these complaints with the prosecutor's office, where they open the cases without conducting any

---

57. Elisabetta Piqué, "La periodista que destapó un escándalo de abusos en la Iglesia de Perú detalla cuál fue el rol de León XIV," *La Nación*, May 15, 2025.

investigation," she says. It was then that the nuncio in Peru, Nicola Girasoli, and Prevost told her that the only way forward was to see Pope Francis to tell him what was happening. Because of COVID-19, she was unable to make that trip until November 2022. In Rome she met with Francis and told him that, beyond the abuse, there was also a lot of bullying by the SVC of farmers whose lands had been stolen, not to mention shady multimillion-dollar deals involving cemeteries donated to bishoprics.

"There is a lot of fear, and you have to do something, Holy Father, because they have been given papal permission and no one is stopping them," Paola told Francis, directly asking him to open an investigation. Thus, Jorge Bergoglio, who had already taken significant steps to intervene with the group in 2018, decided in July 2023 to send Maltese Archbishop Charles Scicluna—the Vatican's top expert on abuse—and Spanish Monsignor Jordi Bertomeu, an official of the Dicastery for the Doctrine of the Faith, on a special mission to Peru similar to what they did in Chile.

The investigation led to the resignation of the archbishop of Piura, José Antonio Eguren, a member of the founding generation of the Sodalitium on April 2, 2024, well before his 75th birthday. By that time, Prevost had already left his beloved Peru. He had been called by Pope Francis to the Vatican to be prefect of the Dicastery for Bishops.

"With the fall of Eguren, it became clear that the work was getting serious, that Francis was coming in with a strong hand, and it was on the following May 30th that the first allegations of a cover-up against Prevost emerged, fabricated by the Sodalitium and completely false. At the same time, the persecution against us increased. So, desperate, we came [to Rome] in October to ask for help because we didn't know where to turn. And the person we met with at the Vatican went to Robert to tell him what was happening," she says.

"He had known us all our lives and conveyed calm. He always conveys calm. He's a pragmatist, and he advised us on this occasion not to see Francis because he was currently engaged in the Synodality Synod, on something else. And he told us: 'Give me time. But I do need reports, write things up for me.'"

Finally, Paola Ugaz, Pedro Salinas, and journalist Elise Allen, also a victim of Sodalitium, were able to see Francis on Monday, December 9, 2024, thanks to Prevost. At that time, he had a bruise on his face from a fall but was "very lucid." Aside from confirming his support for them, as well as for the Scicluna-Bartomeu mission, Francis assured them, "I'm going to close it properly, I'm going to do it well."

"We immediately went to see Robert to tell him. We saw him two more times on that trip," says Paola, who adds that Sodalitium was closed in January, but then Francis fell ill, and it wasn't officially shut down until the following April 14.

Paola, who traveled to Rome to cover the conclave and never imagined that her friend "Robert" would be elected, believes it is necessary to tell this story now. "One of the first people we thank for the closure of the Sodalitium is Robert, because his role was fundamental, right until the very end. Both popes, both Francis and Leo XIV, have supported us greatly, but in our country, in Peru, the injustice remains the same: Pedro (Salinas) has a hearing in June where they are seeking eleven years in prison against him," she laments.

"We wouldn't have spoken of all this either if he [Robert] hadn't become the pope and it was necessary to tell of his role in this story, especially now that totally false and unjust accusations of a cover-up are coming out. But he didn't help the victims in order to make the story known; rather, he did it secretly so they could survive, so that they could be well," Paola emphasized. She recalled that, when Francis was elected in 2013, he was also falsely accused of having been an accomplice to the dictatorship in Argentina, despite the fact that, instead, he had discreetly and secretly helped dozens of people escape the country, risking his own life.[58] "Robert is personable; he quietly helped many victims, pragmatically. because he is a mathematician, a great strategist, speaks perfect Spanish, and knows how Latin America and corruption operate," she says.

Paola states that everything Leo XIV said last Monday, in his first audience with the international press, when he defended freedom of expression and spoke about journalists imprisoned for telling the truth, resonated with her.

"Francis and Leo XIV are not the same; they are different, but what unites them is the fight for good journalism. Both, in their own ways, have defended and continue to defend good journalism and detest toxic journalism, fake news. They fought for good journalism,

---

58. Elisabetta Piqué, *Pope Francis: Life and Revolution* (Loyola Press, 2013), chapter 6.

and I believe that, thanks to them, this story will reach many people. Their support has been real, concrete. If it hadn't been for Francis and Leo XIV, we would be in jail today—and that's no joke."

PREVOST NOT ONLY HELPED victims of abuse while in Peru. He also cared for thousands of migrants, especially those arriving from Venezuela, as revealed in an excellent report by our friend Lucia Capuzzi of *Avvenire*—Betta's colleague covering wars in Israel and Syria—who was sent to Chiclayo to explore the new pope's little-known past.[59]

In the midst of Venezuela's terrible economic crisis that began in 2013, more than nine million people fled the country, crushed by Nicolás Maduro's regime; 1.7 million desperate people arrived in Peru, a fifth of them in Chiclayo, in the north. "In 2018, there were thousands of people, many sleeping on the streets of Chiclayo, en route to Lima: young people, the elderly, women with newborn babies. The authorities didn't even see them. Monsignor Prevost's heart broke. Then he called me and said, 'We have to do something,'" says Augusto Martínez Ibáñez, head of the Human Mobility Ministry that, in the midst of that emergency, established "Don Robert," a pragmatist, in his diocese.

"Father Roberto used his usual method: starting from reality, analyzing it carefully first and foremost, and understanding where and how to act. And then, building a network of various entities to be able to provide effective support," explains Augusto, adding that the mobilization promoted by Prevost encouraged everyone to collaborate. Thus, they were able to provide shelter in premises made available by religious congregations, parishes, and evangelical churches, creating six temporary shelters for migrants in transit. There, the migrants could eat, wash, rest, and receive medical care while waiting to continue their journey. "We also helped some seven thousand families stay, and in this case, the channel Monsignor Prevost opened with the various ministries so that the new arrivals could register and receive temporary work authorization was vitally important."

"We were resigned to staying on the streets, and a friend told me, 'Go to the cathedral,'" Jenior, a Venezuelan woman who left the Caribbean region of Anzoátegui in early 2019 with her husband and

---

59. Lucia Capuzzi, "Il ricordo vivo dei migranti: 'Prevost è stato il solo che non ci ha mai tradito,'" *Avvenire*, May 16, 2025.

two children, ages 10 and 25, recalled with emotion when she spoke with Lucia. They arrived in Chiclayo two months later, where, thanks to her brother, they found a place to live, but were soon evicted, leaving them homeless. Jenior, who works as a kitchen helper, said that she will never forget when, in 2022, Bishop Prevost visited the Albergue de la Via San Vicente, one of the shelters they had created, in Puerto Eten, a fishing village an hour from Chiclayo. "He came over to greet us one by one, and I told him: 'You extended a hand when everyone else looked the other way.'"

Thanks to him and the pastoral care promoted by the Diocese of Chiclayo, in her most desperate moment she was able to go to the cathedral to ask for help. And they gave it to her. They arranged for her to move into a simple prefabricated house in Puerto Eten. "You have no idea how we lived before.... Here we have services and we don't have to pay anything. We can save up to pay off our debts and, slowly, find a bigger house. Now we have residence permits, as well as access to healthcare, and all of this thanks to Monsignor Robert. He doesn't know how many thousands of us he has helped."

MAY 16, FRIDAY [BETTA] _____

## Descendant of Immigrants

WE WAKE UP EARLY. Juan Pablo has a cough and fever. After having been immersed in all the work of the past few weeks, and he has come down with bronchitis. He is supposed to take an exam next week, but he will not be able to. I immediately leave for the pharmacy to buy him some medicine.

We read newspapers. In *Le Figaro*, there's a very interesting interview with French Cardinal Christophe Pierre, nuncio to the United States since April 2016 (whom Gerry and I met in November 2023[60]). He talks about the conclave and reveals details about the pope-elect's psychology and personality, marked by his calmness [*sangfroid*].

---

60. Gerard O'Connell, "Cardinal Pierre on Why the US Bishops Are Struggling to Connect with Pope Francis," *America*, November 2, 2025.

"First, he is American, but he is also Latino. He spent more pastoral time in Latin America than in the United States. Second, he is a religious. Pope Francis was a Jesuit; he is a member of the Augustinians and represents one of the great spiritualities of the Church. Saint Augustine is a monument. And this pope is a pure Augustinian religious. He was twice superior general of this religious order, and in that capacity he lived in Rome for fifteen years. He was then appointed a bishop in Peru. He is a Latino who speaks Spanish like we speak French. He is a canon lawyer, a specialist in internal Church law, and is very well educated. He worked as a grassroots priest in Peru and then assumed the responsibility of bishop in a diocese where conditions were often difficult. In fact, he is Latin American, which is very interesting for the Church," the bishop notes in an interview with Jean-Marie Guénois,[61] whom we've known for many years.

What is his psychology like? "He seems very calm, he smiles a lot.... I can't speak about the electoral process, but during it, I was impressed by him.... I saw an inner man, who saw the wind coming, but didn't yet know which way it would blow, and that's how the Holy Spirit works, and then the chosen one accepted what was coming with impressive serenity. It all happened in a matter of minutes: you're a bishop, a cardinal, and now you're pope. Why had Pope Francis entrusted him with the enormous task of appointing bishops? There are traces of the Holy Spirit here too. He comes from Latin America, like Francis. He already has a vast pastoral and intellectual background. When it came to finding someone for this important position of appointing the world's bishops, Francis chose this man because he had already seen his qualities. A quality a pope needs is that of knowing how to surround himself with good people. You can't govern alone," he says.

Asked about Leo XIV's style, both in substance and form, Cardinal Pierre recalls that he met him in his role at the Dicastery for Bishops, "because the job of an apostolic nuncio is to prepare the files for the appointment of bishops. The pope appoints them, but we are the ones who prepare the appointments by gathering information on possible candidates and sending the recommendations to Rome," he ex-

---

61. Jean-Marie Guénois, "Mgr Christophe Pierre: 'Ce nouveau pape a beaucoup de sang-froid,'" *Le Figaro*, May 15, 2025.

plains, adding that "this new pope is very composed, calm, profound, cultured, sees things coming, and is serene. I perceive great serenity in him, and I have seen it again in recent days. When you experience a change like this, there are many things to worry about or be anxious about. I have truly seen great serenity. When you have known someone with whom you have worked and they become pope in a matter of minutes...you see them in white, everything has changed, but they have not changed."

How does he interpret the first words of this pontificate, marked by "peace" and the insistence on "Christ" in a tense geopolitical context? "First of all, we were all surprised by his choice of name. There was the symbolism of the name Benedict, then Francis, and here comes Leo XIV, who follows Leo XIII, the pope of the beginning of the Church's social doctrine, of the industrial revolution, of the moment in which the Church adapted to modernity. That is the first aspect. Regarding the theme of peace, we remember Pope Francis's fight against the madness of war and against the arms race, overcoming the logic of war, which is imprisoning the world and from which there is no escape. So there will be continuity in this area. Regarding the Church's social doctrine, he reminds us that Catholicism is not an intimate religion, but rather one that impacts reality. Finally, his reference to Christ goes against the ideologization of faith."

SPEAKING OF PEACE, during his first speech before the diplomatic corps accredited to the Holy See,[62] on his eighth day as pontiff, Leo XIV once again makes it clear that peace is a priority, along with truth and justice.

He emphasizes that these are "the three key words that constitute the pillars of the Church's missionary action and the diplomatic work of the Holy See: peace, truth, justice.

"I hope that this [peace, truth, justice] can happen in all contexts, starting with those that suffer the most, such as Ukraine and the Holy Land," he says in the spectacular Clementine Hall before the ambassadors of the 184 states that have diplomatic relations with the Holy See. The states that do not yet have such relations are China, Saudi

---

62. "Corpo Diplomatico Accreditato Presso La Santa Sede," Sala Stampa della Santa Sede, May 16, 2025.

Arabia, Afghanistan, North Korea, Bhutan, Brunei, Comoros, Laos, Maldives, Somalia, Tuvalu, and Vietnam.

However, the situation is changing with Vietnam, as the Holy See now has a permanent representative in Hanoi. The government had invited Pope Francis to visit the country, and on June 30, Vice President Vo Thi Anh Xuan will pay a courtesy visit to Pope Leo XIV and reiterate the invitation.

Following this visit, the Vietnamese online newspaper affiliated with the government would write : "Pope Leo XIV expressed his gratitude and reaffirmed his desire to visit Vietnam to deepen his connection with the Vietnamese Catholic community and further consolidate relations between the Vatican and Vietnam."[63]

Pope Leo XIV begins his speech to the ambassadors by expressing his gratitude for the numerous messages of congratulations received following his election, as well as the condolences sent on the occasion of Pope Francis's death, even from countries with which the Holy See does not maintain diplomatic relations. "This is a significant expression of esteem, which encourages the deepening of mutual relations," he states.

He reminds them that "papal diplomacy is an expression of the very catholicity of the Church. In its diplomatic activity, the Holy See is inspired by a pastoral outreach that leads it not to seek privileges but to strengthen its evangelical mission at the service of humanity. Resisting all forms of indifference, it appeals to consciences, as witnessed by the constant efforts of my venerable predecessor, ever attentive to the cry of the poor, the needy and the marginalized, as well as to contemporary challenges, ranging from the protection of creation to artificial intelligence."

Highlighting the presence of diplomats from most of the world's countries, Leo XIV renews the Church's—and his own—aspiration to reach out and embrace every people and every person on this Earth, yearning for and in need of truth, justice, and peace.

"In a certain sense, my own life experience, spent between North America, South America, and Europe, highlights this aspiration to transcend borders to encounter different people and cultures," he

---

63. "Pope Leo XIV Welcomes Vietnam's Invitation for Future Visit," Vietnamnet.vn, July 1, 2025; "Pope Leo XIV Receives Vice-President of Vietnam," www.vaticannews.va, June 1, 2025.

notes, recalling that, having served as prior general of the Augustinians, he visited many countries around the world and says that he will now have the opportunity to travel to many others, in order to "build new bridges."

Underlining the three key words that guide both the Church's missionary action and the diplomatic work of the Holy See, Leo XIV begins with peace. "Peace is above all a gift, the first gift of Christ. But it is an active, passionate gift that affects and involves each one of us, regardless of cultural origin or religious affiliation, and that first and foremost requires work on oneself," he says. "Peace is built in the heart and from the heart, eradicating pride and grievances, and measuring language, because one can also hurt and kill with words, not only with weapons," he warns.

In this context, he describes the contribution that religions and interreligious dialogue can make as "fundamental" for peace building and here he emphasizes the importance of full respect for religious freedom.

He issues a call to governments for "revitalizing multilateral diplomacy and those international institutions that have been desired and conceived primarily to resolve conflicts that may arise within the international community."

"Certainly, the will to stop producing instruments of destruction and death is also necessary, because, as Pope Francis recalled in his last *Urbi et Orbi* message, 'peace is also impossible without true disarmament, and the need of each people to provide for its own defense cannot be transformed into a general race for rearmament.'"

Elaborating on the second key word—justice—he reminds his listeners that "seeking peace requires practicing justice." He then explains that he chose to call himself Leo XIV "with Leo XIII in mind, the pope of the first great social encyclical, *Rerum Novarum*."

Furthermore, he insists, "Every effort should be made to overcome the global inequalities—between opulence and destitution—that are carving deep divides between continents, countries and even within individual societies. This can be achieved above all by investing in the family, founded upon the stable union between a man and a woman, 'a small but genuine society, and prior to all civil society.'"

In addition, he reminds the ambassadors that "No one is exempted from striving to ensure respect for the dignity of every person, especially the most frail and vulnerable, from the unborn to the elderly, from the sick to the unemployed, citizens and immigrants alike."

On a more personal note, he tells them, "My own story is that of a citizen, the descendant of immigrants, who in turn chose to emigrate. All of us, in the course of our lives, can find ourselves healthy or sick, employed or unemployed, living in our native land or in a foreign country, yet our dignity always remains unchanged: it is the dignity of a creature willed and loved by God."

What Leo, the second pope after Francis to be descended from migrants, doesn't say but what we have since learned is that as cardinal, Prevost was one who pushed for Pope Francis to write the Letter to the Bishops of the United States of America on immigration at a time when the Trump administration had started an immigration crackdown and was moving ahead with mass deportations.[64] In that letter, Francis told the bishops "the rightly formed conscience cannot fail to make a critical judgment and express its disagreement with any measure that tacitly or explicitly identifies the illegal status of some migrants with criminality." Moreover, he said, "The act of deporting people who in many cases have left their own land for reasons of extreme poverty, insecurity, exploitation, persecution or serious deterioration of the environment, damages the dignity of many men and women, and of entire families, and places them in a state of particular vulnerability and defenselessness."

Addressing the third key word—truth—Leo warns that "truly peaceful relationships cannot be built, also within the international community, apart from truth. Where words take on ambiguous and ambivalent connotations, and the virtual world, with its altered perception of reality, takes over unchecked, it is difficult to build authentic relationships, since the objective and real premises of communication are lacking.

"For her part," he says, "the Church can never be exempted from speaking the truth about humanity and the world, resorting whenever necessary to blunt language that may initially create misunderstanding. Yet truth can never be separated from charity, which always has at

---

64. "Letter of the Holy Father Francis to The Bishops of the United States of America," February 10, 2025, www.vatican.va; Gerard O'Connell, "Pope Francis to US Catholic Bishops: Oppose Mass Deportations," *America*, February 11, 2025.

its root a concern for the life and well-being of every man and woman."

Furthermore, "From the Christian perspective, truth is not the affirmation of abstract and disembodied principles, but an encounter with the person of Christ himself, alive in the midst of the community of believers. Truth, then, does not create division, but rather enables us to confront all the more resolutely the challenges of our time, such as migration, the ethical use of artificial intelligence and the protection of our beloved planet Earth. These are challenges that require commitment and cooperation on the part of all, since no one can think of facing them alone."

The speech, his first before the diplomatic corps, comes on the eve of the arrival in Rome of two hundred delegations from around the world for the solemn Mass to inaugurate Leo's pontificate, scheduled for Sunday. As happened during Francis's funeral—when Donald Trump and Volodymyr Zelensky unexpectedly held a face-to-face meeting inside St. Peter's Basilica, considered by many to be "a miracle" by the Argentine pope—another meeting of global leaders is expected, with the possibility of bilateral meetings also.

The White House announces that Trump will not attend the inauguration and that the US delegation will be led by Vice President JD Vance and Secretary of State Marco Rubio, both Catholics. It is possible that Leo XIV will hold a bilateral meeting with Vance, who was the last political leader to meet with Francis on Easter Sunday.

WITHOUT PAUSING, Leo XIV receives various collaborators in audience: his friend, Father Alejandro Moral Antón, prior general of the Augustinians; Cardinal Daniel Sturla, archbishop of Montevideo, Uruguay; Argentine Cardinal Víctor Manuel "Tucho" Fernández, prefect of the Dicastery for the Doctrine of the Faith; and Philippine Cardinal Luis Antonio Tagle, pro-prefect of the Dicastery for Evangelization.

Tagle—whom Gerry and I know well and who was among the conclave's frontrunners—offers some interesting insights in an interview with the Vatican media. "Before major events of global impact, various speculations, analyses, and predictions arise. The conclave was no exception. It's true that I participated in two conclaves, which I consider a true blessing. In the 2013 conclave, Pope Benedict XVI was still alive, while in the 2025 conclave, Pope Francis had already passed away. We must take into account the difference in context and atmosphere. I would also add that, although each of the two conclaves was a unique and unrepeatable experience, there were constant elements,"[65] he says. "In 2013, I wondered why we had to wear choral vestments during the conclave. Later, I learned and experienced that the conclave is a liturgical event, a time and space for prayer, for listening to the Word of God, to the promptings of the Holy Spirit, to the groanings of the Church, of humanity, and of Creation, for personal and communal purification of motivations, and for worship and adoration of God, whose will must reign supreme. Both Pope Francis and Pope Leo were elected on the second day," he notes. "The conclave teaches us, as well as our families, parishes, dioceses, and nations, that communion of hearts and minds is possible if we worship the true God."

Since Tagle was seated next to Prevost in the Sistine Chapel, he was a privileged witness to the election. How did the future pope react when the two-thirds quorum was reached? "His reaction was an alternation between smiles and deep breaths. It was one of holy acceptance and sacred concern at the same time. I prayed for him in silence. At the very moment he reached the required number of votes, thunderous applause erupted, similar to the election of Pope Francis," he says.

"The cardinals expressed joy and gratitude to their brother, Cardinal Prevost. But it was also an intimate moment between Jesus and him, which we could not enter and which we should not interrupt. I said to myself: 'Let us allow the sacred silence to envelop Jesus and Peter.'"

Asked about the significance of the election of an Augustinian pope—the first, following a Jesuit, also a first—Tagle emphasizes that "Saint Augustine and Saint Ignatius had many things in common. Both had a worldly journey and experienced a restlessness that drove them to adventurous pursuits. Then, at the time God determined, they found in Jesus what their hearts desired: 'Beauty ever ancient and ever new,' 'Eternal Lord of all things.' The Augustinian and Ignatian schools are born from a common foundation: the grace and mercy of God, which frees the heart to love, serve,

---

65. Alessandro Gisotti, "Cardinal Tagle Reflects on Pope Leo XIV as a Missionary Shepherd," www.vaticannews.va, May 16, 2025.

and go out on mission. Maintaining his Augustinian spirit, Pope Leo will echo the Ignatian spirit of Pope Francis. I believe the entire Church and all of humanity will benefit from their gifts. After all, Saint Augustine and Saint Ignatius (and all the saints) are the treasure of the entire Church.

"Without denying the primacy of grace in Pope Leo's ministry, I believe that his human, cultural, religious, and missionary formation can give a unique face to his ministry. But this is true for all popes. The Petrine Ministry of confirming brothers and sisters in the faith in Jesus, the Son of the living God, remains constant, but it is lived and exercised by each pope in his unique humanity. Pope Leo's multicontinental and multicultural experience will certainly aid him in his ministry and benefit the Church. People in Asia love the pope as pope, no matter what country he comes from. He is loved not only by Catholics, but also by other Christians and followers of non-Christian religions," he adds.

Finally, he confesses that he did not live peacefully throughout the entire period leading up to the conclave, during which he appeared as one of the leading candidates and during which he received many attacks. "Not being someone who enjoys being in the spotlight, I found the attention directed at me quite disconcerting," he admits. "I tried to muster my spiritual and human strength to avoid being drawn into it. I meditated a great deal on the words of the apostolic constitution *Universi Dominici Gregis* regarding the 'most grave duty incumbent upon [the cardinals] and, therefore, on the need to act with right understanding for the good of the universal Church, having only God before their eyes.'"

IT'S ANOTHER DAY OF WORK with Gerry, during which we interview Brazilian Cardinal Steiner, whom we meet in a lobby of Vatican Radio. We continue talking with various editors interested in the idea of a book about the conclave, about which we have gathered and will continue to gather a lot of information.

We go out to eat at Da Costanza, a restaurant near our house, with Chris Lamb. We not only talk, but also toast Leo while we eat *"fritto misto di pesce"* (fish fritters) with baked potatoes, nicely paired with the house white wine.

## MAY 17, SATURDAY [GERRY]
*A Different Style*

AFTER A CAPPUCCINO AND *CORNETTO* BREAKFAST at Angelo's Bar Farnese, a classic, we head to the Vatican to meet with a Latin American cardinal who just sent Betta a WhatsApp message saying he has time to see us at 10 AM. He's staying at the Augustinian Generalate, currently in the world's spotlight. We chat, but he prefers not to give us an interview.

Meanwhile, Leo, on the eve of assuming his Petrine Ministry tomorrow, once again gives clues as to what his papacy will be like. He makes clear the importance of the Church's social doctrine, of critical thinking in a world of fake news and little dialogue, and of giving voice to and listening to the poor, "the treasure of the Church and of humanity, bearers of discarded points of view, but indispensable for seeing the world through God's eyes.

"I recommend giving voice to the poor," he says, when receiving in audience the members of the Centesimus Annus Pro Pontifice Foundation, a group that takes its name from the encyclical written by John Paul II on the centenary of Leo XIII's *Rerum Novarum*, and whose purpose is to study and disseminate Catholic social doctrine.

In his speech,[66] Leo explains the role of the Church's social doctrine—which must be part of a dialogue and does not seek to raise the banner of possessing the truth—and warns against "indoctrination," which he defines as "immoral." Furthermore, he considers "in-depth analysis and study," as well as encountering and listening to the poor, to be "fundamental." And he emphasizes the need to educate people in "critical thinking."

He affirms that "those born and raised far from the centers of power should not merely be taught the Church's social doctrine; they should also be recognized as carrying it forward and putting it into practice. Individuals committed to the betterment of society, popular movements, and the various Catholic workers' groups are an expression of those existential peripheries where hope endures and springs anew."

---

66. Address of His Holiness Pope Leo XIV to Members of the "Centesimus Annus Pro Pontifice" Foundation, May 17, 2025, www.vatican.va.

The pope recalls that "Pope Leo XIII—who lived in a historical period of transcendental and disruptive transformations—had already proposed contributing to peace by stimulating social dialogue between capital and labor, between technologies and human intelligence, between different political cultures, between nations."

He reminds his listeners that "Pope Francis used the term *polycrisis* to evoke the dramatic nature of the historical situation we are experiencing, where wars, climate change, growing inequalities, forced and contrasting migrations, stigmatized poverty, disruptive technological innovations, and precarious employment and rights converge." And he asserts that, "in such important matters, the Church's social doctrine is called to provide interpretive keys that bring science and conscience into dialogue, thus making a fundamental contribution to knowledge, hope, and peace.

"Social Doctrine teaches us to recognize that more important than the problems themselves, or the answers to them, is how we confront them, with evaluative criteria and ethical principles and with openness to God's grace," he adds.

The pope continues, "You have the opportunity to show that the Church's social doctrine, with its specific anthropological approach, seeks to encourage genuine engagement with social issues. It does not claim to possess a monopoly on truth, either in its analysis of problems or its proposal of concrete solutions. Where social questions are concerned, knowing how best to approach them is more important than providing immediate responses to why things happen or how to deal with them. The aim is to learn how to confront problems, for these are always different, since every generation is new, and faces new challenges, dreams, and questions."

He states that this is a fundamental aspect of building a "culture of encounter" through dialogue and social friendship, and he acknowledges that "for the sensibilities of many of our contemporaries, the words 'dialogue' and 'doctrine' sound opposite and incompatible." Therefore, he considers it "urgent" to demonstrate, through the Church's social doctrine that there is another, and promising, meaning to the term "doctrine," whose synonyms can be "science," "discipline," or "knowledge."

"Understood in this way," he says, "doctrine appears as the product of research, and hence of hypotheses, discussions, progress and setbacks, all aimed at conveying a reliable, organized and systematic body of knowledge about a given issue. Consequently, a doctrine is not the same as an opinion, but is rather a common, collective, and even multidisciplinary pursuit of truth."

Addressing the members of this social doctrine foundation in the magnificent Clementine Hall of the Apostolic Palace, Pope Leo affirms that "indoctrination is immoral. It stifles critical judgment and undermines the sacred freedom of conscience, even if erroneous. It resists new notions and rejects movement, change or the evolution of ideas in the face of new problems. 'Doctrine,' on the other hand, as a serious, serene and rigorous discourse, aims to teach us primarily how to approach problems and, even more importantly, how to approach people. It also helps us to make prudential judgments when confronted with challenges. Seriousness, rigor and serenity are what we must learn from every doctrine, including the Church's social doctrine."

Then he considers that, within the framework of the ongoing digital revolution, "the mandate to educate in critical thinking must be rediscovered, articulated, and cultivated, countering opposing temptations, which can also affect the ecclesial body."

He then recalls the Second Vatican Council, which declared that it is the Church's permanent duty to observe the signs of the times and interpret them in the light of the Gospel. Finally, he invites everyone to "participate actively and creatively in this exercise of discernment, contributing to the development of the Church's social doctrine together with the People of God in this historical period of great social upheaval, listening and dialoguing with all.

"There is today a widespread need for justice, a demand for fatherhood and motherhood, a profound desire for spirituality, especially among young people and the marginalized, who do not always find effective channels for expressing themselves. There is a growing demand for the Church's social doctrine to which we must respond," he concludes to sustained applause.[67]

It's clear that Leo, who chose this name with Leo XIII in mind, presents himself as a pope who lives in the midst of a new revolution under way—the technological or digital revolution—and sees the urgent need for the Church to address it, drawing on its legacy of social doctrine and developing new ways of responding to the challenges posed by the digital age.

---

67. Elisabetta Piqué, "León XIV llamó a darles la palabra y a escuchar a los pobres, 'tesoro de la Iglesia y de la humanidad,'" *La Nación*, May 17, 2025.

ASIDE FROM MAKING THESE STATEMENTS, Pope Leo XIV continues with a busy schedule of meetings. According to the Vatican, he will receive in audience the archbishop of Bologna and president of the Italian Episcopal Conference, Matteo Zuppi—one of the Italian papal candidates before the conclave; Venerando Marano, president of the Vatican Tribunal; the young Italian Cardinal Giorgio Marengo, apostolic prefect of Mongolia; and the Portuguese Cardinal José Tolentino de Mendonça, prefect of the Dicastery for Culture and Education.

Meanwhile, the Vatican is preparing to welcome 156 delegations from around the world and more than 250,000 faithful to St. Peter's Square for the investiture ceremony of Pope Leo XIV. The most important seats for world leaders will be reserved for Italy, with head of state Sergio Mattarella and Prime Minister Giorgia Meloni; Peru—where Robert Prevost was a bishop and holds citizenship—with President Dina Boluarte; and then the United States, the pontiff's country of birth, with Vice President JD Vance and Secretary of State Marco Rubio.

Also expected to be present are heads of state such as Ukraine's Volodymyr Zelensky, Israel's Isaac Herzog, and Colombia's Gustavo Petro, as well as representatives of royalty, including King Felipe VI of Spain and Queen Máxima of the Netherlands, who was unable to attend Francis's funeral.

ALTHOUGH NOT YET OFFICIALLY CONFIRMED, and in another sign of his inner freedom and personal style, it is an open secret that the new pope will return to live in the papal apartment in the Vatican's Apostolic Palace, as previous pontiffs did, thus resuming a tradition that was interrupted for twelve years and thirty-nine days by Pope Francis.[68]

Since 1903, when Pius X moved into the third floor of the Apostolic Palace, all popes until Jorge Bergoglio had lived there. Since the fourteenth century, previous popes have always lived in other areas of the Apostolic Palace and the Vatican; for example, where the museums are now.

After being elected on March 13, 2013, the then-unknown archbishop of Buenos Aires, who had gone to the Santa Marta residence to

---

68. Elisabetta Piqué, "León XIV volverá a vivir al departamento papal del Palacio Apostólico," *La Nación*, May 17, 2025.

participate in the conclave, decided to stay there. After visiting the apartment in the Apostolic Palace, he said that that living in that sort of "gilded cage" would have caused him "psychiatric problems" and that he preferred living in a community.

Santa Marta, a guesthouse for clergy within the Vatican walls, permanently houses some prelates of the Roman Curia and temporarily receives others during their stays in Rome. Although he was initially assigned room 207 by lottery, Pope Francis later moved to the slightly larger suite 201, which includes a small living room, a desk, a bedroom, and a bathroom.

It was in Santa Marta that the "pope from the end of the world" kept a parallel private agenda in the afternoons, managed only by himself and, more recently, by his private secretaries. In fact, living there meant greater scope for action and freedom for him, since in the apartment on the third floor of the Apostolic Palace he would have been more confined and controlled, like living in a funnel.

According to what several cardinals told us, the question of where the new pope would live was raised during the general congregations. Now it appears that Leo, who has his own personality and manners, has decided to live in the Apostolic Palace. Beyond the fact that this is a matter of tradition, they said that the decision also has to do with security and the costs of protecting the pope.

Although for now Robert Francis Prevost continues to live in a 150-square-meter apartment in the Palazzo del Sant'Uffizio in the Vatican, according to *Corriere della Sera*, restoration work has already begun on the papal apartment in the Apostolic Palace.[69]

The most urgent work focuses on the renovation and modernization of the bathrooms, as well as the repair of damp stains on the walls of some rooms. Although Benedict XVI had already carried out some work to control water leaks, after twelve years the problem has reappeared. The furniture in the pope's room and his desk will also be replaced. Just as Pope Francis gradually occupied other rooms on the second floor of Santa Marta as offices for his secretaries, his successor will need the entire space of the papal apartment on the third floor of the Apostolic Palace. It has ten rooms—including a doctor's office, a

---

69. Ester Palma, "Papa Leone e i lavori nell'appartamento del Palazzo Apostolico: bagni da rifare e arredi nuovi, potrebbe entrarci fra un mese," *Corriere della Sera*, May 15, 2025.

chapel, a kitchen, and a dining room—with ornate salons and sixteenth-century marble floors. Francis used the apartment only to appear from his office window on Sundays for the Angelus or Regina Caeli prayers. Therefore, the rest, unused, needs to be renovated, because it had been abandoned, we were told.

AS EXPECTED, this move, coupled with the fact that Leo presented himself to the world after his election wearing a red *mozzetta* and a golden pectoral cross in the style of Benedict XVI, and that he abandoned Francis's white Fiat 500 and opted for a black SUV, has caused great satisfaction in the more conservative sectors of the Church. They applaud all of the above, and also the fact that he gave a blessing in Latin at the end of his first audience with journalists. From the very beginning, they have tried to pigeonhole and appropriate the figure of the new pope, presenting him as a counterpoint to Francis.

Although there are still early days and we must let him settle in and take his first steps, most of the cardinals we spoke with agree that, beyond style and manner, there is essentially much of Francis in Robert Francis Prevost. "I am confident that we made the right decision—that the Holy Spirit made the right choice through us—because we are very happy with the messages we have received from him," Filipino Cardinal Pablo "Ambo" Virgilio David, president of his country's episcopate, tells us.[70] "We feel that Leo XIV will truly uphold Francis's vision, especially his call for the Church to be a synodal Church in mission. We don't expect him to be a carbon copy or a clone of Francis, because he has a completely different personality, but I think he has many original things to contribute, given his entire experience: it is a combination of North American and South American experience and his universal experience as superior general of the Augustinians.

"I base my understanding of where his pontificate is headed on the content of his messages. It's already refreshing to have a pope who is fluent in Italian, English, Spanish, and French. And he is a good communicator. And now we're happy with what he's said. I think that is the important thing. It's understandable that the pope is

---

70. Elisabetta Piqué, "Una 'gran síntesis: cómo interpretan los cardenales los primeros gestos de León XIV," *La Nación*, May 18, 2025.

the supreme pontiff, and the seat of the papacy is in Rome, and I suppose there's some pressure on him to show that, even though he's American, even though he's influenced by South American culture or because he's an Augustinian, he's aware of the Roman nature of the papacy. And I think speaking Italian and praying in Latin is symbolic. After all, the Catholic faith is rooted in Rome. It's more of a symbol than a literal attempt to go back," he says. "I don't think he'll go back to celebrating Mass in Latin as the norm. I don't think he'll ask churches in the Philippines to celebrate all Masses in Latin and stop using the vernacular languages. I do not think he will go that way."

Czech-Canadian Cardinal Michael Czerny, prefect of the Dicastery for Promoting Integral Human Development, agrees, also noting that wearing the red *mozzetta* or returning to the Apostolic Palace can be seen as gestures toward those who felt somewhat disillusioned with Francis.... And those who were not disillusioned with Francis can clearly read or see that he, Leo XIV, is on that same path.

"I interpret it as an expression of his priority. Francis initiated processes, and Pope Leo XIV will carry them forward. That is my premise: the process of reforming the Curia has already been launched; Leo XIV will complete it, and something that will contribute to that is a concrete closeness. He is comfortable with and clearly likes the Curia. He wants to work with it and for it to work with him, and living in the Apostolic Palace is a way of saying that," he concludes.

Asked what he would say to those who now insist that there is no continuity between Pope Francis and Leo XIV because he wore the red *mozzetta*, Brazilian Cardinal Leonardo Steiner, archbishop of Manaus, was blunt: "In the Church there is always continuity; from the Second Vatican Council until now there has been continuity, but there is also discontinuity. Each pope has his own personality, his own formation, his own past, and his own way of being, and this is natural," he explains. "We cannot think of having another Pope Francis, with his own different way of being. But he, Leo XIV, will give continuity, for example, to synodality, and will give continuity to the concern for the least. I often use this expression: 'whoever has once been touched by the poor will never be the same again.' The poor convert us and show us a path to freedom," he added. Finally, he predicted that, just as Pope Francis was a free man, "Leo XIV will be a free man, but in a different way."

Chilean Cardinal Fernando Chomalí, archbishop of Santiago, boldly predicts: "Leo XIV will follow Pope Francis's path in his pastoral work, and Benedict XVI's in his intellectual work: a great synthesis for our times."

IN A SLOW RETURN TO NORMALCY, Betta manages to get back to her usual Saturday tennis class. Eva and Juan Pablo, who usually attend as well, cannot. Eva is crazy about covering the Jubilee of the Confraternities, and Juampy is still sick. Our dear friend Raffa, whom we haven't seen since Easter Sunday, is coming for dinner and wants us to tell her everything about this period of absolute vertigo.... We eat pasta with Betta's famous "Nonna Tina's ragù," with buffalo mozzarella, ham with melon, and finally, sliced peaches.

MAY 18, SUNDAY [GERRY]
*Love and Unity*

WE LEAVE HOME AT 8 AM. Juampy is still ill, so he watches the grand ceremony of the pontifical inauguration on television. Betta and I take a taxi to Piazza del Risorgimento because everything is blocked off, as it was during Francis's funeral. Luckily, that same bar near where Cardinal Müller lives is open and we have breakfast with the classic cappuccino and a *cornetto*. We then go to the Vatican Press Office, which can only be accessed through the back from Via Rusticucci.

The hundreds of thousands of faithful who have come to St. Peter's Square have had to wake up very early to deal with extraordinary security measures—street blockades and metal detectors. The atmosphere is one of enormous expectation, because everyone knows that Leo XIV, before the Mass of inauguration of the pontificate, will make his first appearance in a popemobile, his first drive among the crowd, which lasts about twenty minutes and unleashes enormous excitement.

"Long live the Pope! Leone, Leone! USA! USA!" are the shouts of joy that rise from the square, where flags from all over the world, although mostly the red and white of Peru, can be seen. Leo not only greets the colorful sea of people of all ages with a smile, raising his arms, waving and blessing people, but also greets all those along the Via della Conciliazione, in the midst of a festive atmosphere.

With Betta, of course, we leave the Press Room to immortalize that moment. A climate of euphoria reigns also among the Vaticanistas, but among them, some Italians make comments that leave us speechless: "Finally he wears cufflinks with his shirt!"

IN A HISTORIC AND SOLEMN ATMOSPHERE, as at Francis's funeral, the powerful of the earth are present, with 156 delegations. They include Presidents Volodymyr Zelensky of Ukraine, Isaac Herzog of Israel, Michael D. Higgins of Ireland, Andrezj Duda of Poland, Vice President of the United States JD Vance, Prime Ministers François Bayrou of France, Mark Carney of Canada, Anthony Albanese of Australia, and the new German Chancellor Friedrich Merz. Also present are heads of royal families, including King Felipe and Queen Letizia of Spain and Queen Máxima of the Netherlands. European Union Commission President Ursula von der Leyen and President of the European Parliament Roberta Metsola of Malta are also among those present.

So too are thirty-nine leading representatives of the Christian churches, chief among them ecumenical patriarch of Constantinople Bartholomew, and representatives of the other world religions including Muslims, Hindus, Buddhists, Sikhs, Zoroastrians, and others too. Thirteen leaders of Jewish communities from around the world are also present. Led by Chief Rabbi of Rome Riccardo Di Segni, they include Argentine Rabbi Abraham Skorka, an old friend of Jorge Bergoglio, currently at Georgetown University in Washington.

THE SOLEMN RITE FOR THE BEGINNING of the Petrine Ministry begins when Leo XIV descends to the tomb of St. Peter, in the Vatican basilica, where the pallium and the fisherman's ring have been placed. He is accompanied by the patriarchs of the Eastern Churches. He stops there in prayer. Then, accompanied by the beautiful singing of the Sistine Choir in Latin and carrying the pastoral cross that was used first by Paul VI and then by his successors including Francis, he climbs back up and follows the procession of two hundred cardinals that escort him to St. Peter's Square.

There, in the course of the eucharistic celebration, after the proclamation of the Gospel, the specific rites for the beginning of the Petrine Ministry take place. First the imposition of the pallium by the senior cardinal deacon present, Mario Zenari, nuncio in Syria (who replaces the French cardinal, Dominique Mamberti, who has suffered health problems). This is followed by the giving of the fisherman's ring, which is placed on his finger by the Filipino Cardinal Luis Antonio Tagle, who had encouraged and accompanied him like no one else during the rapid conclave, and represents Asia. At that moment everyone notices that Robert Francis Prevost, when looking at that ring, is visibly moved, almost to the point of tears. Finally, there is the moment of the promise of obedience to the new successor of Peter on the part of ten representatives of the People of God, and in their name: three cardinals (including Frank Leo representing North America), a bishop from Peru, two representatives of the international unions of religious superiors (Sr. Oona O'Shea and Father Arturo Sosa SJ), a married couple and two young people.

Leo XIV does not hide his emotion, and an ovation breaks out in the Plaza to which he responds smiling, grateful.

THE MASS IS CONCELEBRATED IN LATIN with 200 cardinals, 750 bishops, and 3,000 priests. After thanking all those who have come to Rome for the ceremony, Leo XIV begins his homily,[71] given in Italian. As he has been doing since he was elected, he starts by mentioning his predecessor.

"In recent days, we have experienced a particularly intense time. The death of Pope Francis has filled our hearts with sadness and, in those difficult hours, we have felt like those crowds that the Gospel describes 'like sheep without a shepherd.'

"It is precisely on Easter Day that we received his last blessing and, in the light of the resurrection, we face that moment with the certainty that the Lord never abandons his people, he gathers them together when they are scattered and cares for them 'as a shepherd does

---

71. Homily of the Holy Father Leo XIV, May 18, 2025, www.vatican.va; Gerard O'Connell, "Pope Leo XIV at Inaugural Mass: 'This Is the Hour for Love,'" *America*, May 18, 2025.

his flock,'" he says, recalling Francis's last appearance on Easter Sunday and generating applause from the crowd.

Leo then speaks about the quick conclave that elected him on May 8. "Coming from different backgrounds and experiences, we placed in God's hands our desire to elect the new successor of Peter, the Bishop of Rome, a shepherd capable of preserving the rich heritage of the Christian faith and, at the same time, looking to the future, in order to confront the questions, concerns, and challenges of today's world. Accompanied by your prayers, we could feel the working of the Holy Spirit, who was able to bring us into harmony, like musical instruments, so that our heartstrings could vibrate in a single melody," he says.

And, he humbly affirms: "I was chosen, without any merit of my own, and now, with fear and trembling, *I come to you as a brother*, who desires to be the servant of your faith and your joy, walking with you on the path of God's love, for he wants us all to be united in one family.

"*Love and unity*: these are the two dimensions of the mission entrusted to Peter by Jesus," he says. "We see this in today's Gospel, which takes us to the Sea of Galilee, where Jesus began the mission he received from the Father: to be a 'fisher' of humanity in order to draw it up from the waters of evil and death. Walking along the shore, he had called Peter and the other first disciples to be, like him, 'fishers of men.' Now, after the resurrection, it is up to them to carry on this mission, to cast their nets again and again, to bring the hope of the Gospel into the 'waters' of the world, to sail the seas of life so that all may experience God's embrace.

"How can Peter carry out this task?" he asks. "The Gospel tells us that it is possible only because his own life was touched by the infinite and unconditional love of God, even in the hour of his failure and denial," he says. And he goes beyond, to tell the vast crowd in the square and a global audience of countless millions following on television and the social media: "The ministry of Peter is distinguished precisely by this self-sacrificing love, because the Church of Rome presides in charity and its true authority is the charity of Christ. It is never a question of capturing others by force, by religious propaganda or by means of power. Instead, it is always and only a question of loving as Jesus did.

"The Apostle Peter himself tells us that Jesus is 'the stone that was rejected by you, the builders, and has become the cornerstone.' Moreover," he says, "if the rock is Christ, Peter must shepherd the flock without ever yielding to the temptation to be an autocrat, lording it over those entrusted to him. On the contrary, he is called to serve the faith of his brothers and sisters, and to walk alongside them, for all of us are 'living stones,' called through our baptism to build God's house in fraternal communion, in the harmony of the Spirit, in the coexistence of diversity." Here again, as in other talks, he quotes Saint Augustine: "The Church consists of all those who are in harmony with their brothers and sisters and who love their neighbor.

"Brothers and sisters, I would like that our first great desire be for a united Church, a sign of unity and communion, which becomes a leaven for a reconciled world," he exhorts.

The pope from the Americas denounces the fact that "in this our time, we still see too much discord, too many wounds caused by hatred, violence, prejudice, the fear of difference, and an economic paradigm that exploits the Earth's resources and marginalizes the poorest.

"For our part," he says, "we want to be a small leaven of unity, communion and fraternity within the world. We want to say to the world, with humility and joy: Look to Christ! Come closer to him!" he exhorts, drawing applause from the 150,000 people present.

The first Augustinian pope adds, "Welcome [Christ's] word that enlightens and consoles! Listen to his offer of love and become his one family: *in the one Christ, we are one.* This is the path to follow together, among ourselves but also with our sister Christian churches, with those who follow other religious paths, with those who are searching for God, with all women and men of good will, in order to build a new world where peace reigns!

"This is the missionary spirit that must animate us: not closing ourselves off in our small groups, nor feeling superior to the world. We are called to offer God's love to everyone, in order to achieve that unity which does not cancel out differences but values the personal history of each person and the social and religious culture of every people," he explains.

"Brothers and sisters, this is the hour for love! The heart of the Gospel is the love of God that makes us brothers and sisters. With my predecessor Leo XIII, we can ask ourselves today: If this criterion 'were to prevail in the world, would not every conflict cease and peace return?'" Leo XIV asks, quoting the encyclical *Rerum Novarum* of his namesake predecessor.

"With the light and the strength of the Holy Spirit, let us build a Church founded on God's love, a sign of unity, a missionary Church that opens its arms to the world, proclaims the word, allows itself to be made 'restless' by history, and becomes a leaven of harmony for humanity. Together, as one people, as brothers and sisters, let us walk toward God and love one another," he concludes, drawing enthusiastic applause from the crowd.

AT THE END OF THE MASS, before reciting the Marian prayer of the Regina Caeli, Pope Leo XIV thanks all those present, Romans and faithful from so many parts of the world, who participated in the ceremony.[72]

He thanks especially the official delegations from many countries, as well as the representatives of the churches and ecclesial communities and of the other world religions. He also greets the thousands of pilgrims who have come from every continent for the Jubilee of the Confraternities. "Dear brothers, I thank you for keeping alive the great patrimony of popular piety," he tells them.

He again recalls his Argentine predecessor: "During Mass, I strongly felt the spiritual presence of Pope Francis accompanying us from heaven."

He then expresses again his concern about the ongoing conflicts in the world, with special emphasis on the humanitarian situation in Gaza and the suffering of the Ukrainian people. "In the joy of faith and communion, we cannot forget our brothers and sisters who are suffering because of war. In Gaza, the surviving children, families, and elderly are reduced to starvation. In Myanmar, new hostilities have cut short innocent young lives. Finally, war-torn Ukraine awaits negotiations for a just and lasting peace," he says.

The presidents of Israel and Ukraine, Herzog and Zelensky, are present and listening,

After the Mass, in good spirits, smiling and now dressed again in a white cassock with the red *mozzetta*, Leo XIV stands for an hour and twenty minutes in front of Bernini's majestic *baldachino*, greeting the members of the 156 official delegations from all over the world.

---

72. Pope Leo XIV, Regina Caeli at the Conclusion of the Mass. May 18, 2025, www.vatican.va.

According to protocol, the first to greet him is the president of Italy, Sergio Mattarella, followed by the prime minister, Giorgia Meloni. The Italian delegation is, naturally, the largest delegation, as it is the host country of the Vatican.

Then it is the turn of the president of Peru, Dina Boluarte, who has already been received in a private audience before the Mass, in a gesture of deference to the adopted nationality of the new pope.

Next the pope greets JD Vance, vice president of the pope's native country, a Catholic convert who was baptized a few years ago, and his wife of Indian origin, with whom the pope also has a brief conversation. There are smiles and relaxed gestures, anticipating the audience scheduled for tomorrow, when Vance will hand him a letter from President Donald Trump inviting him to visit the United States.[73]

The US delegation also includes Secretary of State Marco Rubio, also Catholic, and the pope's brother, Louis Prevost, 73, who rose to fame for his pro-MAGA (Make America Great Again) and pro-Trump posts on his social networks. With him, he melts into a strong embrace.

Then it is the turn of the royal houses. Dressed in white—a privilege reserved for Catholic queens—Letizia of Spain and Mathilde of Belgium greet Leo XIV. So does Princess Charlene of Monaco, accompanied by Prince Albert. Queen Máxima of the Netherlands, always very elegant and friendly, opts for a dark outfit with a veil, and attends without her husband, King William.

Later the pope is greeted by several presidents, including Isaac Herzog of Israel, Gustavo Petro of Colombia (who will also be received tomorrow in an audience with the pope), Daniel Noboa of Ecuador, and Santiago Peña of Paraguay, among others. Heirs of various royal houses are also present, such as Princess Victoria of Sweden, Prince Edward of the United Kingdom, and Prince Faisal Bin Sattam of Saudi Arabia.

Afterwards, Leo XIV has a private audience with Zelensky, accompanied by his wife Olena, in the study adjacent to the Paul VI Hall. "It's good to see you again, thank you for your patience," the top leader of the Catholic Church is heard to say in English. Leo and Zelensky will meet again on Wednesday, July 9, at the papal residence in

---

73. Gerard O'Connell, "JD Vance Meets with Pope Leo, Brings Invitation from Trump to Visit the U.S.," *America*, May 19, 2025.

Castel Gandolfo where the pontiff will resume the tradition of resting on the outskirts of Rome for a few days.[74] During that meeting the pontiff will reiterate the Vatican's willingness to host eventual negotiations. Since, according to the Russian news agency TASS, the plane that should have brought Culture Minister Olga Liubimova never arrived due to technical problems, Russia has been represented at the inauguration Mass by Ambassador to the Vatican Ivan Soltanovsky.

Just as during Francis's funeral there had been "the miracle" of an unforeseen meeting alone in St. Peter's Basilica between the Ukrainian president and US President Donald Trump—who weeks earlier had publicly humiliated Zelensky in the White House—this time the inauguration Mass of Francis's successor gives rise to an even greater rapprochement, which could mean a turnaround. Not only did Zelensky shake hands with Vice President JD Vance at the beginning of the Mass, but they then met again at Villa Taverna, the residence of the US ambassador to Italy, together with Secretary of State Marco Rubio.

IT'S ANOTHER SUNDAY of a lot of work, which closes one stage and begins another. Betta and I don't go home right away. Both she and I have several television appearances and interviews. Many ask me how to interpret the beginning of this pontificate. I tell everyone that Leo XIV's commitment to continue on the path of Francis is evident; but it is clear that he will do so in his own way, time, and style. Leo needs time to see, analyze, reflect, assemble his new team. Beyond the vertigo of our times, the Church has its own times.

We return home. Although it is Sunday, we are not going to eat the traditional pizzas because some of Betta's long-time friends—Carolina Preve, Martín Aberg Cob, Maria Duhalde, and Ismael Jaras—have arrived in Rome after visiting the shrine of Medjugorje. Betta cooks some linguine with Argentine *gamberi* and *pomodorini* (ribbon pasta, Argentine shrimps, and small tomatoes). At the table we talk about that mystical experience of theirs and, of course, about the recent conclave. And we raise a toast to Francis, whom we believe is in heaven and to his successor, Leo, the new pope.

---

74. Francesco Merlo, "Pope Meets with Ukrainian President," www.vaticannews.va, July 9, 2025.

# CONCLUSION

THE PAPAL TRANSITION THAT BEGAN on Easter Monday, April 21, with the death of Pope Francis, ended on May 18 with the inauguration of the Petrine Ministry of Leo XIV. It marked a momentous and profoundly emotional moment in the two-thousand-year history of the Catholic Church and in the life of its 1.4 billion members, who experienced immense sadness at the passing of the charismatic, courageous, greatly-loved "pope of the poor" and afterwards enormous surprise and joy at the election, within twenty-four hours, of the first American-born missionary pope who is also a citizen of Peru.

Pope Francis could not choose his successor but, as we explain in this book, he created the conditions that made Leo's election possible. It was his last surprise.

He began by creating a College of Cardinals that is without precedent in the history of the Church. Conscious that the axis of the Catholic Church had moved to the global south, where most of its members—some 72 percent—now live,[1] Francis broke with the traditional ways of choosing cardinals. He set out to reduce the number of European and Italian cardinals and named cardinals from the world's peripheries and from countries that never had one before. By the time of his death, the College of Cardinals had a record number of members: 252 from ninety-six countries, of whom 135 from seventy-one countries were electors, and he had created 80 percent of the electors that would vote for the man to succeed him.

One year after becoming pope, he chose Chicago-born missionary Robert Francis Prevost, a man who had by then spent some twelve

---

1. *Annuario Pontificio* (Vatican Yearbook) 2025. More than 72% of the world's Catholics live outside Europe, predominantly in South and Central America (41.2%), Africa (20%), and Asia (11%). Europe has 20.4%.

years of his life in Peru and another fifteen in Rome, to be apostolic administrator and soon after bishop of Chiclayo, a poor diocese in Peru's northwestern region. Francis had first come to know him when the American, then prior-general of the Augustinian order, visited him in Buenos Aires where he was archbishop in the early part of this century.

After sending Prevost as bishop to Peru, the Jesuit pope continued to be briefed on his progress there and came to know how courageously, humbly, creatively, and in a synodal way Prevost was carrying out that difficult mission. In July 2019, Francis appointed him a member of the Congregation for the Clergy, and in November 2020, a member of the Congregation for Bishops.

In January 2023, Pope Francis decided to call this missionary bishop to Rome to head the important Vatican office (dicastery) for bishops. Then, in September 2023, he created him a cardinal. Over the two-year period from April 2023 to his hospitalization in mid-February 2025 the pope and cardinal came to know each other very well through weekly meetings related to Prevost's role as prefect in the Dicastery for Bishops, and the American became one of Francis's most trusted advisors.

Observing how well Prevost was performing in his role as head of that important Vatican office, just two months before he died, Francis gave him further endorsement and visibility within the College of Cardinals by promoting him to the elite rank of cardinal bishops. While this promotion may have meant little to outsiders, to Vatican insiders it was the clearest sign that Prevost enjoyed the pope's confidence.

As pope, Francis could do no more to influence the conclave. It was now up to the cardinals to make their free choice.

Before entering the conclave, we heard several cardinals say, "God has made his choice from all eternity; it is up to us to discern who that person is."

In writing this book, we learned that by the time the 133 cardinals from seventy countries entered the Sistine Chapel to elect the new pope, more than 20 of them, unknown to the outside world, had already identified Prevost as the one most qualified to be pope. After considering the other possible candidates—and there were several—they had come to the conclusion that this humble, low-profile American missionary cardinal, though very different in character and style from the Argentine pope, would be the one most likely to continue Francis's legacy of reforming the Roman Curia, building a synodal, missionary church that reaches out to all people, without exception, to bring the good news of Jesus Christ to them, to promote justice, fraternal harmony, and peace in the polarized, war-torn, climate-hit world of the twenty-first century. Moreover, because of his global missionary experience and pragmatic approach, they saw him as one who could be capable of healing the internal divisions and polarization in the Church and of fostering greater unity.

Within twenty-four hours, using human intelligence and with the assistance of the Holy Spirit, an overwhelming majority of the cardinal electors, many of whom hardly knew each other, in total freedom, reached the same conclusion and elected Robert Francis Prevost as the 267th successor of St. Peter.

Just as in 2013, when many electors did not know much about Cardinal Bergoglio or what kind of pope he would be, but had heard from others who knew him well that he was the man best suited to be pope, and so voted for him, the same appears to be true of the May 2025 conclave. Many electors did not have in-depth knowledge of Cardinal Prevost, but having spoken with others who knew him and having discerned the movement of the Spirit in the early ballots, they concluded that this was indeed the man God wanted to lead the Catholic Church at this moment in history.

In this book, we have tried, in a short space of time, to reconstruct how all that happened. It has been a challenging, fascinating work, like trying to create a mosaic, of putting together the many and various pieces of information that we have gleaned from cardinals, not all of whom are mentioned here.

Moreover, as two journalists who have had the extraordinary privilege of being friends of Jorge Mario Bergoglio for more than twenty years, including throughout his twelve-year-long-pontificate, we are convinced that Francis in heaven rejoiced when the cardinals in conclave elected Prevost as pope.

It is interesting to note that in his interview with Elise Ann Allen, Pope Leo XIV recalls that Francis said that at some future time the pope may dispense with the secrecy of the Sistine Chapel. He admits however: "At this point, I don't want to even dispense myself. There were a couple of things during that time that would make for a great book...."

We believe—and hope—we've made some of these things known in these pages, but only those who participated in the conclave can confirm this.

# INDEX

Abdelsalam, Mohamed, 237
abuse scandals
   2019 summit, 75
   Apuron, 74
   Belo, 74
   Cipriani, 73
   Figari, 257
   Francis's handling of, 15, 75
   McCarrick, 101
   Prevost's handling of, 141, 152, 198, 256–58, 260
   Red Hat Report, 104
   sanctions, 34, 37, 74
   Tagle's handling of, 100, 102
   victims, 75, 100–102, 141, 260
   *Vox estis lux mundi*, 76
Acutis, Carlo, 40, 53
Advíncula, José, 61, 99
Agasso, Domenico, 110, 129
Alazraki, Valentina, 235, 255
Albanese, Anthony, 278
Albert II, 283
Alfieri, Sergio, 31–33
Allen, Elise Ann, 7, 43, 136, 198, 258, 287
Allen, John, 7
Ambarus, Benoni, 30
Ambongo Besungu, Fridolin, 108–9, 124
Ambrosi, Roberto Apo, 161
American Jewish Committee (AJC), 242
*Amoris Laetitia*, 94, 151
Anyolo, Philip, 107
apostolic constitution. See *Universi Dominici Gregis*

Apostolic Signatura. *See* Supreme Tribunal of the Apostolic Signatura
Apuron, Anthony, 74
Arborelius, Anders, 15, 131
Arinze, Francis, 65
Augustine of Hippo, 137, 190, 214, 234, 241, 262, 268–69, 281
Aveline, Jean-Marc, 113, 117, 122, 124, 149–50, 154, 169–70, 175, 177–78
Ayala, Mónica, 173

Babel synod, 152
Baggio, Fabio, 164
Baker, Nigel, 111
Baldisseri, Lorenzo, 39
Barbarin, Philippe, 113, 122
Barreto, Pedro, 256
Bartholomew I, 43, 278
Bayrou, François, 278
Beauchemin, Geneviève, 5
Becciu, Giovanni Angelo, 33–35, 37–40, 65, 71–73
Becquart, Nathalie, 197
Belo, Carlos Ximenes, 74
Benedict XVI, 5, 15, 28, 38, 56, 60, 76, 79–80, 84–85, 90, 92, 107–8, 110, 121, 125, 130, 132, 147, 160, 186, 207, 229, 235, 245–46, 249, 255, 263, 267, 274–75, 277
Bergoglio, Jorge Mario. *See* Francis, Pope
Bernini, Gian Lorenzo, 23, 42, 55, 159, 162, 240, 282

Bertomeu, Jordi, 100, 258
Besungu, Fridolin Ambongo, 108, 127
Better Church Governance Project, 104
Biden, Joe, 43
Bilotta, Annalisa, 6
Binaghi, Alberto, 253
Bishop Accountability, 100–102
Bo, Charles Maung, 68
Bo, Juan Vicente, 153
Bochatey, Alberto, 229–31
Bokalic, Vicente, 119
Boluarte, Dina, 273, 283
Bonaparte, Pauline, 55
Brady, Sean, 111
Brambilla, Simona, 83
Brandmüller, Walter, 104
Bruni, Matteo, 33–34, 38–39, 62–65, 71, 73, 76–77, 85–87, 106–7, 116, 119, 133, 142–44, 192–93
Building Bridges program, 220
Burch, Brian, 151
Burke, Greg, 69, 117–18
Burke, Raymond, 83, 85, 104, 126
Bustillo, François, 113

C9, 200
Caballero Ledo, Maximino, 86
Cabrejas, Cristina, 6, 50, 58, 153, 212, 231
Cabrejos, Miguel, 257
Camilla, Queen, 20
Cañizares Llovera, Antonio, 77, 107–8
Cantalamessa, Raniero, 63, 163, 166–67, 172, 209
Capaccioli, Mariana, 173
Capdevila, Inés, 4
Capuzzi, Lucia, 260–61
Caram, Lucía, 6
Caricato, Cristiana, 9
Caritas Internationalis, 117, 134, 148, 175
Carney, Mark, 278
Castillo, Carlos, 141, 256
Castro, Nelson, 56
Centesimus Annus Pro Pontifice Foundation, 270
Charlene, Princess, 283

Charles III, 20
China-Vatican relations, 17–18, 60, 66, 85, 105, 147
Chomali, Fernando, 153, 277
Chow, Stephen, 66–67, 103–4, 166–67, 169, 180, 183, 199
Cicioni, Ety, 186
Cipolla, Carmine, 125
Cipriani, Juan Luis, 73–74, 85
Clement V, 72
Clement VII, 164
Cobo, José, 58–59
College of Cardinals, 12, 63, 87, 121, 144, 285–86
*College of Cardinals Report, The*, 103
Collins, Thomas, 111, 210
*Comment l'Amérique veut changer de pape* (Senéze), 105
Communion and Liberation movement, 150
Community of Sant'Egidio, 80, 112–13, 129, 150
*Conclave*, 38, 78, 107, 144, 204
conclaves
  1276, 185
  1958, 152
  1978, 152
  2005, 7, 66, 80, 122, 174
  2013, 10, 43, 78, 110–11, 121–22, 138, 142, 149, 153, 159, 169, 172, 174, 178, 182, 267–68, 287
  attempts to influence, 99, 103–4, 112, 125
  Becciu case, 33, 37–38, 65, 72
  eligibility for, 63
  information leaks, 134, 161, 167
  mechanics of stoves, 171
  rules for scheduling, 8, 14, 33
conservative sectors, 34, 66–67, 80, 91, 104, 115, 151, 169–70, 238, 275
Cooper, Anderson, 48
cordate, 87, 114
Corradini, Luisa, 43, 178
Cor Unum, 108
COVID-19. *See* pandemic
Cruz, Juan Carlos, 6
Cuda, Emilce, 18, 21, 160, 218
Cullen, Shay, 102

Cupich, Blase, 140, 180, 198, 209, 225–26, 231
Curia. *See* Roman Curia
Czerny, Michael, 41, 87–88, 184, 276

Damilano, Marco, 114
Da Silva, Ricardo, 135
David, Pablo Virgilio, 61, 98–99, 102, 115, 117, 152, 154, 164, 275
De Jesús, Maravillas, 244
De la Salle, John Baptist, 254–55
Dew, John, 111
*Dialogue of Salvation, The* (Avenline),113
Dicastery for Bishops, 112, 117, 132, 137–38, 140, 188, 198, 202–3, 226, 230, 252, 258
Dicastery for Promoting Integral Human Development, 41, 88, 110, 276
Di Nardo, Daniel, 209
Di Segni, Riccardo, 242, 278
Dogbo, Ignace Bessi, 131
Dolan, Timothy, 124–25, 175–76, 209, 211
Domínguez, Iñigo, 73
Don Ben. *See* Ambarus, Benoni
Doyle, Anne Barrett, 100–101
Duda, Andrezj, 278
Dulle, Colleen, 40, 208
Dunbar, Patrick, 160
Duquet, Léonie, 24
Duterte, Rodrigo, 61, 102, 117

Eastern Churches, 39, 47, 248, 250–51, 278
ecumenical dialogue, 116, 144
Edward, Prince, 283
Eguren, José Antonio, 258
*Election of Pope Francis, The* (O'Connell), 182
Elizabeth II, 48
El-Tayeb, Ahmed, 237
Episcopal Conference, 109
Erdő, Péter, 15, 91, 124, 126–27, 151, 167–71, 173, 175–78
Estrada Herrera, Lizardo, 241

evangelical churches, 140, 260
*Evangelii gaudium*, 45, 116

Farrell, Kevin, 4, 12, 22–23, 28–29, 34, 38, 50, 64, 74, 86, 133, 169, 215, 225
Fazio, Mariano, 191, 253
Felipe VI, 43, 273, 278
Fernández
  Eva, 3, 235
  Víctor Manuel, 34, 96–98, 119, 267
Fernández Artime, Ángel, 83, 135
Ferrão, Filipe Neri, 111
*Fiducia Supplicans*, 67, 108–9
Figari, Luis Fernando, 256–57
Figari slaves, 257
Filoni, Fernando, 39, 85, 181–83
Fisichella, Salvatore, 253
Fitzgerald, Michael, 111, 208
Fontan, Clara, 145, 173
Francis, Pope
  and abuse cases, 15, 73, 75–76, 101–2
  assessment of pontificate, 14–16
  and Becciu case, 33–34, 37–40, 65, 72
  Cardinal Re homily, 44–46
  and Caritas Internationalis, 148
  and China, 85
  and Church social doctrine, 263
  commitment to poor, 13, 41–42, 97–98
  death, 3–8, 11–12, 14, 17, 77, 126, 179, 188, 225, 233, 242, 264, 279, 285
  detractors, 82–84, 87–92, 103–6, 127, 151
  on discernment, 93
  election, 44, 55, 268
  and Emilce Cuda, 218
  final days, 8–10, 16–17, 20, 98
  funeral, 18–24, 26, 28–30, 35, 39–41, 43–49, 56, 59, 63, 112
  and Gaza, 243–44
  health issues, 108
  hospitalization, 6, 21, 31–32, 39, 55, 286
  on immigration, 266

291

imposes sanctions, 73–74
interment, 49
and Jewish communities, 242
legacy, 66–70, 75–76, 203
and Madonna Salus Populi Romani, 55
media response to death, 14–15
mourners' comments about, 25, 27, 30, 41
and Muslims, 237
and Robert Prevost, 136–39, 149, 229, 286
in Santa Marta, 274–75
similar possible successors, 15, 56, 89, 131
and social media, 246–47
and Sodalitium, 256–59
support for women, 36
and synodality, 94–95, 144–45, 151–52, 216–17, 230–31
tomb, 53–54, 73, 212, 218, 239
and Vatican II, 94
wake, 18–21
work ethic, 98
Francis of Assisi, 44, 57
*Fratelli Tutti*, 46, 67, 237
Fucili, Paolo, 160
Fujimori, Alberto, 73, 230

Galeazzi, Giacomo, 35
Gallagher, Paul, 225
Gänswein, Georg, 245
García Ovejero, Paloma, 56, 69–71, 117–18
Gatchalian, Michal, 101
*Gaudium et Spes*, 87
Gaza (*see also* Palestinians), 28, 68, 132, 151, 223, 233, 237, 242–44, 251, 282
German Synodal Path, 140
Ghobrial, Adrian, 172, 193
Giansoldati, Franca, 128
Girasoli, Nicola, 258
Gomes, Sebastian, 210, 238
Grabois, Juan, 41
Gracias, Oswald, 200–201, 216
Grech, Mario, 82, 116, 151, 169, 175
Greek Orthodox community, 244

Gregory, Wilton, 209
Gregory I, 222
Gregory the Great. *See* Gregory I
Gregory XI, 150
Gugerotti, Claudio, 39, 250
Guille, Guillermo Idiart, 178
Guo Jiakun, 17–18

Habsburg, Eduard, 127
*Half Monks, Half Soldiers* (Ugaz), 256
Hardjoatmodjo, Ignatius Suharyo, 145
Herlin, Arthur, 122
Hernández, Irene, 10, 14, 25, 34–36, 42–43, 53, 57, 90, 123, 186–87, 221, 231–32, 238
Herzog, Isaac, 273, 278, 282–83
Higgins, Michael D., 278
Hollerich, Jean-Claude, 81–82, 116, 146, 152, 199
Human Fraternity. See *Fratelli Tutti*
humanitarian initiatives, 69, 150, 171, 223, 282

Ignatius of Antioch, 207
Ignatius of Loyola, 49, 268–69
Innocent V, 185
International Eucharistic Congress, 151
International Red Cross, 243
Irene Hernández, 69
Islam, 67, 149, 208, 237
Israel, 206, 242–43, 245, 260, 282
    Gustavo Petro, 283
Italian-Albanians, 248

Jatta, Barbara, 142
Jeanningros, Geneviève, 24
Jewish communities, 24, 242, 278
John Paul II
    and abuse cases, 101
    and Apostolic Constitution, 38, 184–85
    approval ratings, 15
    canonization, 15
    and communism, 220

critiques of, 91
death, 5, 7, 25, 80, 160
and Eastern churches, 250
election, 152
final years, 8
and freedom of Church, 132
funeral, 47
and traditionalism, 125, 130
John XXIII, 124, 152
Jubilee, 2025, 116, 253
Jubilee of Bands and Popular Entertainment, 212, 222, 225
Jubilee of Mercy, 110
Jubilee of Teenagers, 40, 53–54
Jubilee of the Confraternities, 277, 282
Jubilee of the Eastern Churches, 248
Jubilee of the Sick, 21, 32
Julius II, 164

Kasper, Walter, 126, 131
Kikuchi, Tarcisio Isao, 113–14, 134
Koovakad, George Jacob, 164, 167, 174, 183
Krajewski, Konrad, 39, 86

Lacroix, Gerald Cyprian, 111, 135, 210
Lamb, Christopher, 4, 7, 103, 106, 269
*Latae sententiae*, 134
*Laudato Si*, 46, 88
Leo, Frank, 95, 111, 210, 279
*León XIV, Ciudadano del mundo misionero del siglo XXI*, 136
Leo XIII, 54, 184, 192, 230, 250, 263, 265, 270–72
Leo XIV
  and abuse cases, 198, 260
  American identity, 132, 199–200, 226
  announcement of election, 188
  audience with dignitaries, 283–84
  candidacy, 139–41
  and Chiclayo, 117, 132, 137, 149, 191, 198, 202, 214, 229, 252–53, 256–57, 260–61, 286
  chooses name, 184, 192, 211

  chooses personal secretary, 252
  confirms Curia, 207
  detractors, 152
  and Eastern Churches, 248–51
  election, 183–84, 187–89, 200, 203–4, 208, 213, 242, 287
  episcopal motto, 137
  family, 204
  first address, 189, 191–92
  first homily, 205
  first night as pontiff, 197
  and Francis, 136–37, 149, 286
  and Grand Imam of Al-Azhar, 237
  handling of abuse cases, 141, 152, 198, 227, 256–58, 260
  inauguration Mass, 277, 284
  investiture, 273, 278–79
  and Jewish community, 242
  joins Curia, 136
  and journalists, 232–33
  and Latin America, 132, 199, 218, 220, 229–30, 260
  as leading candidate, 118, 132, 148–49, 169–70, 173–78, 180–81, 183, 198
  and LGBTQ+ community, 211
  made cardinal, 138–39
  as major superior, 135
  as missionary, 149, 229–30, 256
  Parolin article after election, 213–14
  and polarization of US Church, 226
  reactions to election, 201–4, 208, 211, 238–39, 276
  Regina Caeli, 222, 224–25
  reopens papal apartments, 225, 274–75
  in Room of Tears, 185
  and royal houses, 283
  and social doctrine, 270, 272
  and social media, 246–47, 253
  and Sodalitium, 257–59
  speech to cardinals, 216–17
  as successor to Francis, 125, 201, 231, 256, 277
  supporters, 140–41, 154, 171, 181, 209, 220
  trip to Turkey, 236

and Trump, 211, 227, 267
*Urbi et Orbi*, 217
and Vietnam, 264
visits Francis's tomb, 218
and Zelensky, 283
Letizia, Queen, 43, 278, 283
Leung, Rodney, 194
LGBTQ+ community, 26, 67, 92, 210–11
Liberman, Luis, 24
Little Sisters of Jesus, 24
Liubimova, Olga, 284
Long Garcia, JD, 40
López Romero, Cristóbal, 57
Luciani, Albino. *See* John Paul I
Lula da Silva, Luiz Inácio, 47, 132
*Lumen Gentium*, 87
Lustiger, Jean-Marie, 122
Lutheran Church, 140

Macron, Brigitte, 47
Macron, Emmanuel, 43, 47, 112–13
Maduro, Nicolás, 132, 260
Mafi, Soane Patita Paini, 111
Makrickas, Rolandas, 55
Mamberti, Dominique, 64, 74, 129–30, 188, 279
Mangin, Florence, 113
Manico, Lisa, 7
Manos Abiertas Foundation, 119
Maradiaga, Oscar, 141
Marano, Venerando, 273
Marans, Noam, 242
Marcó, Guillermo, 145
Marengo, Giorgio, 63, 273
Marroni, Carlo, 108
Martin, James, 210–11
Martínez Brocal, Javier, 18
Martínez Ibáñez, Augusto, 260
Marx, Reinhard, 64, 74, 85, 140, 181
Mathilde, Queen, 283
Mattarella, Sergio, 273, 283
Máxima, Queen, 273, 278, 283
McCarrick, Theodore, 101
McCarthy, Neil, 193, 210
McElroy, Robert, 164, 182–83, 198–99, 209
McElwee, Joshua, 235

McKinless, Ashley, 4, 238
Megen, Hubertus Matheus Maria van, 107
Melloni, Alberto, 34
Meloni, Giorgia, 81, 273
Mendonça, José Tolentino de, 273
Menor, Darío, 143
Merz, Friedrich, 278
Metropolitan Anthony, 43
Metsola, Roberta, 278
migrants, 36, 49, 88–89, 93, 149, 211, 239, 260, 266
Milei, Javier, 43, 238
Missa Pro Eligendo Pontifice, 63
missionary synodal Church, 62
Montagna, Diane, 103
Montanari, Ilson de Jesús, 163, 171, 183
Morabito, Rosanna, 27
Moral Antón, Alejandro, 224, 241, 267
Müller, Gerhard, 90–93, 104, 126, 146, 277
Munsterman, Hendro, 115
Muslim Council of Elders, 237
Muslims, 57, 237, 244–45
world religions including, 278

Nadeau, Barbie Latza, 7
Nassau, Juli, 18, 49, 78
Netanyahu, Benjamin, 242
Nichols, Vincent, 111, 203
Njue, John, 77, 107–8
Noboa, Daniel, 283
non-electors, 108, 128, 214
*Nostra Aetate*, 242
novemdiales, 40, 94, 96, 128–29
Nusca, Antonello, 6
Nzapalainga, Dieudonné, 110

Ogliari, Donato, 63, 76
O'Malley, Sean, 153, 174, 179, 253
Omella, Juan José, 202–3
Opus Dei, 73, 191, 253
Orbán, Viktor, 151
Ordinary Jubilee (2025), 116, 253
*Ordo Exsequiarum Romani Pontificis*, 49

*Ordo Rituum Conclavis*, 77, 163, 165
*Orientale lumen*, 250
*Orientalium dignitas*, 250
Orthodox churches, 144, 244–45
O'Shea, Oona, 279
Osoro Sierra, Carlos, 182
Ouellet, Marc, 117, 138, 140, 218

Paglia, Vincenzo, 150
Palacio y Pérez-Medel, José Luis del, 137
Palestinians, 242, 244. *See also* Gaza
pandemic, 247, 249
papabile, 66, 81, 89, 108, 110, 113, 139, 145, 148, 151, 174, 198
papal absolutism, 16
*Para leer a Francisco* (Cuda), 218
Parolin, Pietro
 and abuse cases, 100–101
 alleged fainting, 107–8
 and Becciu case, 37–40, 72
 and Cardinal Stella, 83–85, 87, 89–90, 114, 127, 236
 detractors, 122
 and German Synodal Path, 140
 as leading candidate, 14–15, 53, 63, 65, 70–71, 78–82, 115, 118, 127–30, 146–50, 158, 160–61, 170–71, 173, 177–78, 187
 presides over conclave, 163, 165, 167, 169, 176, 182–84
 rumors of election, 187, 189
 supposedly asks supporters to vote for Prevost, 181
 writes article after Leo XIV elected, 212–14
Pasinya, Laurent Monsengwo, 109
Paul III, 162, 164
Paul VI, 64, 89, 92, 158, 278
Pecci, Gioacchino Vincenzo Raffaele Luigi. *See* Leo XIII
Pedicino, Gabriele, 241
pedophilia. *See* abuse scandals
Péguy, Charles, 209
Pell, George, 151
Pellizón, Daniel, 23
Pen, Edward, 103
Peña, Santiago, 283

Peña Parra, Edgar, 81, 225
Pérez, Ernesto, 10
Peruvian Episcopal Conference, 136–37, 200, 229, 256–57
Pesce, Francesco, 124
Petrine Ministry, 179, 269, 278–79, 285
Petrini, Raffaella, 86
Petro, Gustavo, 132, 273
Pierre, Christophe, 113, 141, 209, 261–62
Pironio, Eduardo, 86
Pius X, 273
Pius XII, 129
Pizzaballa, Pierbattista, 15, 63, 80, 118, 124, 129, 151, 161, 169, 245, 251
plan B, 152–53
Poli, Mario, 119, 127
Pontifical Commission for Latin America (PCAL), 18, 117, 138, 160, 218
Pontifical Commission for the Protection of Minors, 64, 74
Pontifical Council for Justice and Peace, 88, 110
Porras Cardozo, Baltazar Enrique, 143
*Praedicate Evangelium*, 83
pre-conclave meetings, 33, 36, 40, 44, 57, 74, 91, 103, 116, 133
Prevost, John, 204
Prevost
 Louis, 283
 Robert. *See* Leo XIV
Pro Eligendo Pontifice masses, 77, 118, 133, 153, 157, 160

Radcliffe, Timothy, 111, 135, 181
Raddatz, Martha, 225
Ratzinger, Joseph. *See* Benedict XVI
Ravasi, Gianfranco, 202
Ravelli, Diego, 163, 166–67, 183, 185
Re, Giovanni Battista, 12, 38, 63, 118, 157, 215
Red Hat Report, 104
Regina Caeli, 123, 192, 208, 221, 223–25, 275, 282

Regoli, Roberto, 34–35
Reina, Baldassare, 47, 92–94, 146
*Rerum Novarum*, 184, 192, 256, 265, 270, 281
Ribat, John, 111
Riccardi, Andrea, 112–13
Rimaycun, Edgard Iván, 252–53
Rinaldi, Andrea, 23, 32
Ring-Eifel, Ludwig, 140
Robles, Kevin Christopher, 238
Roche, Arthur, 111, 203
Roman Curia, 12, 24, 81–83, 97–98, 105–6, 116–17, 122, 136, 143–44, 149, 207–8, 218–19, 276
Romanelli, Gabriel, 243, 245
Rossi, Ángel, 119, 184, 238–39
Rubio, Marco, 267, 273, 283–84
Ruffini, Paolo, 83
Rutelli, Francesco, 54

Sako, Louis Raphael, 164, 183, 249
Salerno, Fabio, 23
Salinas, Pedro, 256–59
Sánchez, Sergio, 40–41
Sandri, Leonardo, 79
San Martín, Inés, 239–40
Sant'Egidio. *See* Community of Sant'Egidio
Santillán, María Laura, 238
Sapienza, Leonardo, 225
Sarah, Robert, 104, 108, 126
Sawyer, Sam, 5, 40, 42, 208, 247
Scannone, Juan Carlos, 218
Scaramuzzi, Iacopo, 131
Schönborn, Christoph, 56, 86
Scicluna, Charles, 100, 258
Scola, Angelo, 78–79, 150
Scriven, Gail, 212
Second Vatican Council. *See* Vatican II
Secretariat of State (Vatican), 12, 37, 81, 84, 101, 122, 147, 187, 227
Sékou Touré, Ahmed, 108
Senéze, Nicolas, 105
sensus fidei, 216
Sevryuk, Anthony. *See* Metropolitan Anthony
sexual abuse. *See* abuse scandals

Shevchuk, Sviatoslav, 251
Sideman, Yaron, 242
signal jammers, 161
Sinner, Yannik, 253
Sixtus IV, 164
Skorka, Abraham, 278
social doctrine, 192, 256, 263, 270–72
Sodalitium Vida Cristiana, 256–59
Soltanovsky, Ivan, 284
Soria, Manuel, 224
Sosa, Arturo, 279
*Spotlight*, 257
Steiner, Leonardo Ulrich, 200, 216, 269, 276
Stella, Beniamino, 82–84, 87, 89, 114, 126–27, 236
*St. Gallen Mafia, The*, 103
stoves, mechanics of, 171
Strappetti, Massimiliano, 16–17, 23, 31–32, 55
Sturla, Daniel, 267
Supreme Tribunal of the Apostolic Signatura, 64, 83, 85
Survivors Networks of Those Abused by Priests (SNAP), 141
Suu Kyi, Aung San, 68
SVC. *See* Sodalitium Vida Cristiana
synodal Church, 60, 94, 121, 131, 141–42, 145, 152, 191, 217, 230, 275
synodality, 58, 86, 91, 94–95, 106, 116, 120, 144, 149, 151, 211, 216–17, 250, 276
Synod of Bishops, 91, 151, 197, 250
Synod on Synodality, 16, 60–61, 81–82, 94, 116, 200, 217, 239, 258
Synod on the Amazon, 16
Synod on the Family, 108

Tagle, Luis Antonio
  and abuse cases, 100–102
  attacks against, 148, 152
  and Caritas crisis, 117, 148, 175
  and Francis, 71
  as leading candidate, 15, 61, 64, 71, 117, 128, 146, 148–49, 170, 183
  and Leo XIV, 183, 267–68, 279
Taquini, Cristina, 10, 50, 123, 212

Tarantelli, Renato, 93
Therese of Lisieux, 21
Tobin, Joseph William, 126, 135, 209, 226
Tramontano, Andrea, 160–61
Tridentine Mass, 105
Trott, Christopher, 111
Trump, Donald, 43, 47–48, 56, 117, 125, 132, 211, 220, 227, 230, 267, 283–84
Tscherrig, Emil Paul, 167–68
Turkson, Peter, 88, 110, 169, 174

Ugarte, Robertino Funes, 56
Ugaz, Paola, 236, 256–59
*Universi Dominici Gregis*, 12, 38, 63, 79, 134, 159, 165, 168, 181, 183–85, 269
*Urbi et Orbi*, 10, 16, 32, 192, 217, 265

Vance, JD, 247, 267, 273, 278, 283–84
Vatican II, 6, 16, 34, 62, 66, 87, 94, 216, 242, 272, 276

Vérgez Alzaga, Fernando, 86
Versaldi, Giuseppe, 72
Vesco, Jean-Paul, 146
Vian, Giovanni Maria, 14–15, 38
Victoria, Princess, 283
Viganó, Carlo Maria, 104
Villalón, Juan Cruz, 3, 17, 21, 23, 55
viri probati, 16
Von der Leyen, Ursula, 278
*Vos estis lux mundi*, 76, 227

Winfield, Nicole, 194
Wooden, Cindy, 126
World War II, 223

Zanetti, Piergiorgio, 23
Zelensky, Volodymyr, 43, 46–48, 56, 267, 273, 278, 282–84
Zen, Joseph, 12, 59–60, 84–85
Zenari, Mario, 167–68, 279
Zollner, Hans, 74–76, 102
Zuppi, Matteo, 15, 79, 113, 124, 129, 143, 150–51, 169, 171, 273

www.ingramcontent.com/pod-product-compliance
Lightning Source LLC
Chambersburg PA
CBHW071709180426
43192CB00052B/2215